The Complete
Home Freezer

The Complete Home Freezer

Mary Norwak

BOOK CLUB ASSOCIATES · LONDON

Designed by Paula Hawkins
Illustrated by Richard Armstrong

Text filmset in 11/12 pt Ehrhardt by
Keyspools Limited, Golborne, Lancs.
Printed in Singapore by Toppan
Printing Co. (S) Pte. Ltd.

ACKNOWLEDGEMENTS

The Publisher and Author want to record their thanks to the many people whose research has contributed to the information in this book.

Their thanks are also due to the following for pictures and relevant material:
Alcan Polyfoil Ltd; Angel Studio; British Bacon Curers' Federation; British Meat Service; Birds Eye Foods Ltd; H. P. Bulmer Ltd; British Sugar Bureau; Food Advisory Service, Cadbury-Typhoo Ltd; Cherry Valley Farms Ltd; Danish Agricultural Producers; Dutch Dairy Bureau; Electrolux Ltd; Flour Advisory Bureau; Frigicold Ltd; Frozen Food Committee; Kellogg Company of Great Britain Ltd; Bejam Bulk Buying Ltd; Lea and Perrins Ltd; New Zealand Lamb Information Bureau; Oxo Ltd; R.H.M. Foods Ltd; Tabasco Sauce (Horlicks) Ltd; Philips Electrical Ltd; G.E.C. (Domestic Appliances) Ltd; Walls (Ice Cream) Ltd; Young's Seafoods Ltd.

They would also like to thank, in particular, John Dixon for much co-operation in taking the photographs specially commissioned for this book, and Richard Armstrong for the diagrams. Thanks are also due to Mrs Gwen Conacher of the Electricity Council and Mrs D. E. M. Short of Van den Bergh's Ltd for specially-undertaken research.

Contents

INTRODUCTION

The number of households owning a home freezer has grown rapidly and is still growing.

Whether the freezer was originally bought as an aid to economy or as a status symbol, it represents a new way of life. Perhaps no other piece of household equipment has so totally revolutionised our domestic and eating habits. The freezer has given us a safe way of preserving vegetables, meat, fish, dairy produce and cooked dishes in our homes for the first time. It has cut down the constant and tiresome chores of shopping and cooking, simplified preserving methods and increased the range of foods which we are prepared to sample. The freezer has helped working women and mothers of families, and has encouraged the men of the household to take a greater interest in the food which is bought and prepared for them, because they can see positive results from this piece of equipment and like to bring their analytical minds to the task of filling and using it to best advantage.

The interest and discussion engendered by the use of the freezer have already created their own 'old wives' tales'. Wherever freezer owners meet, they talk about methods of purchasing and preserving food; and many misconceptions are passed on, often the fault of ill-written instruction books or half-digested information. Too often, freezing is made to sound much more complicated than it is.

This book gathers together the most authoritative information on the subject. Nobody using it need be frightened of home freezing, nor be alarmed by apparent difficulties. A little time given to reading it and to studying the topic will soon be repaid in greater saving of time and money and more delicious and varied food.

Tables of Weights, Measures and Temperatures

FLOUR, SIFTED	3 TABLESPOONS	1 OZ
CASTER OR GRANULATED SUGAR	2 TABLESPOONS	$1\frac{1}{4}$ OZ
ICING SUGAR, SIFTED	3 TABLESPOONS	1 OZ
BUTTER OR MARGARINE	2 TABLESPOONS	$1\frac{1}{4}$ OZ
CORNFLOUR	2 TABLESPOONS	1 OZ
GRANULATED OR POWDERED GELATINE	4 TEASPOONS	$\frac{1}{2}$ OZ
GOLDEN SYRUP OR TREACLE	1 TABLESPOON	1 OZ
FLOUR, SIFTED	1 CUP	5 OZ
CASTER OR GRANULATED SUGAR	1 CUP	9 OZ
ICING SUGAR, SIFTED	1 CUP	5 OZ
BUTTER OR MARGARINE	1 CUP	9 OZ
CORNFLOUR	1 CUP	8 OZ
GOLDEN SYRUP OR TREACLE	1 CUP	1 LB

All the spoons referred to in this book are British Standard teaspoons and tablespoons, which hold the amounts of liquid given above. They are measured with the contents levelled off, i.e. all the spoonfuls are level spoonfuls.

The cup is a British Standard measuring cup which holds 10 fluid oz or an Imperial $\frac{1}{2}$ pint.

The standard measuring cup in Australia and the USA holds 8 fluid oz, so that 1 cup holds 4/5th of the quantities given above.

60 DROPS	1 TEASPOON
3 TEASPOONS	1 TABLESPOON
4 TABLESPOONS	$\frac{1}{2}$ GILL
1 GILL	$\frac{1}{4}$ PINT
4 GILLS	1 PINT
2 PINTS	1 QUART
4 QUARTS	1 GALLON

OVEN TEMPERATURES

	Fahrenheit	Celsius	Gas
VERY COOL	225°F	110°C	$\frac{1}{4}$
VERY COOL	250°F	130°C	$\frac{1}{2}$
VERY COOL	275°F	140°C	1
COOL	300°F	150°C	2
WARM	325°F	170°C	3
MODERATE	350°F	180°3	4
FAIRLY HOT	375°F	190°C	5
FAIRLY HOT	400°F	200°C	6
HOT	425°F	220°C	7
VERY HOT	450°F	230°C	8
VERY HOT	475°F	240°C	9

SUGAR BOILING TEMPERATURES

1	SMALL THREAD	102°C	215°F
2	LARGE THREAD	103°C	217°F
3	SMALL PEARL	104°C	220°F
4	LARGE PEARL	106°C	222°F
5	SMALL BLOW	110°C	230°F
6	LARGE BLOW OR FEATHER	112°C	233°F
7	SMALL BALL	114°C	237°F
8	LARGE BALL	119°C	247°F
9	SMALL CRACK	143°C	290°F
10	LARGE CRACK	154°C	310°F
11	CARAMEL	177°C	350°F

DEEP FAT FRYING TABLE

Food	Bread Browns in	Fat Temp	Oil Temp
RAW STARCHY FOODS— DOUGHNUTS, FRITTERS, CHIPS (1st FRYING)	1¼ MINUTES	325°–340°F 170°C	340°F 170°C
FISH IN BATTER	1¼ MINUTES	325°–340°F 170°C	340°F 170°C
FISH IN EGG AND CRUMBS	1 MINUTE	360°F 185°C	360°F 185°C
SCOTCH EGGS	1 MINUTE	350°F 180°C	350°F 180°C
REHEATED FOODS, POTATO STRAWS, CHIPS (2nd FRYING)	40 SECONDS	380°F 190°C	390°F 195°C

Part I BASIC FREEZER INFORMATION

CHOOSING A FREEZER

There are four factors involved in choosing a freezer, and these must be assessed carefully when making such a large and important purchase. If the wrong type of freezer is chosen for a household, it may be many years before the mistake can be rectified. Although its use will soon show whether a freezer is fully suitable for any given family, it is obviously better to plan ahead with the aid of other people's experience, and avoid making a mistake.

Size A freezer which is too small will soon become irritating. Experience will stimulate greater use of the freezer, and it is wise to buy one which may seem at first glance rather too large.

(a) It is generally agreed that 2 cu. ft. capacity should be allowed for the food of each person in a family, with an additional 2 cu. ft. to allow for awkwardly-shaped packages, bulk buying, entertaining and home produce, but with today's increased range of commercially-prepared foods and the growth of bulk buying, this figure is somewhat unrealistic. For instance, the recommended size is 10 cu. ft. for a four-person family, but in practice this size of family may well need a 16 cu. ft. freezer if they have a large garden or entertain a lot.

(b) From this, it will be seen that the size of the freezer cannot entirely be assessed from the regular consumption of a family. For instance, if bulk purchases are to be made, a larger freezer may be necessary. Meat, for instance, takes up a great deal of space when bought in bulk. An economical purchase may contain 180 lb meat, often in awkwardly-shaped packages. Bulk market purchases of fruit or vegetables, or glut home-grown produce can easily give 200 lb. food to be stored, although this can be arranged in neater packages. It is therefore sensible to work out the likely annual consumption of food and the amount to be stored, before deciding on the size of the freezer.

(c) The size of the freezer may be determined by the place in which it must stand. A larger cabinet can usually be bought if it is to stand in a garage or outhouse. Chest freezers all used to be rectangular in shape, but some are now being designed as squares, which makes them more compact, and therefore more convenient for indoors.

Capacity Size and capacity are sometimes confused when a freezer is bought. Usually the capacity of a freezer is given in cu. ft., but this does not give much of a clue to the amount of food which can be stored.

(a) Calculate storage space by multiplying each cu. ft. by 30 to give storage capacity in *lb. per cu. ft*. In practice, odd-shaped packages and lightweight packs may take up a large area, so that the actual storage capacity is somewhat reduced. Sixteen 1-pint cartons or 20 lb. meat or poultry occupy about 1 cu. ft. In an upright freezer, the shelves encourage a tidier arrangement of packages, which tends to increase storage space.

(b) If it is hoped to use the freezer to preserve fresh produce and home-cooked food, it is important to study the amount of fresh food which can be successfully frozen in 24 hours. Most manufacturers state this amount in their leaflets, generally giving it as one-tenth of the total storage capacity. This figure is vital for anyone with a garden which can produce fresh foods for the freezer, or who wishes to buy meat in bulk, since it tells them how much to pick or purchase at one time.

Type of Freezer A proper home freezer is capable of operating at 0°F (−18°C) always. It can freeze within 24 hours, without any significant change in the temperature of food already stored, a specified quantity of fresh or cooked food. In addition, a freezer has the ability to store food for relatively long periods – months or even a year – rather than just a few weeks. Freezers in countries with hot climates are tropicalised and behave in all ways like freezers in Europe. They may not, however, carry British Star markings and a would-be purchaser should check recommended storage times for food packs before buying.

(A) STAR-MARKED FROZEN FOOD COMPARTMENT

Frozen-food compartments on most British refrigerators are marked with stars in accordance with British Standards Specification No. 3739. This indicates recommended storage times for individual packets of commercially-frozen foods.

★ (one star) operates at −6°C or 21°F and stores bought frozen food for one week and ice cream for one day.

★ ★ (two star) operates at −12°C or 10°F and stores bought frozen food for one month and ice cream for two weeks.

★ ★ ★ (three star) operates at −18°C or 0°F and stores bought frozen food for three months and ice cream for one month. Very small quantities of fresh or cooked food can also be home-frozen down to −18°C or 0°F, following individual manufacturers' instructions.

(B) FOUR STAR MARKING

This symbol, consisting of a rectangular frame containing a large six-pointed star, and three small six-pointed stars in a curved frame distinguishes a true freezer compartment from the type above. The large star symbolises the food freezing capacity, and the three smaller stars (as used on frozen food storage compartments) indicate that most commercially-frozen foods can be stored up to three months. Manufacturers using this symbol must indicate in their instructions the maximum weight of food which can be frozen in 24 hours.

(C) CON-SERVATORS

These are cabinets designed only for the storage of foods already frozen. They cannot be adjusted to sufficiently low temperatures for freezing food from the raw state. These were formerly bought as second-hand bargains from shops and factories, but should not be bought as freezers. They can be useful for the additional storage of such items as animal food.

13

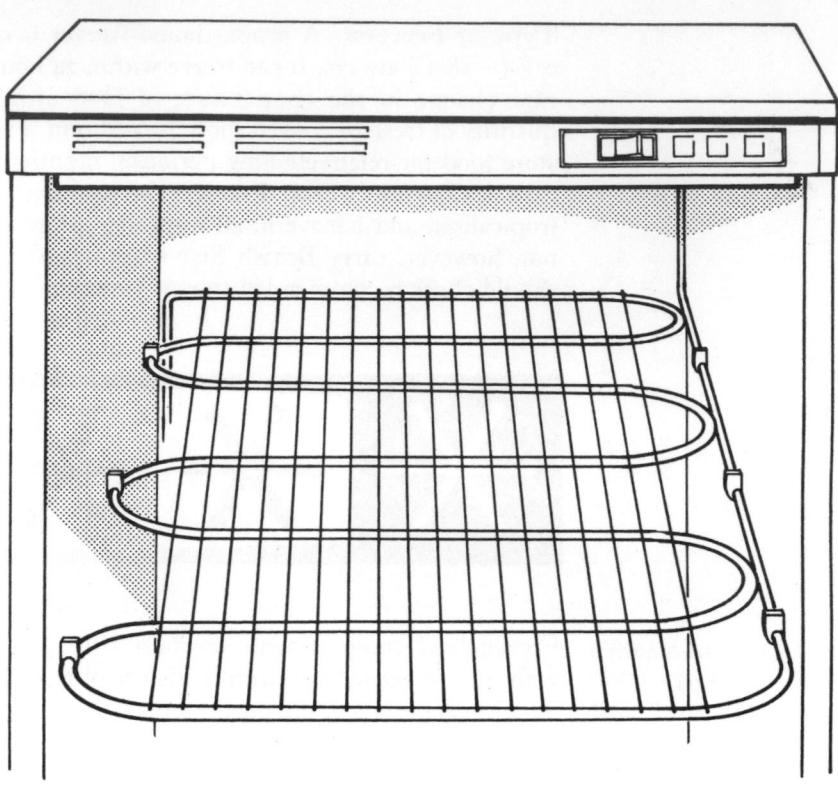

(D) CHEST FREEZERS These, as stated, occupy a large floor area, although the new square designs are more suitable for the house. They are excellent for bulk storage, but should be fitted with dividers and baskets for easy arrangement of the smaller packages. Short or fat people may find them difficult to use, as it is awkward to lift heavy packages from the bottom of chest cabinets. Check before purchase that a chest freezer has a self-balancing lid, magnetic lid seal and plenty of baskets, and an easily-controlled fast-freezing compartment. A lock is useful for a cabinet placed outside.

(E) UPRIGHT FREEZERS These are neatly designed, and easy to use for freezing fresh food, and for organising contents. The weight is concentrated in a small area, so floor safety must be checked before purchasing one. See that there are plenty of shelves and door fittings.

(F) COMBINATION REFRIGERATOR-FREEZERS It is important to check the star-markings on combination models, since many people are sold refrigerators with so-called 'freezers' which are in fact only frozen food storage compartments. A true refrigerator–freezer may consist of a small freezer on top of a larger refrigerator, or equal-sized refrigerator and freezer. These may be installed side-by-side, or stacked, and it usually makes for easier use if the refrigerator is stacked on top of the freezer. There is today a slight trend towards preferring a large freezer combined with a small refrigerator, since many people find that a well-used freezer renders a refrigerator almost obsolete except for storing of dairy produce.

A FAST-FREEZING COMPARTMENT A fast-freezing compartment is now fitted to most chest freezers, divided from the main cabinet by a panel and controlled by a special switch. This switch cuts out thermostatic control so that the motor runs continuously. This ensures that heat is removed from fresh food as quickly as possible, and already-frozen foods do not rise in temperature when the freezer is opened. A light indicates that the motor is running continuously and the fast-freezing compartment is in action. In an upright freezer, the shelves with electric coils are the ones used for fast-freezing fresh food.

THE WARNING LIGHT It is important to choose a freezer which has a warning system. Some freezer warning lights are connected with the thermostat and stay on as long as the cabinet temperature does not rise above a few degrees from the normal operating temperature. Some cabinets have a light which comes on when the electricity supply is connected and switched on, and a failure of the light indicates that something is wrong. If a freezer has no warning system, an insurance claim for food wastage may be disallowed if it stops working. See page 20 below.

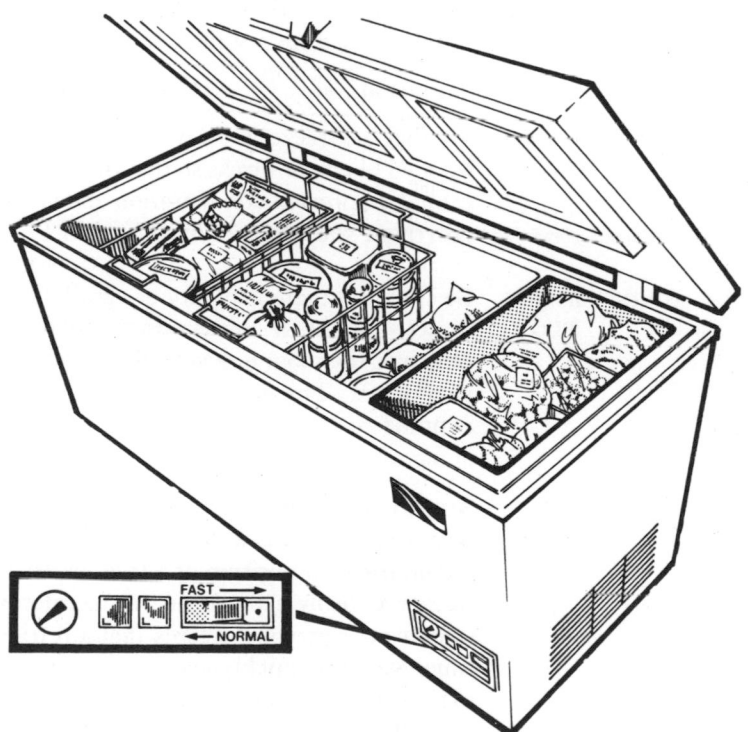

Some manufacturers give a freezer thermometer with the cabinet. If not, it is worth purchasing this small item to hang on a freezer shelf or basket. The thermometer can indicate not only the temperature inside the freezer, but safe and unsafe storage zones for frozen food. If a freezer is placed in a sun-room, for instance, the outside temperature may be higher than normal, and it is worth keeping a check that the motor is working to maintain a constant temperature inside the cabinet.

INSTALLING A FREEZER

A freezer should clearly be kept in a place where it is easily accessible for regular use, where it will not need much maintenance and where it will run economically. Ideally, a home freezer should be installed in a dry place with a 2 in. space all round it to allow the air to circulate. The surrounding temperature should not sink below 4°C, and should never be too cold. The freezer should therefore be placed in a dry, cool and airy position, such as the part of a kitchen farthest from the stove, in a large airy larder, a dry garage or outhouse or a utility room, spare-room or passage. Preferably, the freezer should be in good natural or artificial light, and have a table near it for ease of packing and unpacking.

(A) IN THE
KITCHEN

See that the freezer is not placed near the cooker, near a radiator or a boiler. Also avoid an unventilated cupboard, and see that the freezer stands away from a wall. Use a suitable covering if the cabinet is to be used as a work-top.

(B) IN THE
GARAGE

See that the freezer is away from the wall, and also see that it is raised on wooden blocks or bricks so that there is air-space beneath the floor of the cabinet to prevent condensation and spoilage of the cabinet. Use a thick polythene sheet to prevent the cabinet being damaged by damp or dust.

(C) IN A SPARE-
ROOM

Be sure that there is plenty of ventilation, and that the cabinet is out of direct sunlight. A conservatory or sunroom is often used for a freezer, but since the room is designed to catch the sun, it will obviously become very warm. This may affect the freezer, and will certainly add to the running costs.

Avoiding Noise   Many new freezer owners find their cabinets seem to be noisy, and it is as well to understand the reasons for this before deciding on the final position of a freezer. It is necessary to appreciate that a freezer is really a powerful refrigerator which operates in exactly the same way. Everyone accepts that a refrigerator 'cuts in and out' and in time everyone quickly gets used to the associated low hum. The noise may seem worse in a freezer however, especially if it is standing on a stone floor, which acts like a sounding-board. A piece of felt or rubber-

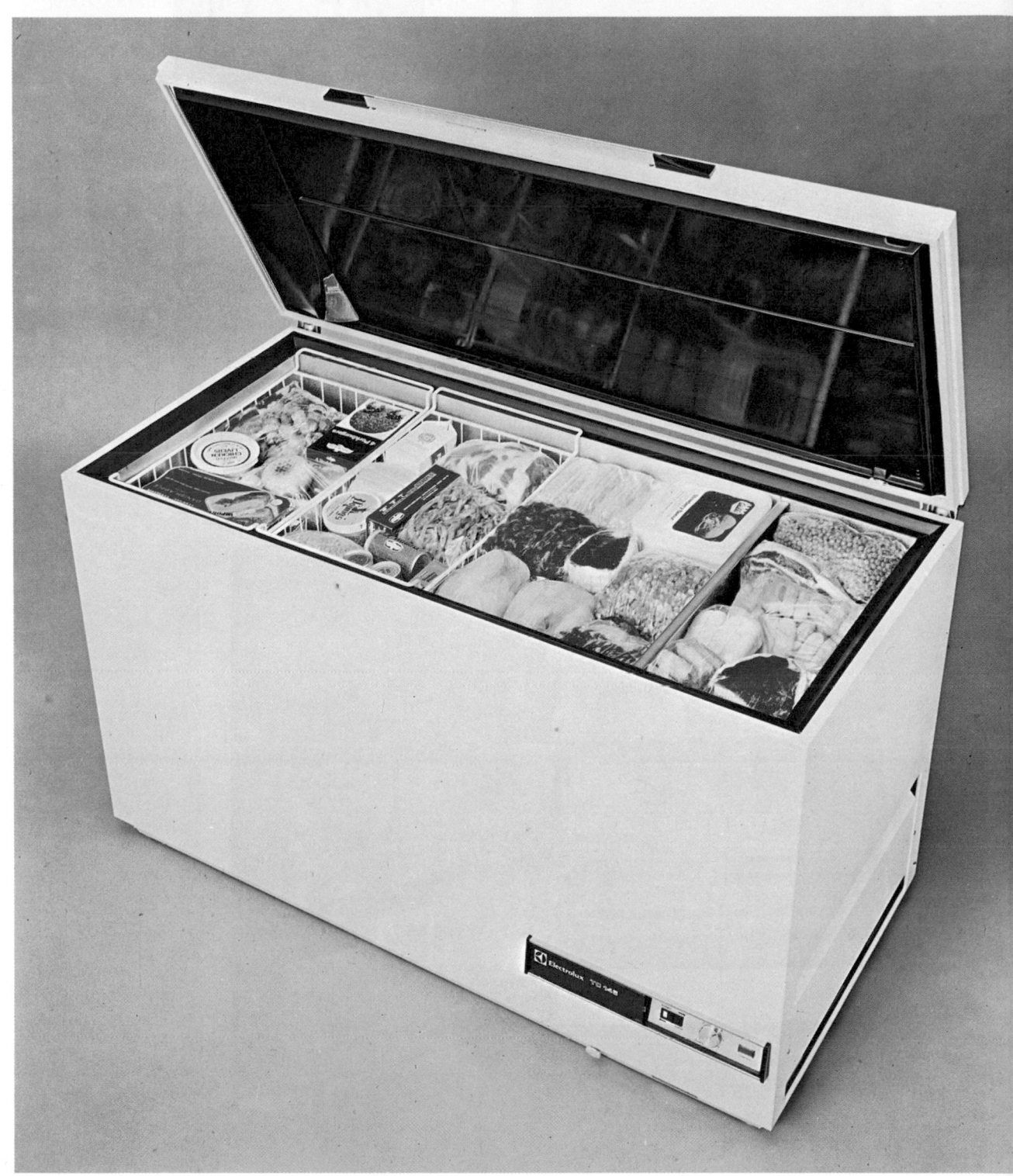

A chest freezer. Note the compact arrangement of the packages in the baskets.

A combination refrigerator–freezer with equal-sized compartments, easy to use for slow thawing.

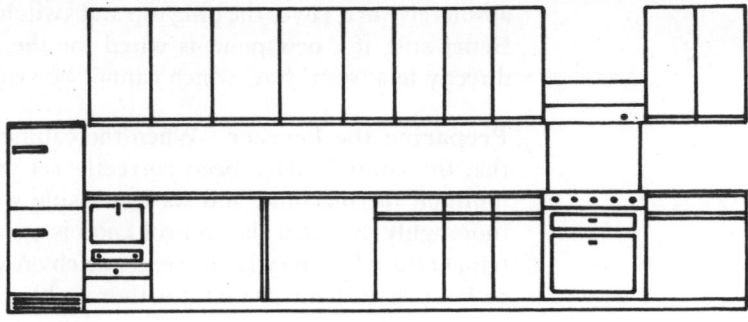

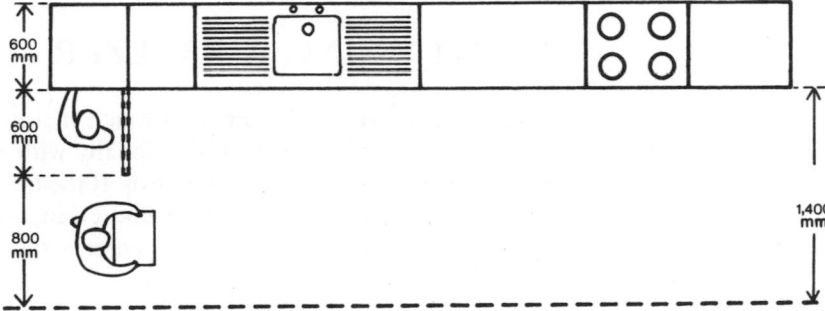

*Site the freezer clear of
the wall, well away
from a cooker or fire*

600 mm

600 mm

800 mm

1,400 mm

backed vinyl placed under the freezer will help to solve the problem.

An uneven floor can also cause noisy vibration, and the freezer must stand absolutely level. It should also be well away from walls, especially if it is in an enclosed space, as these can intensify sound.

The freezer runs much better if it is at least three-quarters full. With a solid mass of food packages inside, the temperature remains much more stable, and the motor usually only needs to cut in occasionally to keep the temperature steady, and will be much quieter when it does. However, if the freezer is in a warm steamy kitchen, a lot of this steamy warmth has to be counteracted every time the freezer is opened, so the motor acts more often and more noisily.

If the freezer is proving noisy, therefore, check the following points: (a) is the freezer in a reasonably cool dry place? (b) is it standing absolutely level? (c) is it in an open situation? (d) does it stand on sound-absorbing material? (e) is it set correctly, according to the manufacturer's instructions? (f) has the fast-freeze control been left on accidentally? (g) is it reasonably full?

The Correct Power Point   Be sure there is a suitable power point for the exclusive use of a freezer. Freezers should be connected to a nearby fused power socket. It should never be run off an adaptor, nor be unplugged to accommodate another appliance, however briefly. It is all too easy to forget to replace the plug or to switch on again. To make absolutely sure, cover the plug top and switch with strong adhesive tape. Better still, if a new point is wired for the freezer, have it connected directly to a 'spur' box, which cannot be switched off.

Preparing the Freezer When the cabinet has been installed, check that the controls have been correctly set and tested by the supplier. Turn off the machine, and wash it inside with plain warm water. Dry thoroughly. See that the control knob is switched to the recommended temperature for everyday use and switch on again. Leave the cabinet for 12 hours before use so that it is thoroughly chilled before being packed with frozen food.

MAINTAINING A FREEZER

A freezer cabinet should not need much maintenance. The outside of the cabinet should be washed occasionally with warm soapy water, and polished with an enamel surface polish. If the freezer has to be turned off for a period, make sure it is empty and clean, and leave the lid or door open (be sure that no children can enter a room or outhouse where a freezer is standing empty and open).

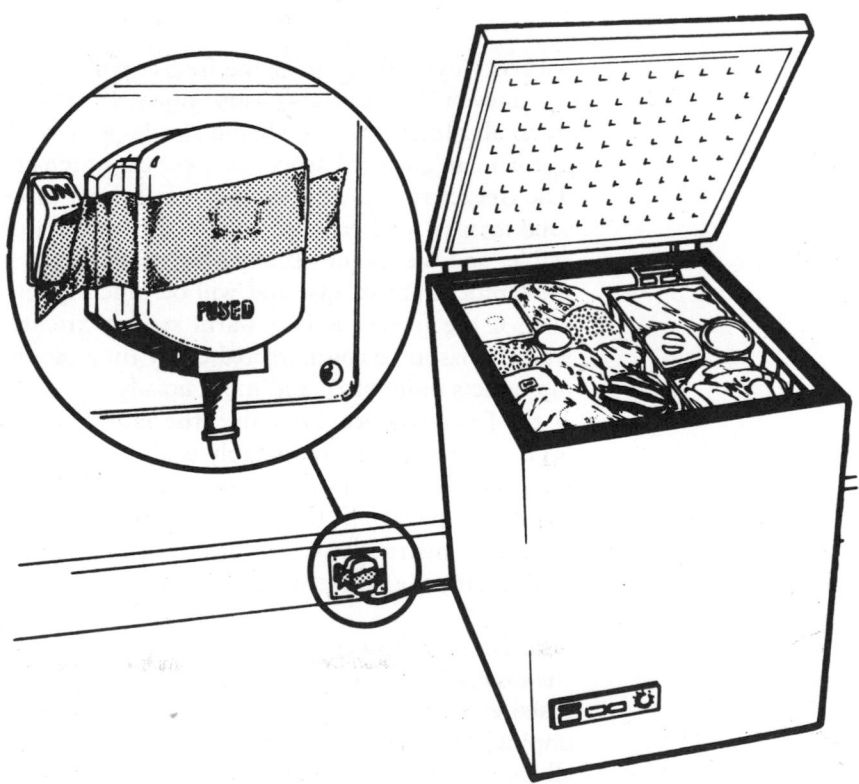

Defrosting   A freezer should be defrosted once or twice a year when food stocks are low and frost is about $\frac{1}{4}$ in. thick. An upright freezer may need defrosting more often as frost tends to build up quicker when it is opened. To avoid frequent defrosting, it is worth spreading a little newspaper on top of frozen packages and scraping down ice regularly with a plastic or wooden spatula. The ice will fall into the paper, and can be removed easily and quickly.

Before defrosting, make sure any food packages in the freezer are very cold. This can be done by putting on the fast-freeze switch the day before defrosting. Take the food from the freezer and pack it closely in a refrigerator; or wrap it in layers of newspapers and blankets and keep it in a cold place.

Disconnect the freezer from the electricity supply. Put newspaper or a piece of towelling on the floor of the freezer and scrape the sides with a wooden or plastic tool, not with a wire brush or sharp implement. A bowl of cold or just-warm water can be placed in the freezer to speed up the melting of ice, but the cabinet may be damaged by really hot water, heaters or lamps. Leave the cabinet open while defrosting, and mop up drips with a clean cloth from time to time.

When defrosting is complete, wash the inside of the cabinet with a solution of 1 tablespoon bicarbonate of soda in 1 quart water. Rinse with clean water and dry very thoroughly. Do not use any soap, detergent or caustic cleaners. Switch the control to the coldest setting and run the motor for 30 minutes. Put back the packages, and return the control to normal setting after 3 hours. Do not try to freeze any fresh food for 24 hours after defrosting.

Use defrosting time to check the packages in store. See that wrappings are intact, and plan to use up any long-stored food quickly, storing it in a basket or on a special shelf as a reminder.

Moving House   Some removal firms will handle a loaded freezer cabinet, but this is only possible if the move does not involve overnight stops. If the move is to be a long one, use up the food stock and clean the cabinet. Follow normal preparation procedure for the cabinet before restocking with food.

If a removal can be completed in one day, food can be taken with it. Run stocks as low as possible, and put on the fast-freeze switch 24 hours before the move so that the food is very cold. Have the freezer loaded last and unloaded first, and see that there is a position and power point ready at the new house, and that the electricity supply is switched on.

Power Failure   If a power failure is indicated, follow a simple checking procedure. It is rare for anything to go wrong with a freezer motor, but it is a good idea to check ahead with the freezer supplier whether he has arrangements for storing or replacing food if it should happen. Normally, the loss of power is due to a fault in the house or to bad weather, and food in the freezer will last in good condition for at least 12 hours while the fault is remedied. It will keep better in a well-insulated cabinet full of food.

If failure does occur, check (a) has the switch been turned off by mistake? (b) has a fuse blown? (c) is the power failure general and has the Electricity Board been informed?

If the failure is due to none of these causes, contact the supplier or service engineer. Whatever the reason for the failure, do not touch the freezer motor, or open the lid or door.

When the power has been restored, check the condition of stored packages. Thawed food can be cooked and then refrozen. If in any doubt about the condition of the food, consider the type of food, the condition of the packaging, and the length of the breakdown, and discard any packs you are doubtful about.

If fruit, vegetables, pastry, bread and cake packs are only slightly soft, the packs can be refrozen, but the quality of the food will not be so good, and flavour and colour may suffer. These re-frozen packages should be used up quickly.

The door or lid of the freezer is best left closed for at least 2 hours after the power supply is restored.

Insurance The loss of food or breakdown of a freezer is not normally covered in household or comprehensive insurance policies, so a separate policy is needed.

This insurance policy will cover food against various kinds of loss, but not against the accidental switching off of the machine, nor against a power failure through industrial action. There may also be clauses concerning the installation of a warning light or bell. See page 15 above. Any freezer insurance policy must be carefully read.

In this connection it is important to see that the freezer plug is never removed for another appliance to be used. As I have said, the plug and switch should also be covered with adhesive tape to avoid accidental switching-off.

An insurance policy will ensure there is no loss of money spent on raw materials and packaging and of time spent in preparation. Only a small premium is usually required.

THE COST OF RUNNING A FREEZER

Many factors have to be taken into account when assessing the running costs of a freezer. In addition to the initial purchase and installation costs, allowance must be made for insurance, depreciation, running costs, and the actual cost of the food stored.

PURCHASE AND
INSTALLATION
COSTS

A larger freezer will initially be cheaper to purchase per cu. ft. as well as being cheaper to run. In addition to the purchase cost, allowance should be made if it is necessary for a special switch or a warning device to be installed.

In assessing costs, an accountant would also take into consideration the loss of interest on the capital used to buy the freezer and the first stock of food. One must also allow for the cost of insurance and of depreciation over the 'life' of the freezer, which is usually about 15 years.

FOOD COSTS
The greatest savings made with the freezer are in preserving one's own produce of various kinds: home-grown vegetables and fruit, home-reared poultry, family-caught fish and game, and home-baked foods, all of which cost time rather than money, give one big savings; the time spent would normally be reckoned as leisure rather than salaried time. However, allowance should be made for preparation time, and for the cost of special packaging or equipment such as a large mixer for cakes or a large blanching saucepan. Preparation time in particular is usually under-assessed when working out the cost of freezing; it may not be heavy in cost if it can be fitted into the normal household cooking routine, but it is expensive if whole extra days or evenings are spent in butchering meat or preparing vegetables and fruit. Some families would save more by purchasing already-frozen food.

When assessing the cost of commercially-packed food, it can be assumed that the average person consumes 4–5 lb. per week, which works out at three 300 lb. freezer loads in a year for a family of four. Taking into account electricity and general running costs, this can cost up to 5p (10 cents) per lb. for storage, so the freezer must save at least this amount per lb. to be worth while.

When working out costs, the cost of special bulk purchases such as meat must be carefully checked to allow for variations in quality and for wastage.

One should, however, remember that, even if the freezer does not actually reduce the cost of living, it usually raises the standard of the food eaten because greater attention is paid to purchasing; and of course the more expensive commercially-packed out-of-season foods can be balanced by inexpensive glut garden produce.

ELECTRICITY COSTS
The cost of running a freezer will be affected by the size of the cabinet, the warmth of the room in which the freezer stands, the number of times the cabinet is opened daily, and the length of time it is kept open. The amount of fresh food being frozen can also affect running costs, and the temperature of the food when it is put inside the freezer.

There is little difference in the cost of running an upright and a chest freezer. A little more cold air 'escapes' from an upright freezer, but this is negligible in running costs. The larger freezers are usually more economical to run than small ones, since the packages provide insulation. A larger freezer can be more economical to run, although unit costs may vary in different areas.

As a rough guide, a 6 cu. ft. freezer uses 0.3 kw per cu. ft. per 24 hours. 12 cu. ft. uses 0.25 kw in the same time; 18 cu. ft. uses 0.2 kw per cu. ft. in the same time. Put in the most simple terms, the usual estimate of running a freezer is to allow 2 units per cubic foot per week. This can be roughly translated into annual monetary terms by multiplying the number of units per cu. ft. used per week by the cubic capacity of the freezer. The resulting figure is the total amount of electricity used and the cost can easily be worked out from it.

The cost of running the fast-freeze switch is infinitesimal. It does not use any more electricity; it simply prevents the thermostat switching on and off, so the same amount of electricity is being used steadily. The overall cost of using the fast-freeze switch periodically is included in the usual estimate of running cost i.e. 2 units per cu. ft. per week.

Part II ORGANISING THE FREEZER

To make the best use of a freezer, it is important to assess the family's food needs before placing the initial orders. Every family will have its own special requirements and priorities: some may use the freezer mainly to save money on meat; others may only be interested in freezing home-grown vegetables and fruit; yet others may have little time or inclination to prepare their own food, but have money to spend on commercially frozen raw materials and cooked dishes. It is best to consider all the types of food which can be stored in the freezer, and to allocate space according to family needs.

TYPES OF FOOD TO FREEZE

(a) **Meat**. Many households want to save money by buying meat in bulk, usually beef, lamb, pork and poultry. Meats include also meat-based convenience foods which are quickly prepared, such as sausages or beefburgers, and offal and bacon.

(b) **Fish and Shellfish**. These are useful for preparing family main meals and for entertaining. They are usually bought ready-frozen and in smaller quantities than meat, and include quick-cooking convenience foods such as fish fingers and fishcakes. Include them in the space allocation for meat.

(c) **Dairy Produce**. Most dairy produce is bought fresh, but it is sensible to freeze surplus cheese from a party, one or two pots of thick cream, surplus egg yolks or whites, or cheap butter when available. Include these in the space allocation for prepared foods, as quantities are usually small.

(d) **Fruit and Vegetables**. These may be home-grown, market-bought in bulk, or commercially frozen. Packs may be an awkward shape so allow plenty of space.

(e) Prepared and Cooked Dishes. Pastry dishes, bread and cakes, ice cream, sandwiches, sauces, soups, puddings and cooked meat or fish dishes come into this category. Include, too, any leftovers to be used in further cooking, such as breadcrumbs, cooked rice or pasta.

PLANNING FREEZER CONTENTS

Family preferences are very important when planning the contents of a freezer, and it is also important to keep in stock a variety of foods to assist with menu-planning. The following points should be considered:

(a) The type of food which the family enjoys and which is eaten frequently. It is useless to take up freezer space with a glut of rhubarb, for instance, if nobody particularly likes it.

(b) The type of meal commonly eaten. Some families like a lot of pastry dishes which are worth freezing; others need plenty of cakes and sandwiches. Again, some families mainly use roasting and grilling cuts of meat while others need or enjoy plenty of the cheaper stewing cuts.

(c) The monthly or annual budget. An overall assessment of money spent on fresh food and groceries will indicate whether more money will be saved by buying meat in bulk, growing more vegetables, or home-baking cakes, puddings and pies.

(d) A monthly consumption of types of foods will enable major items to be fitted into the freezer in proportion to the space available.

(e) The variety of menus. Variety in menu-planning is one of the greatest benefits of the freezer, and this should be allowed for in deciding what foods to stock.

Space Allocation Plan A good general plan is to allow:—
> **Half the storage capacity:** Meat, Fish and Dairy Produce
> **Quarter of the storage capacity:** Fruit and Vegetables
> **Quarter of the storage capacity:** Prepared Dishes

Households with a large garden may want to use up to half the storage capacity for fruit and vegetables, cutting down on the space for meat, fish and dairy produce. A family who likes to entertain may find it convenient to use up to half the storage capacity for prepared dishes, again by cutting down on meat, fish and dairy produce storage. A country family will probably put most emphasis on home-grown fruit and vegetables, local poultry and fish, and a wide variety of baked goods for teatimes, picnics or packed meals and for family suppers. For a town family with little or no garden, the wife, who may be working, will be more interested in quick-cooking cuts of meat and fish, prepared dishes for quick meals, and more elaborate dishes for entertaining. In whatever way the space is to be allocated however, a rough division of the freezer storage capacity into quarters will allow calculations to be made so that the correct quantities of items such as meat can be ordered.

Often a frozen item such as fish or fruit is to be used in a recipe in place of
fresh raw material. Because commercially frozen products are specially
prepared, cleaned, and trimmed, there can be a considerable difference
in their weight compared to market-bought food, so it is useful to know
comparative weights when allocating freezer space:

	Weight of frozen fish	Comparable weight of market-bought fish
Cod	13 oz	1 lb. 12 oz
Haddock	13 oz	1 lb. 12 oz
Plaice	13 oz	1 lb. 10 oz
Kippers	7½ oz	1 lb. 7 oz
	Weight of frozen juice	Equivalent in fresh fruit
Orange	6 fl. oz	Juice of 12 oranges
Grapefruit	6¼ fl. oz	Juice of 6–8 grapefruit
	Weight of frozen vegetables	Comparable weight of market-bought vegetables
Peas	10 oz	1 lb. 12 oz
Broad Beans	10 oz	2½ lb.
Brussels Sprouts	10 oz	1 lb.
Sliced Green Beans	9 oz	1 lb.
Spinach	12 oz	1½ lb.

HIGH QUALITY STORAGE LIFE

It is important that food stored in the freezer should not remain static; a
good turnover should be maintained. Many foods can be stored for
months in the freezer, but if they are kept too long colour, flavour and
texture suffer. 'High Quality Storage Life' is the longest time food
should be stored so that it is still perfect in every way when used. Cooked
dishes in particular should be used within this storage time. Commercially-frozen packs should not be stored for longer than 3 months,
and ice cream is best stored for no longer than 1 month.

It is a waste of valuable freezer space to store food beyond the end of the
recommended storage life.

Remember that the wrong packaging material, bad packing and air
spaces in the packs will affect the keeping qualities of frozen food. Salt,
spices, herbs, onion and garlic flavours and fats also shorten the keeping
time of foods as well as affecting flavours.

	Item	High Quality Storage Life Number of Months
MEAT	Beef	12
	Ham and Bacon (whole)	3
	Ham and Bacon (sliced)	1
	Lamb	9
	Minced Beef	2
	Offal	2
	Pork	6
	Sausages and Sausage Meat	1
	Veal	9
POULTRY	Chicken	12
	Duck	6
	Giblets	3
	Goose	6
	Poultry Stuffing	1
	Turkey	6
GAME	Feathered Game	10
	Hare	6
	Rabbit	6
	Venison	12
FISH	Oily Fish (Herring, Mackerel, Salmon, Trout)	2
	Shellfish	1
	White Fish (Cod, Haddock, Plaice, Sole)	6
VEGETABLES	Asparagus	9
	Beans	12
	Brussels Sprouts	10
	Carrots	10
	Fresh Herbs	10
	Part-Fried Chips	4
	Peas	12
	Spinach	12
	Tomatoes	6
FRUIT	Apricots	6
	Cherries	7
	Currants	10

Item	High Quality Storage Life Number of Months
Fruit Juices	9
Fruit Purées	5
Gooseberries	10
Melon	9
Peaches	6
Plums	6
Raspberries	12
Rhubarb	12
Strawberries	12

DAIRY PRODUCE		
	Double Cream	6
	Eggs	12
	Fresh Butter	6
	Hard Cheese	3
	Ice Cream	3
	Salted Butter	3
	Soft Cheese	6

BAKERY GOODS		
	Baked Bread, Rolls and Buns	2
	Breadcrumbs	3
	Danish Pastry	1
	Decorated Cakes	3
	Fried Bread Shapes	1
	Fruit Pies	6
	Meat Pies	3
	Pancakes (unfilled)	2
	Pastry Cases	3
	Pizza	1
	Plain Cakes	6
	Sandwiches	2
	Savoury Flans	2
	Unbaked Biscuits	4
	Unbaked Bread, Rolls and Buns	2
	Unbaked Cakes	2
	Unbaked Pastry	3

COOKED DISHES		
	Casseroles and Stews	2
	Curry	2
	Filled Pancakes	1
	Fish Dishes	2
	Meat in Sauce	2
	Meat Loaf	1

Item	High Quality Storage Life Number of Months
Pâté	1
Roast Meat	1
Sauces	2
Soufflés and Mousses	2
Soup	2
Sponge Puddings	3
Stock	2

PACKAGING AND PACKING MATERIALS

Correct packaging is very important in preparing food for the freezer. The packaging must protect the food from drying out, from air which will cause deterioration, and from the crossing of smells and flavours. In addition, the packaging material must be easy to handle, must not be liable to split, burst or leak, and must withstand the low temperature at which the freezer is maintained.

Good packaging materials must therefore be (a) moisture-vapour-proof (b) waterproof (c) greaseproof (d) smell-free (e) durable (f) easily handled (g) economically stored (h) resistant to low temperatures.

It is important to buy only such materials as have been tested and proved satisfactory in a freezer. Basic packaging comes in the form of sheet wrappings, bags, waxed and plastic boxes, and should be complete with sealing tape, twist-ties and labels which will withstand low temperatures.

IMPROVISED PACKAGING It is possible to use many everyday containers such as plastic boxes, glass jars, discarded grocery packs and ice cream packs if they have been tested under freezer conditions and proved satisfactory. They must of course be completely clean, and conform to the general requirements listed above.

PACKAGING; STORAGE AND CLEANING Packaging items must be stored carefully. They should be stacked in a dry pest-proof place, preferably packed in polythene to exclude dust. Most items can be washed, dried and stored in sterile condition for future use. Boiling water should not be used for washing; it is better to use a sterile solution such as that used for sterilising babies' bottles. Bags and boxes to be re-used should be carefully examined for punctures, tears or fractures before packing.

Packing Materials The choice may be made from wrappings and containers made from foil, polythene and waxed materials.

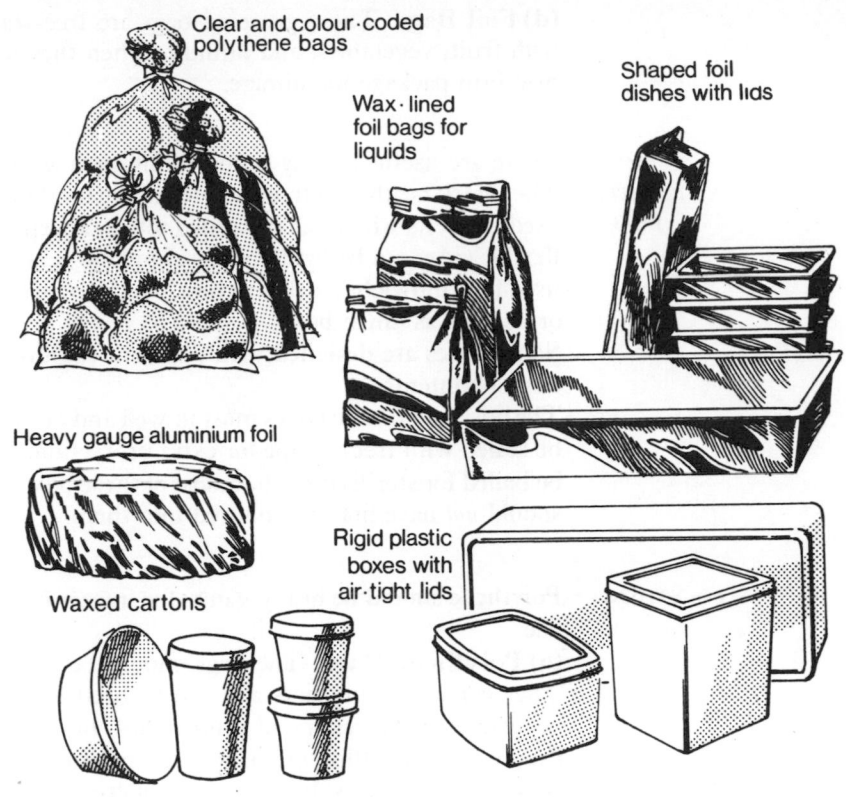

Clear and colour·coded
polythene bags

Wax·lined
foil bags for
liquids

Shaped foil
dishes with lids

Heavy gauge aluminium foil

Waxed cartons

Rigid plastic
boxes with
air·tight lids

FOIL   Foil is one of the most useful wrappings for the freezer. If used carefully,
it can be cleaned and used again. Food can often also be cooked in the
same foil used for freezer storage.

(a) **Sheet Foil.** Heavy-duty foil specially made for freezer use is
useful for wrapping awkward parcels of food, for meat and poultry
(especially with projecting bones) and for cakes. It can also be used to
make lids for containers. Ordinary household foil should be used double
thickness. Foil should be wrapped thickly round bone ends to prevent
puncturing of other containers.

(b) **Foil Trays, Dishes and Pie Plates.** Pie and pudding dishes,
patty pans and compartmented trays for freezing whole meals are all
obtainable. The food can be cooked in these dishes, then covered with a
foil lid or over-wrapped in polythene or freezer paper for storage.

(c) **Foil Deep Dishes.** Deep containers are useful for cooked dishes
such as casseroles or shepherd's pie. These are obtainable with their own
lids, so that the food can be prepared and packed in one dish, which is
also used for heating the meal for serving. These are made in many sizes,
from individual portion sizes up to sizes suitable for large families or for
entertaining.

(d) Foil Bags. These gusseted bags are free-standing, and easy to fill with fruit, vegetables, and liquids. When they are closed, they make a neat firm package for storage.

RIGID
PLASTIC
BOXES

These are useful for any liquid items such as soup and fruit in syrup. They stack neatly in a freezer, and can be used many times. They can be used for stews which can be turned into a saucepan for thawing, since the flexible sides can be lightly pressed to help removal. If plastic boxes are used for sandwiches, cakes or pies, they can be taken straight to a picnic or be used as lunch boxes.

Some boxes are designed with different coloured lids to aid identification of contents.

The lids of all plastic boxes must fit well and be airtight. The lids can also be sealed with freezer tape for extra protection. Some freezer boxes can be boiled for sterilisation, but most of these boxes cannot stand heat, and should *not* have hot food poured into them.

POLYTHENE

Polythene should be heavy-gauge for freezer use. It is cheap and easy to use.

(a) Polythene Bags. The bags should be gusseted for easy packing. They come in many sizes and can be used for meat, poultry, fruit and vegetables, pies, cakes and sandwiches, but should be overwrapped if they will be handled often, to prevent tearing. Strong-smelling food should also be overwrapped to prevent cross-contamination. Bags can be sealed with heat or a twist fastening, and air must be excluded.

(b) Polythene Sheeting. This sheeting is useful for wrapping meat, poultry and large cakes or pies, but it must be sealed with freezer tape. Sheeting can also be used for dividing small pieces of meat, fish, cakes etc. to be stored in solid containers.

WAXED
CONTAINERS

These were originally used a great deal for freezer storage, but are being superseded by plastic boxes. They are useful for fruit and for liquids, but they stain and hold smells, and are not always easy to use a second time. Tubs with screwtops have been discontinued; flush airtight lids are used. Square and rectangular boxes with fitted lids can be used for asparagus, carved meat, and fruit. Tall containers with tuck-in lids are useful for free-flowing fruit and vegetables, and stack well in the freezer. Food which may leak can be packed in waxed cartons with polythene liners.

FREEZER PAPER

This strong puncture-proof paper is available packed on rolls with a dispensing box and metal tearing edge. It does not become brittle in the freezer, and is highly resistant to fats and grease. The paper strips off easily when the food is frozen or thawed. Freezer paper is particularly useful for meat and poultry. It has a coated inner surface, but the uncoated outer surface can be written upon.

FREEZER ACCESSORIES

(a) **Labels.** These should be special labels made for freezer use, stuck on with gum which is resistant to low temperatures; tie-on labels may get torn off during storage. Different coloured labels can be used to aid rapid identification of foods.

(b) **Felt-Tip Pens.** This type of ink does not fade in the freezer. A Chinagraph pencil can be used if preferred, or a wax crayon.

(c) **Bag Fasteners** made of covered wire can be used to give a simple closure to polythene bags. Some are combined with labels.

(d) **Freezer Tape.** A number of types of freezer tape are available, all treated with special gum which is resistant to low temperatures so that there is no loosening or curling.

GLASS JARS

Screw-topped preserving jars, bottles and honey jars can all be used for the freezer but must be tested first. The empty jar should be packed into a polythene bag and frozen overnight; if the jar breaks, the pieces will be held in the bag. Glass jars should not be filled to the brim; headspace must be allowed when packing the food in them, to allow for contents which may expand and break the jar. They can be used for soups and stews; if the food is likely to be needed in a hurry, it should be packed into jars without 'shoulders', so that the contents will slip out easily when still only partly thawed.

Packing the Food   Besides choosing 'freezable' packaging, make sure that the method of packing is suitable for any particular food, and for the type of freezer. Most food can be packed in a number of alternative ways. A cake can be packed in a rigid plastic box, in a polythene bag or sheeting, in sheet foil or freezer paper. In an upright freezer with shelves, a bag or sheet wrapping is adequate as the cake can be easily stored without crushing; in a chest freezer, a rigid box is preferable. Experience will soon show which packaging is most suitable for any particular food, for the housekeeping budget and storage conditions.

Suitable Packing Materials   The most commonly-used packaging materials for various types of food are tabulated overleaf.

PORTIONS

Food for the freezer should always be packaged in usable portions. It is important to decide in advance when each item is likely to be used, for what type of meal and for how many people. Some people need many one-person portions; others need portions packed for serving three or four people; still others need bulk packs for large families or staff. Sometimes a mixture of package sizes is needed; for instance, a housewife may need single portions for her own lunch or a baby's meal, while needing larger packages for family use and entertaining.

LOOSE PACKING

Fruit and vegetables can be frozen individually, then poured into a container. This means that large packs can be stored, but a small quantity can be shaken out for use without having to chop up a frozen

31

The most usual packagings for various foods are indicated thus ★

Food	Waxed or rigid plastic containers	Foil containers	Foil sheeting	Polythene bags or sheeting
Fresh Meat			★	★
Fresh Poultry and Game			★	★
Fresh Fish			★	★
Cooked Meat and Fish Dishes	★	★	★	★
Fresh Vegetables	★			★
Fresh Vegetables (brine pack)	★			
Fresh Fruit (unsweetened or dry sugar pack)	★			★
Fresh Fruit (syrup pack)	★			
Butter, Margarine and Fats		★	★	★
Cheese			★	★
Milk and Cream	★			
Eggs	★	★		
Soups and Sauces	★	★	★	★
Bread, Cakes and Biscuits			★	★
Pastry and Pies		★	★	★
Desserts	★	★	★	★
Ice Cream	★		★	

A two-section freezer, tidily packed to save wasting space, with food for a big party.

Foil-wrapping of a stuffed fish for storage; behind, casserole-packed frozen fish steaks after thawing and cooking.

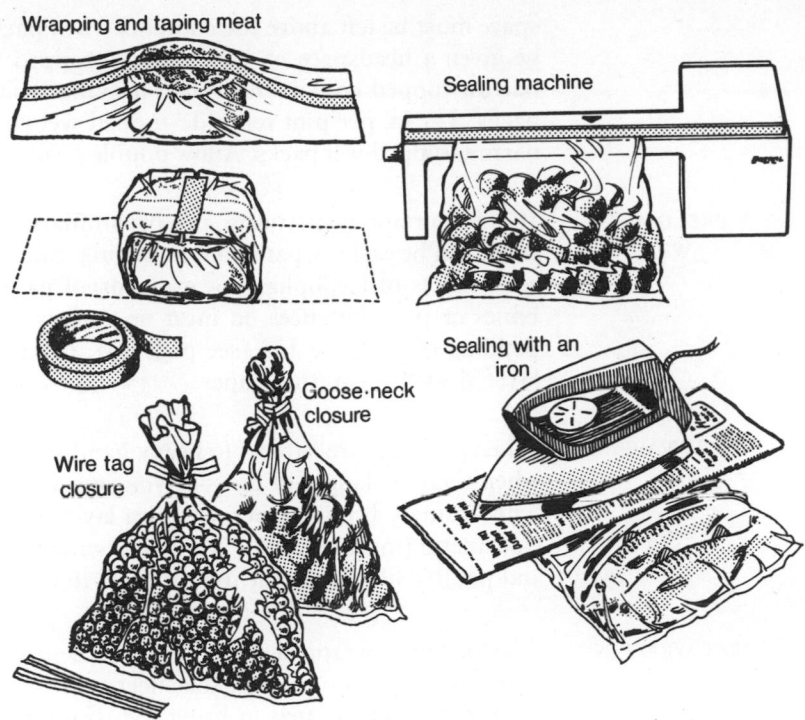

Wrapping and taping meat

Sealing machine

Sealing with an iron

Goose-neck closure

Wire tag closure

block or thaw a large quantity. This is done by freezing the fruit or vegetables uncovered on a metal or plastic sheet on the floor of the freezer or in the fast-freeze compartment, before putting them into containers or bags. Some freezers have a special freezing shelf for this type of fast-freezing. Iced cakes and fragile pies or flans are also usefully frozen by this method so that they become solid before packing and do not crush.

EXCLUDING AIR Whether food is frozen on trays and then packed, or packaged before freezing, it is most important to exclude air from all packages. Air pockets *must* be eliminated to prevent deterioration of the contents. Air is most easily pressed out of soft packages with the hands. Air pockets in cartons can usually be released by plunging a knife into the contents two or three times. We used to remove air from bags by inserting a drinking straw, holding the closing tightly and sucking out air until the package held close to the food, but this is now considered to be unhygienic, and a special pump can be used instead. Air can also be excluded by immersing the bag almost up to its neck in a bucket of cold water. The weight of the water forces all the air out, giving a vacuum-type result. The bag must be thoroughly dried before freezing.

HEADSPACE Liquids expand when frozen, and if cartons are packed to the lid, the result will be that the lid will be forced off in the freezer. Liquids such as soup and fruit in syrup are particularly affected by this problem, and a space must be left above the contents when packing them. Soup should be given a headspace of $\frac{1}{2}$ in. in wide-topped containers, and $\frac{3}{4}$ in. in narrow-topped containers. When packing fruit, allow $\frac{1}{2}$ in. for all dry packs; $\frac{1}{2}$–1 in. per pint for wide-topped wet packs; $\frac{3}{4}$–1 in. per pint for narrow-topped wet packs. Allow double headspace for quart containers.

PRELIMINARY
WRAPPING
It is important to attend to any preliminary wrapping of food so that items can be easily separated for thawing. Sliced meat should be layered with sheets of Cellophane or greaseproof paper to separate the slices; bones or protuberances on meat or poultry should be covered with a padding of paper or foil (see page 29); cakes without icing should be layered with separating paper.

OVERWRAPPING
When packages are subject to heavy handling and possible puncture, or when there is danger of cross-flavouring, they should be overwrapped with ordinary brown paper, an extra layer of foil or polythene, or with stockinette (mutton cloth). An inside wrapping of stockinette on meat and poultry helps prevent freezer burn during long storage.

SHEET WRAPPING
The food to be wrapped should be in the centre of the sheet of packaging material. Draw two sides of the sheet together above the food and fold them neatly downwards to bring the wrappings as close to the food as possible. Seal this fold, then fold ends like a parcel to make them close and tight, excluding air. Seal all folds and overwrap if necessary. This is sometimes called the 'druggist's wrap' or 'chemist's wrap'.

BAG WRAPPING
Bags must be completely open before filling, and food must go down into corners, leaving no air pockets. A funnel is useful to avoid mess at the top of the bag. Bags can be sealed by heat or twist closing. For easier handling and storage, bags may be placed in other rigid containers for filling and freezing, then removed in a more compact form.

HEAT SEALING
Polythene bags may be sealed by applying heat. This can be done with a special sealing iron or machine, but can also be handled with a domestic iron. When using a domestic iron, a thin strip of brown paper should be placed between the iron and the top of the polythene bag. It is important that all air should be excluded before sealing. Heat sealing gives a neat package which can be stored easily.

TWIST TYING
All air should be extracted from the bag, and then a plastic-covered fastener twisted round the end of the bag. The top of the bag should then be turned down over this twist, and the fastener twisted again round the bunched neck of the bag. This gives a neat parcel, and ensures an air-tight seal. It is sometimes known as a 'goose-neck closing'. Rubber bands are not recommended for this type of closing, as they perish at freezer temperatures.

TAPE SEALING	Special freezer tape must be used. It should be applied to all containers with lids which do not have a special airtight seal, and to sheet-wrapped items. Tape should join the lid and container on cartons and plastic boxes, with an additional piece of tape over the lid to reach down the sides. On sheet-wrapped items, all folds must be taped so that all air is excluded.	
BRICK FREEZING	When a large quantity of liquid such as stock or soup has to be frozen, freezer space can be wasted by using irregularly shaped containers. It is most practical to freeze this type of liquid in 'brick' form. The liquid can be poured into loaf tins of a convenient size, frozen, removed from the containers, and wrapped in freezer foil or polythene for easy storage.	
ICE CUBE FREEZING	The same method can be used for freezing small quantities of liquid such as concentrated soups, sauces, fruit and vegetable purées, leftover tea and coffee, herbs, syrups and juices. The liquid should be poured into the ice cube trays and frozen without covering. Each cube should then be wrapped in foil and packed in quantities in a polythene bag for easy storage. The cubes can also be sprayed with soda water and packed in bulk, and will not stick together. Each cube will generally be enough for a single serving of the food.	

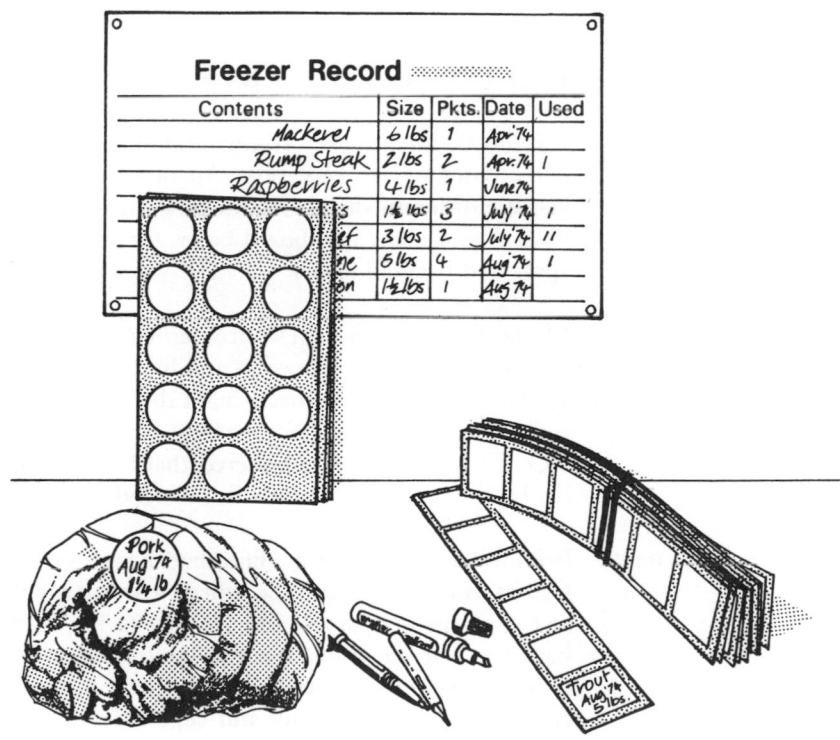

Freezer Record

Contents	Size	Pkts.	Date	Used
Mackerel	6 lbs	1	Apr'74	
Rump Steak	2 lbs	2	Apr'74	1
Raspberries	4 lbs	1	June74	
	1½ lbs	3	July'74	1
	3 lbs	2	July'74	11
	5 lbs	4	Aug'74	1
	1½ lbs	1	Aug'74	

LABELLING AND RECORDING

Labelling and Recording   All items in the freezer should be labelled carefully, as many frozen items look alike after storage, particularly meat. Label with the name of the food, size of package in portions or by weight, and date of freezing. If possible include the date by which food should be eaten. (See 'High quality storage life', page 25.) Add details of additional seasonings or other ingredients which must be added for serving, and of any planned accompaniments.

Labels must be written in felt pen, wax crayon or Chinagraph pencil, as other types of pen or pencil fade in the freezer. Labels can be written on tie-labels (which save additional closing wires), on labels treated with special adhesive which will stand sub-zero temperatures, or on paper tucked into transparent packages. It is easier to put stick-on labels on a package before filling it with food.

RECORDING

It is difficult to remember to keep records of food in the freezer, but it is essential to maintain some sort of record so that food is used in rotation while it is still of high quality. A plastic shopping list which can be wiped clean is easy to use. A book or card index is more difficult to maintain regularly. Record the food frozen, the number and size of packages, the date of freezing, the date by which food should be eaten, and the number of packets removed.

KEEPING THE FREEZER TIDY

It is much easier to use a freezer and maintain a regular turnover of food if the contents are kept tidy. An upright freezer is easier to organise because different shelves or drawers can be used for the various types of food. Avoid using cardboard boxes for storage as these take up a lot of space and become messy.

BASKETS AND
DIVIDERS

Plastic-covered wire mesh freezer baskets are available for hanging across the top of chest freezers and for use for stacking. Dividers are also available. This means that a main division can be made between meat and vegetables, for instance, or between raw materials and cooked foods. NOTE: It must be remembered that baskets can be heavy to lift from the bottom of freezers when full of food.

BAGS

Brightly-coloured mesh shopping bags are useful for keeping the freezer tidy. They can be filled with bag-wrapped food and with awkward-shaped parcels and are easy to lift. Large coloured polythene bags can also be used, but the contents are less easy to distinguish. Different colours of mesh or polythene bags can be used to identify types of food, such as fruit and vegetables.

COLOUR CODING   Identification of food can be greatly aided by using distinguishing colours. Bags, batching bags, labels and rigid boxes are available in six colours, so that one can identify different groups of foods e.g. meat, vegetables, fruit; or a distinction can be made between different types of one food e.g. carrots, peas, beans.

Part III BULK BUYING AND BULK COOKING

BULK BUYING

Most people assume that buying in bulk will lead to a considerable saving in the family budget. Savings depend however on the number of people in the family, shopping and eating habits and the accessibility of shops. Freezer owners in fact find that they save on such hidden factors as public transport fares, or petrol and parking charges for cars, and they save a great deal of shopping time (which represents money). They also find that, although their overall shopping bills may remain the same, they tend to live better, since the price of better cuts of meat or out-of-season vegetables is balanced by freezing cheaper meat or home produce.

FACTORS AFFECTING BULK BUYING

It is a mistake to buy in bulk with price as the only consideration. This can result in poor quality food. For instance a cheap bag of prawns will probably have come from warmer waters and be tasteless compared with cold-water prawns from Greenland or Norway which are initially more expensive. In fact, the customer usually gets exactly what he pays for, and quality rarely combines with cheapness. When choosing a source of supply for buying food in bulk, therefore, it is worth considering the quality of the food, the service offered and the amount of food to be bought at one time.

It is also important to know the storage capacity of the freezer, and to judge how much space will be taken up by bulk purchases. About 20 lb. of frozen food will fit into 1 cu. ft. but a lot depends on the packaging and the shape of the food packages stored.

Some consideration must also be given to high quality storage life. There is little point in buying a gross of fish fingers for instance, if the family cannot eat these up within three months, as quality, flavour and texture deteriorate when the recommended storage life is exceeded.

HOW TO BUY IN BULK

(a) Check on savings of time or money. Before making out bulk orders, check how the family money is spent and where the greatest savings can be made. Some bulk purchases, such as meat, save money. Other purchases, such as bread, save time. Some families hate spending time on shopping or cooking; so these factors should be considered when choosing the types of food to buy in bulk.

(b) Check on quality. Test small quantities of food before placing a large order. It is expensive, in the long run, if a bulk order of four dozen meat pies turns out to be unpopular with the family after one has been eaten. The remaining pies will take up valuable freezer space, and may put the whole family off this type of frozen food for keeps; little is lost by trying an individual item first.

Cheapness can also mean poor quality, so study order lists carefully. There may be half-a-dozen varieties of garden peas, for instance, and what looks like good value on paper can turn out to be very poor value indeed if the quality is low; much of the food may be wasted.

(c) Check on packaging. See that bulk food is properly packed for long-term storage. Food originally prepared for commercial and rapid use may come simply packed in cardboard boxes, or be slung into a polythene bag. A 7-lb. slab of pastry or 10 lb. minced meat clinging together in an enormous lump will be almost useless under home conditions. Be prepared to re-pack large purchases in usable quantities, as soon as the food is purchased. Check also whether it will be more convenient and cheaper in the long run to buy a bulk quantity of individual or family-size portions rather than enormous packs which are difficult to handle and store.

WHERE TO BUY IN BULK

(a) Delivery Services. Some frozen food manufacturers and some freezer centres deliver in bulk to the door. This is a convenient way of ordering food since it can be transferred straight from the refrigerated van to storage, and it is particularly useful in country areas. A minimum order is normally stipulated, and it is worth preparing a bulk order with friends to make the delivery a worthwhile business. Sample small quantities of items which have not been bought before, and check delivery lists carefully to see that the order has been properly filled.

(b) Frozen Food Centres. These are found in many towns, and are useful for buying a wide variety of foods in both family and commercial pack sizes. They are useful places for trying new items before placing bulk orders, and the customer has the advantage of seeing and comparing the types of food. Try to choose a centre which is near a good parking space, and from which food can be taken home quickly. It is better to stick to reputable shops where the turnover is quick and the storage conditions are good. Some centres buy mainly on price and quality may be poor. Try to find the best shopping day for freezer centres when they take their main deliveries. It is not always a good idea to shop at a freezer centre on a Friday or Saturday, when most other people are shopping; stocks of popular items may be low, so that a planned list cannot be completely filled and valuable shopping time is wasted. Check also on highly seasonal items, particularly fruit. Popular fruits such as redcurrants and raspberries tend to be in short supply after a while, so if the family likes them, stock up in the summer when first supplies come in, since these fruits have a long storage life.

(c) Specialist Producers. Meat in particular is sold by specialist producers, either frozen or prepared for freezing. Such firms operate delivery services or express postal services, or food can be collected. The quality is usually high.

(d) Local Shops, Markets and Farms. Local shops and markets can usually supply fruit by the case and vegetables by the sack at reduced rates, as can local growers. A check should be kept on quality, as food may remain in shops for some days before sale. It is not a good idea to buy in this way if time is short, as there is a lot of labour involved in preparing a sack of vegetables for the freezer. Farmers often supply vegetables, fruit, meat or poultry, and fruit or vegetables are often very cheap if picked by the customer. Fish and shellfish are worth buying direct from the boat or from a seaside shop which has daily supplies. Home-baked bread, cakes and pies can often be obtained from local shops, W.I. stalls, etc. and some housewives undertake bulk cooking for the freezer.

WHAT TO BUY IN BULK

What to Buy in Bulk All types of food can be bought in bulk, but there is skill in choosing foods which the family will like and eat in quantity, and in balancing the quantities and types of food to be stored. Some savings may be in time, while other savings will be directly financial.

BREAD AND CAKES Considerable time is saved by buying baked goods in bulk. This is an opportunity to buy crusty loaves; bread made from special flours; rolls and baps; sliced loaves for sandwiches and toast; buns; crumpets; malt and fruit loaves and cakes.

CONVENIENCE FOODS Food which has been prepared to save cooking and serving time is useful for quick meals, and particularly for in-between meals such as high tea for children which may not be required for the whole family. There are considerable savings in bulk packs of beefburgers, fish fingers, fish-cakes, sausages, and thin cuts of meat and fish. Check the different kinds for variations in flavour and texture to see which are most popular with the family.

PREPARED DISHES
Prepared pies, casseroles, puddings and gourmet dishes are useful for families which have little time for cooking. They should be bought in sizes most convenient for family use or for entertaining. Party dishes which need elaborate ingredients or lengthy cooking time are also useful. It is a good idea to buy small sizes first to see if they are acceptable.

FRUIT AND VEGETABLES
Farm or market produce can be home-frozen but takes time for preparation. It may be more useful to buy commercially-frozen fruit and vegetables in large packs. Particularly useful are such items as chips, mushrooms, green and red peppers, onions and mixed casserole vegetables. These are all in constant use in the kitchen, but are not always on hand in an accessible shop; nor are they particularly easy to prepare for freezing at home. Small quantities for recipe use can be shaken out of loose-packed commercial bags.

ICE CREAM
Ice cream in bulk containers is useful for a family of children. The quality soon deteriorates if a container is frequently opened and 'scooped', and the product has a relatively short high quality storage life. So it may be more practical to buy bulk supplies of smaller packs, or of individual ices such as lollies and chocolate bars which are easy to serve and have a longer storage life.

POULTRY
Whole birds and poultry pieces are very useful for adding variety to family menus, and prices are usually reasonable. They are very useful for converting into cooked dishes for the freezer for both family use and entertaining. Some farms and shops prepare free-range birds in quantity for home-freezing; others supply commercially-frozen poultry in bulk. It is best to pack giblets and livers separately in bulk for the freezer, as they do not store well inside birds, and are useful on their own for many recipes.

MEAT
Meat is usually the most expensive item in the family budget, and is one of the most useful raw materials to buy in bulk. Bulk meat needs careful buying, and it is worth studying the problems before making an expensive purchase.
It is usually most practical to buy enough meat for the family's needs for three months, which is a reasonable turnover time and about the cheapest length of time to store the meat, allowing for the running costs of a freezer. It is a great mistake to purchase a quarter of beef, a pig and a lamb all at the same time, as novice freezer-owners tend to do. This overloads the freezer at the expense of other items, and pork in particular may deteriorate if kept beyond the recommended high quality storage

41

life period. It is better to combine with one or two other families to get the advantage of bulk purchase with a variety of types of meat and different cuts.

Whole carcasses are ideal for those who will cook and eat cheaper cuts. Otherwise these will be wasted, and the roasting and grilling cuts will prove more expensive in the end. If a family only likes the better cuts, it is better to make a bulk purchase of these, or to buy a good variety pack of different meats. There will not be much financial saving, but there will be shopping convenience and no wastage. In bulk carcass buying, there may be considerable wastage in bones and suet; prices must be checked carefully to be sure the actual price of the meat used is not in excess of that quoted by the supplier.

Many experts do not recommend the home-freezing of meat at all. This is because meat must be frozen very quickly to retain its high quality, and commercial blast-freezing techniques give better results. If you do freeze meat at home, it is important to set the freezer correctly and only to freeze the recommended quantities at one time, and to label meat very carefully with the name of the cut and its possible uses. It is often better to choose the meat and have it frozen by the supplier. This does not apply, of course, to home-killed meat, or home-caught game and fish such as pheasants and salmon.

When buying meat, choose good quality, and see that it has been properly hung. See also that a list is made of all the cuts in the order and their possible uses (see FREEZING PROCESSES: MEAT), and also that they are packed in usable quantities. Get the meat properly prepared in the form in which it is wanted, either joints, steaks, casserole meat or mince. These specific points on our four principle meats are worth noting:—

(a) **Beef** is a really bulky purchase. A forequarter will account for about 100 lb. and a hindquarter is even larger. The forequarter is more manageable, but consists mainly of slow-cooking cuts. Boned joints take up far less space in the freezer. The bones will account for about one-quarter of a bulk purchase, but can be made into concentrated stock for freezing (the butcher should be asked to saw them in reasonable pieces for the saucepan). Suet can be used for a wide variety of puddings, and can also be rendered down for fat. Check whether bones and suet are included in the overall price and if they will be delivered with the meat. Have the slow-cooking meat cut into slices and/or cubes for easy use, and ask for plenty of lean mince in 1 lb. packs which are very useful. Try to convert some of the cuts straight into pies or casseroles when they are delivered; this will save freezer space and provide some useful meals for quick use.

(b) **Veal** is not very often available in bulk, and is not very successful in the freezer, since it tends to lose flavour in storage conditions. If veal is bought, see that it is carefully divided into prepared boned roasting joints, escalopes and chops, and pie veal, etc. Remember that some veal bones, e.g. breast tendrons, are a delicacy.

(c) Lamb is worth buying. A small lean one will weigh 25–30 lb. with little waste. Decide if you want chops in roasting joints or divided. If the cheaper chops and breast of lamb are not liked, it may be better value simply to buy roasting joints and bags of chops.

(d) Pork has a shorter storage life than other meats and should not be purchased in over-large quantities. Half a pig will weigh about 50 lb. and consists mostly of roasting and frying joints. The head and trotters may be included, but freezer space should not be wasted on them. They are better used at once in brawn or a dish which requires meat jelly.

BULK COOKING

It can be all too easy to become a slave to the freezer, endlessly shopping and cooking to keep the white box topped up. It is important to take advantage of the fact that this is the only way of safely preserving cooked dishes. Cooking should be organised ahead so that two or three ready meals are always 'in hand' in the freezer. The great thing is to avoid inflicting the same kind of food on the family for weeks ahead, so new bulk purchases should be slightly different from the one recently made, and the cooked dishes used to vary those already in hand.

One of the greatest advantages of bulk cooking is that quantities of raw materials, such as bulk-bought meat, can be converted into cooked dishes as soon as they have been bought, saving considerable space. Stewing steak, for instance, can be made into casseroles and pies; mince can be converted into individual pies and shepherd's pies; chicken pieces can be used with a whole variety of sauces; offal can be made into casseroles and pate.

For most people, it is best to double or treble quantities of such dishes as casseroles, using one immediately and saving the other portions for future use with added seasonings. Batch-baking is also sensible, to take full advantage of oven heat. It takes little more effort to make two cakes instead of one, or five dozen scones instead of one dozen. The same goes for pâtés, ice creams etc. (See DINNER PARTY MENU 3, page 230.)

THE RIGHT EQUIPMENT

It pays to have the right-sized equipment and one or two labour-saving machines to use in conjunction with the freezer. Normal household equipment may not be suitable for bulk cooking.

(a) Large saucepans are useful not only for making stock, but for blanching vegetables, preparing fruit and meat. A large flat pan is useful for cooking ingredients in fat at the first stages of many recipes.

(b) Large casseroles are another essential. At least one 6–8 pint size is needed for bulk cooking, or a large double roaster.

(c) A pressure cooker speeds up the cooking of meat and poultry in particular. It can also double as an ordinary large pan.

(d) An electric mixer with attachments is invaluable in cooking for the freezer. The mixer itself is useful for making all types of cakes, and for beating ice cream and whipping up puddings. The blender attachment, or an independent blender, is useful for soups, purées and sauces. A mincer attachment aids the making of mince and sausages from bulk-bought meat, and speeds up pâté-making. A slicing attachment is handy for preparing vegetables, and a dough-hook is useful for yeast doughs for bread, buns and pizza.

An adequate oven is necessary to take batch-baking, etc. If a new one is being purchased, see that there is plenty of oven space, and if possible buy a cooker with a fan-assisted oven. This ensures that heat is circulated and a steady baking temperature is maintained throughout the oven. Cooks who have an Aga or similar stove with two ovens are fortunate, as different types of dishes can be cooked at the same time.

What to Cook for Freezing   Before cooking foods for freezing, it is wise to assess which items are worth freezer space. Briefly, these are:

(a) Dishes which need long cooking or long and tedious preparation.
(b) Dishes made from seasonal foods.
(c) Dishes which can be made in large quantities with little more work (i.e. three cakes instead of one; double or treble casseroles).
(d) Dishes for special occasions, such as parties or holidays.
(e) Convenience foods for invalids, small children, unexpected illness.

Part IV FREEZING PROCESSES

STORAGE TEMPERATURES

Commercial food freezing takes place at $-34°C$ ($-30°F$), and the food is stored commercially at $-29°C$ ($-20°F$). This is the temperature to which a home freezer can be adjusted to cope with freezing fresh food. For storage in a home freezer, the normal running temperature should be $-18°C$ ($0°F$). Above this temperature, frozen food will only keep for a limited time i.e. up to three months in a three-star storage compartment ($-18°C$ or $0°F$); up to one month in a two-star storage compartment ($-12°C$ or $10°F$); up to one week in a one-star storage compartment ($-6°C$ or $21°F$).

At $-40°C$ ($-40°F$) there is no loss of nutrients in frozen food. At $-23°C$ ($-10°F$) the loss is negligible. At $-12°C$ ($10°F$) or higher, the loss is accelerated, and rancidity and off-flavours can set in.

It is important that the correct temperatures for home-freezing and for storage of frozen food are observed, and a thermometer should be used in a home freezer, and checked regularly.

The Fast-Freeze Switch   As stated, most freezers are now fitted with a special freezing compartment with its own control switch. This may be called fast-freeze or super-freeze, or some other name, but it simply means that the use of this switch will override the thermostat. At normal setting, the freezer is designed to cut out at a temperature which will ensure that the food stored in it is all at, or below, the temperature of $-18°C$ ($0°F$). This is the best setting for long term storage to ensure that the food remains in perfect condition. By using the special control, the thermostat is prevented from cutting out at this temperature so the freezer goes on working and the temperature continues to fall. It does not freeze faster, but allows the temperature to go on dropping so that the newly-introduced food can itself become solidly frozen without raising the temperature of the food already there.

Instructions are given in the manufacturer's booklet with each freezer, and the time for setting the control before freezing varies between 2–5 hours. Packages should be loosely spread out in the fast-freeze compartment during the freezing process. It is impossible to give a definite time for the freezing process, as it depends on the size, shape and thickness of the packages and their contents. Dishes with a high sugar content, such as mincemeat or fruit in syrup, take longer to freeze solid than a thin portion of meat. Once each packet is frozen solid, it may be removed to the storage compartment of the freezer and stacked with already frozen food. As soon as all packages in one batch of food are solidly frozen, the control switch may be returned to normal setting.

SMALL
QUANTITIES OF
FOOD

Many people hesitate to use the fast-freeze switch for small items as they feel this is expensive. There is no health risk involved if the switch is not used for a small quantity of food, although the texture may be less than perfect. It is not absolutely essential to use the switch for small amounts up to 1 lb. weight when frozen individually. If a large proportion of fresh food at normal room temperature is introduced into the freezer (perhaps the normal 1/10th of total capacity), this will affect the temperature of the food already in the freezer. It is wise to use the freezer control switch, and although it is not really necessary for small packages, it is probably advisable.

GENERAL
FREEZING
PROCEDURE FOR
FAST FREEZING

(a) Adjust fast-freeze switch or freezer control for recommended time before freezing begins.
(b) Check that the quantity of food to be frozen will not overload the freezing capacity of the cabinet (generally 1/10th of total capacity may be frozen).
(c) Place packs to be frozen against the wall or floor of the freezer, not against already frozen packs.
(d) Leave food to freeze solid, which may take up to 24 hours.
(e) Stack packages among already frozen food.
(f) Return switch to normal working temperature.

BASIC FREEZING RULES

Choose quality

High-quality food with good flavour will repay freezing. Poor food will not magically improve when frozen and stored, and it is important to choose food for its quality rather than for its cheapness. Time has to be spent in preparing food for freezing, and packaging and freezer space costs money, so that good food should be chosen which keeps its quality, flavour and nutritive value.

Check quantities
Be sure to check the quantity of fresh food which may be frozen at any one time; generally, this is about one-tenth of the freezer's total capacity during 24 hours. If you overload the freezer with fresh food, it will not freeze quickly and well. At the same time, the temperature of the already-frozen food stored in the cabinet will be affected, which can lead to a deterioration in flavour, texture and colour. Generally, the danger of overloading occurs when large quantities of meat are purchased, or when there is a glut of fruit and vegetables.

Work cleanly
Hygiene is very important in a kitchen where food is being prepared for freezing. Clean utensils and a cool atmosphere are vital, and packaging materials must be clean. Only small amounts of food should be prepared at one time, and food should not be left standing in the kitchen before being cooled quickly for freezing. All food must be completely fresh, in peak condition, and must be frozen as quickly as possible after picking or shopping.

Prepare carefully
Prepare, pack and seal food carefully, labelling each package and recording all items in the freezer. Pack only in usable portions, rather than in bulk packs which need dividing constantly; but be prepared to pack such items as fruit and vegetables in a variety of package-sizes according to probable use.

Freeze quickly
Food must be frozen quickly to retain high quality, good texture and flavour and nutritive value. If a fast-freeze compartment is not available, food must be placed against the bottom and sides of the freezer which has been adjusted to its lowest temperature. Fresh food should be well-chilled before being put into the freezer so that it does not raise the temperature of the cabinet nor warm surrounding food.

Thaw carefully
Much frozen food is spoiled by careless thawing and cooking. Thin cuts of meat and fish, and vegetables can be cooked straight from the freezer. Meat joints can be cooked while still frozen, but need 1 hour per lb. cooking time, and the use of foil and a meat thermometer, and it is much more difficult to get a perfect result than when allowing meat to thaw before cooking. Other foods should be thawed slowly, preferably in the refrigerator in wrappings as this saves loss of juices. It is not advisable to speed-up thawing by means of hot water, electric fires or hair dryers which will spoil the texture and flavour of the food.

Observe high quality storage life
While frozen food is stored at $-18°C$ ($0°F$) slow changes are taking

place in colour, texture and flavour. 'High quality storage life' as I have mentioned is judged as the time taken for these changes to be noticeable in comparison with the equivalent fresh food. Opinions vary as to the length of this storage life, in relation to an average person's senses of taste and smell. Foods with a high fat content or with highly volatile ingredients have a shorter storage life than vegetables, for instance, and should therefore only be stored for a relatively short time. Luckily occasional fluctuations in temperature, perhaps during defrosting will not significantly change the quality of the food.

Commercially-frozen foods have a shorter recommended storage life than equivalent home-frozen foods, because they have already been stored by the manufacturers, and also because they may have suffered a number of fluctuations in temperature during distribution.

Be careful about refreezing

Never refreeze cooked dishes which have already been frozen.

Frozen foods which have softened on the surface, but not thawed, in transport from a shop, can go into the freezer without any loss of freezer life. Food which has thawed, but which has not been subjected to a temperature over 10°C (50°F) for any length of time, can be refrozen, but the storage life will be shortened and the food will not be so good to eat, having suffered a loss of flavour, colour and texture. It is much wiser to cook such food and then return the cooked dish to the freezer (e.g. thawed meat and vegetables can be made into a casserole which will freeze well). Bread, cakes, pastry and vegetables can be refrozen if the pack is still cold and intact, but some of the quality *will* be lost. Meat can be refrozen, but loses quality and flavour every time it is frozen again, so it is far better to cook the meat before freezing it again.

FAULTS IN FROZEN FOODS

Food which has been home-frozen carelessly tends to be poorly coloured, and may have an unpleasant flavour or smell; at best, it tends to be tough and tasteless, and will almost certainly have lost some nutritive value. Faults occur when the food has not been correctly packaged, frozen or stored correctly. In the most simple terms, the freezer is a box of cold dry air, and when a package is stored, the cold air attempts to draw the warmth and moisture out of the food. This must happen, but moisture must not be allowed to leave the food. The main faults are:

CROSS-CONTAMINATION   Food with a strong flavour and smell will affect other food in the freezer, and such packages should be carefully overwrapped, and stored for the shortest possible period. Over-blanched green vegetables, cheese and dishes containing onion or garlic are the chief offenders. Broken packages can also allow cross–contamination.

TOP A steamed pudding packed in a foil container for freezing, and reheated in the same container two months later.
ABOVE Various foil pans suitable for freezer use.

This close-up shows clearly the handles which support a top tier of hanging baskets. They are also used for lifting the baskets from here or from the freezer floor.

DEHYDRATION   Drying–out may occur, particularly after a long storage period; the food loses both moisture and juices. Meat often suffers in this way, giving a tough, dry and tasteless result when cooked. Dehydration also results in freezer burn. Only careful wrapping in moisture-proof packaging will avoid the problem.

FLABBINESS   Fruit and vegetables contain a lot of water, and if frozen slowly may be flabby and limp. Fast-freezing is essential if flabbiness is to be avoided. Certain varieties of some fruit and vegetables also freeze badly; the correct varieties for freezing should be chosen.

FREEZER BURN   Discoloured greyish-brown patches on the surface of food taken from the freezer are the result of dehydration. These are not dangerous, but look unsightly. Freezer burn can be avoided by using the correct packaging materials and packing methods.

ICE CRYSTALS   Fast-freezing is essential to avoid the formation of ice crystals in packages of meat, fish, vegetables and fruit. Moisture in the food cells expands when frozen and forms ice which puncture and destroy surrounding tissues. Juices escape from these tissues, particularly in meat, and flavour is removed.

If too much headspace is left in boxes of liquid food such as soup, a layer of ice crystals will form in the space. When the liquid is thawed or heated, it can be shaken or stirred back into emulsion. But storage time and flavour will have been affected.

OXIDATION   Oxygen moves inwards from air to food, causing the mingling of oxygen and food fat cells or oxidation. The cells react together to form chemicals which give meat and fish a bad taste and smell, and fatty foods become rancid. Only moisture-vapour-proof packaging will provide an oxygen barrier and avoid this.

RANCIDITY   When food smells and tastes unpleasant, it may be due to the effect of oxygen on food fat cells (see 'Oxidation' above). Fat foods such as pork, bacon and oily fish are subject to this, besides having a short high-quality freezer storage life. They should also be fast-frozen. Fried foods are not generally recommended for freezer storage.

Salt accelerates the reaction which causes rancidity, so a short storage life is recommended for sausages or minced meat containing salt, for ham and bacon and for salt butter.

Preventing Faults Recurring   If faults have occurred, check your freezing procedures to avoid further disappointments and wastage of expensive food and packaging. Make sure you are carrying out the following:

(a) All food must be prepared without delay. Meat, poultry and fish should be prepared as soon as they are ready, and in cool conditions.

Fruit and vegetables suffer if they are not processed immediately after picking. Cooked dishes should be cooled rapidly for freezing, and left-overs processed as soon as the meal is over.

(b) The food must be packed properly in moisture-vapour-proof wrapping, firmly sealed. Air should be removed from bag and parcel packaging, but a headspace should be left in rigid containers for the expansion of liquids. Strongly-smelling or highly-flavoured foods should be overwrapped. Broken packages should be avoided by wrapping sharp edges, discarding brittle wrappings, and not over-filling containers. (See PACKAGING, pages 28–35.)

(c) The food must be frozen rapidly. Animal products and cooked foods in particular can deteriorate quickly, especially when warm. Fast freezing makes food safer from harmful reactions than slow freezing, and slows up the formation of ice crystals too.

(d) Only the amount of fresh food which can be frozen safely within 24 hours, as specified by the freezer manufacturer, should be frozen at one time. As mentioned, it is the amount which would normally fill one-tenth of the total storage capacity. Overloading of the freezer with more fresh food will result in slower freezing.

(e) The food must be stored at the correct temperature of $-18°C$ ($0°F$). High quality storage life is only ensured when food is stored at this temperature.

(f) The food must be thawed and/or cooked correctly. Rapid thawing results in toughness and loss of texture and flavour. Fruit, bread and cakes can be thawed in the refrigerator or at room temperature, but large pieces of meat, poultry, game or fish, as well as cooked dishes to be eaten cold, should be thawed in their wrappings in the refrigerator, allowing time for a slow thawing process. Vegetables, fish and thin cuts of meat can be cooked directly from the freezer. Pies, casseroles and other cooked dishes can be put straight into the oven from the freezer without thawing, provided they have been frozen in ovenproof ware or foil dishes.

FOODS TO AVOID FREEZING

Nearly all foods freeze well, but there are a few items to avoid completely, or to freeze only with great care. A few other foods cannot be frozen to eat raw, but can be used for cooking.

Foods unsuitable for freezing
Hard-boiled eggs (including Scotch eggs, eggs in pies and in sandwiches).
Soured cream and single cream (less than 40% butterfat) which separate.

Custards (including tarts). The custard mixture of eggs and milk can be frozen uncooked, but there is little point in this.

Soft meringue toppings.

Mayonnaise and salad dressings.

Milk puddings.

Royal icing and frostings without fat.

Salad vegetables with a high water content, e.g. lettuce, watercress, radishes.

Old boiled potatoes (potatoes can be frozen mashed, roast, baked or as chips).

Stuffed poultry.

Food with a high proportion of gelatine.

Whole eggs in shells which will crack (eggs can be frozen in packages).

Foods to freeze with care

Onions, garlic, spices and herbs. They sometimes get a musty flavour in cooked dishes in the freezer, and quantities should be reduced in such dishes as casseroles, and adjusted during reheating. Careful packing will help to prevent these strong flavours spreading to other food, and a short storage life is recommended.

Rice, spaghetti and potatoes should only be frozen without liquid. They become mushy in liquid and should not be frozen in soups or stews.

Sauces and gravy are best thickened by reduction, or with tomato or vegetable purée. If flour is used, it must be reheated with great care, preferably in a double saucepan, to avoid separation. Cornflour can be used but gives a glutinous quality. Egg and cream thickening should be added after freezing.

Bananas, apples, pears, whole melons and avocadoes cannot be successfully frozen whole to eat raw. They can be prepared in various ways for freezer storage (although pears are never very satisfactory). Bananas are not worth while as they are in season at a reasonable price throughout the year.

Cabbage cannot be frozen successfully to eat raw, and is not worth freezing as it occupies valuable freezer space. Red cabbage may be useful to keep frozen, as it has a short season and is never very plentiful.

Celery and chicory cannot be frozen to eat raw. They are useful to freeze in liquid to serve as vegetables. Celery can be used in stews or soup.

Tomatoes cannot be frozen to eat raw, but are invaluable in the freezer to use for soups, stews and sauces, or to freeze as purée or juice.

Milk must be homogenised and packed in waxed cartons. It is hardly worth bothering about as various types of milk can be stored without refrigeration.

51

FREEZING VEGETABLES AND HERBS

All vegetables to be frozen should be young and tender, and they are best picked and frozen in small amounts. Shop-bought vegetables are generally too old to be worth freezing, but a few seasonal delicacies such as aubergines and peppers are worth the trouble of preparing them.

Vegetables to be frozen must be blanched to arrest the working of enzymes (types of protein in foods which speed up chemical reactions). Blanching at high heat stops the enzymes from affecting quality, flavour, colour and nutritive value during storage. Unblanched vegetables can be stored for up to three months in the freezer, but the effect of freezing will be the same as that of an early frost, and they will lose their colour and texture. Unblanched vegetables also require the full cooking time, unlike blanched vegetables which are already partly cooked.

PREPARATION FOR FREEZING
All vegetables must first be washed thoroughly in cold water, then cut or sorted into similar sizes. If more are picked than can be dealt with, they should be put into polythene bags in a refrigerator.

BLANCHING
There are two forms of blanching, (a) by water; (b) by steam. Steam blanching is not recommended for leafy green vegetables which tend to mat together, and it takes longer than water blanching, though it conserves more minerals and vitamins. Blanching should be timed carefully, though inaccuracy will not be disastrous. Too little blanching may result in colour change and in a loss of nutritive value; too much blanching will mean a loss of crispness and fresh flavour.

(a) **Water blanching.** Blanch only 1 lb. vegetables at a time to ensure thoroughness and to prevent a quick change in the temperature of the water. Use a saucepan holding at least 8 pints of water. Bring the water to the boil while the vegetables are being prepared. Put vegetables into a wire basket, chip pan, salad shaker or a muslin bag and completely immerse in the saucepan of fast-boiling water; cover tightly and keep the heat high under the saucepan until blanching is completed. Check carefully the time needed for each vegetable (see below, pages 54–62) and time blanching from when water returns to boiling point. As soon as the full blanching time has elapsed, remove vegetables and drain at once. Bring water to boiling point again before dealing with another batch of vegetables.

(b) **Steam blanching.** Put enough water into the saucepan below a steamer to prevent any risk of it boiling dry. Prepare the vegetables, and when the water is boiling fast put the wire basket or muslin bag into steamer. Cover tightly, and count steaming time from when the steam escapes from the lid. Steam blanching takes half as long again as water blanching (e.g. 2 minutes water blanching equals 3 minutes steam blanching).

COOLING
Cooling must be done immediately after blanching, and it must be very

thorough indeed; before being packed for the freezer, the vegetables should be cool right through to the centre. The time taken is generally equal to the blanching time if a large quantity of cold water is used. It is best to ice-chill this water, and it is a good idea to prepare large quantities of ice the day before a vegetable freezing session is planned. Vegetables which are not cooled quickly become mushy as they will go on cooking in their own heat. After cooling in the water, the vegetables should be thoroughly drained, and preferably finished off on absorbent paper.

PACKING   Pack the cooled food in usable quantities to suit family or entertaining needs (see above, page 31). Vegetables can be packed in bags or boxes; the chosen method will depend on the storage space available, as bagged vegetables are more difficult to keep though obviously cheaper to prepare.

Vegetables are normally packed dry, though wet-packing in brine is believed to prevent some vegetables toughening in storage, and non-leafy varieties can be packed in this way. The vegetables are packed into rigid containers to within 1 in. of the top, and are then just covered with brine, made in the proportion of 2 tablespoons salt per quart of water, leaving $\frac{1}{2}$ in. headspace. It may be found in hard water areas that home-frozen vegetables are consistently tough, and it is then worth experimenting with this brine method.

COOKING   The best results are obtained from cooking vegetables immediately on removal from the freezer. When cooking unthawed vegetables, break the block into 4 or 5 pieces when removing from the carton, to allow heat to penetrate evenly and rapidly.

One or two vegetables such as broccoli and spinach are better cooked partially thawed, and corn on the cob needs complete thawing. Mushrooms should be cooked frozen; they become pulpy when thawed. If vegetables are thawed, they should be cooked at once.

Partial cooking during blanching, and the tenderising process produced by temperature changes during storage, reduce the final cooking time of frozen vegetables. In general, they should cook in one-third to one-half the time allowed for fresh vegetables. Very little water, if any, should be used for cooking frozen vegetables; about $\frac{1}{4}$ pint to 1 lb. vegetables, depending on variety, is plenty. The water should be boiling, the vegetables covered at once with a lid, and as soon as boiling point is reached again, the vegetables should be simmered gently for the required time. Since flavour is always lost into the cooking water, some cooks prefer to steam vegetables, cook them in a double boiler, or to bake or fry them. For baking, the vegetables should be separated and drained, then put into a greased casserole with a knob of butter and seasoning, covered tightly and baked at 350°F (Gas Mark 4) for about 30 minutes. For frying, the vegetables remain frozen, and are put into a heavy frying pan containing 1 oz melted butter. The pan must be tightly covered and the vegetables cooked gently until they separate, then cooked over moderate heat until cooked through and tender, being turned as required to prevent burning.

Here are notes on preparing, packing, storing and cooking various kinds of vegetables. The blanching times given are for water blanching:

Artichokes (Globe)

Preparation   (a) Remove outer leaves. Wash, trim stalks and remove 'chokes'. Blanch in 8 pints water with 1 tablespoon lemon juice for 7 minutes. Cool and drain upside down. Pack in boxes. (b) Remove all green leaves and 'chokes'. Blanch artichoke hearts for 5 minutes.

Serving   (a) Cook in boiling water for 5 minutes. (b) Use as fresh artichokes for special dishes.
High Quality Storage Life   (a) 12 months, (b) 12 months

Artichokes (Jerusalem)

Preparation   Peel and cut in slices. Soften in a little butter, and simmer in a chicken stock. Rub through a sieve and pack in boxes.

Serving   Use as a basis for soup with milk or cream and seasoning.
High Quality Storage Life   3 months

Asparagus

Preparation   Wash and remove woody portions and scales. Grade for size and cut in 6 in. lengths. Blanch 2 minutes (small spears); 3 minutes (medium spears); 4 minutes (large spears). Cool and drain. Pack in boxes.

Serving   Cook 5 minutes in boiling water.
High Quality Storage Life   9 months

Aubergines

Preparation   Use mature, tender, medium-sized. (a) Peel and cut in 1 in. slices. Blanch 4 minutes, chill and drain. Pack in layers separated by paper in boxes. (b) Coat slices in thin batter, or egg and breadcrumbs. Deep-fry, drain and cool. Pack in layers in boxes.

Serving   (a) Cook 5 minutes in boiling water, (b) Heat in a slow oven or part thaw and deep-fry.
High Quality Storage Life   (a) 12 months, (b) 1 month

Beans (Broad)

Preparation   Use small young beans. Shell and blanch for 1½ minutes. Pack in bags or boxes.

Serving   Cook 8 minutes in boiling water.
High Quality Storage Life   12 months

Beans (French)

Preparation   Remove tops and tails. Leave small beans whole; cut larger ones into 1 in. pieces. Blanch 3 minutes (whole beans); 2 minutes (cut beans). Cool and pack in bags.

Serving   Cook 7 minutes in boiling water (whole beans); 5 minutes (cut beans).
High Quality Storage Life   12 months

Beans (Runner)

Preparation   Do not shred, but cut in pieces and blanch 2 minutes. Cool and pack.

Serving   Cook 7 minutes in boiling water.
High Quality Storage Life   12 months

Beetroot

Preparation   Use very young beetroot, under 3 in. across. They must be completely cooked in boiling water until tender. Rub off skins and pack in boxes, either whole or cut in slices or dice.

Serving   Thaw 2 hours in container in refrigerator. Drain and add dressing.
High Quality Storage Life   6 months

Broccoli

Preparation   Use green, compact heads with tender stalks 1 in. thick or less. Trim stalks and remove outer leaves. Wash well and soak in salt water for 30 minutes (2 teaspoons salt to 8 pints water). Wash in fresh water, and cut into sprigs. Blanch 3 minutes (thin stems); 4 minutes (5 minutes thick stems). Pack into boxes or bags, alternating heads.

Serving   Cook 8 minutes in boiling water.
High Quality Storage Life   12 months

Brussels Sprouts

Preparation   Grade small compact heads. Clean and wash well. Blanch 3 minutes (small); 4 minutes (medium). Cool and pack in bags or boxes.

Serving   Cook 8 minutes in boiling water.
High Quality Storage Life   12 months

Cabbage (Green and Red)

Preparation   Use crisp young cabbage. Wash and shred finely. Blanch $1\frac{1}{2}$ minutes. Pack in bags.

Serving   Cook 8 minutes in boiling water. Do not use raw.
High Quality Storage Life   6 months

Carrots

Preparation   Use very young carrots. Wash and scrape. Blanch 3 minutes for small whole carrots, sliced or diced carrots. Pack in bags or boxes.

Serving   Cook 8 minutes in boiling water.
High Quality Storage Life   12 months

Cauliflower

Preparation   Use firm compact heads with close white flowers. Wash and break into sprigs. Blanch 3 minutes in 8 pints water with 1 tablespoon lemon juice. Cool and pack in lined boxes or bags.

Serving   Cook 10 minutes in boiling water.
High Quality Storage Life   6 months

Celery

Preparation   (a) Use crisp young stalks. Scrub well and remove strings. Cut in 1 in. lengths and blanch 2 minutes. Cool and drain and pack in bags. (b) Prepare as above, but pack in boxes with water used for blanching, leaving $\frac{1}{2}$ in. headspace.

Serving   Use as a vegetable, or for stews or soups, using liquid if available. Do not use raw.
High Quality Storage Life   6 months

Chestnuts

Preparation   Bring chestnuts in shells to the boil. Drain and peel off shells. Pack in boxes or bags.

Serving   Cook in boiling water or milk, according to recipe.
High Quality Storage Life   6 months

Chicory

Preparation   Wash well and remove outer leaves. Blanch 3 minutes and cool in cooking liquid. Pack in the blanching liquid in boxes, leaving $\frac{1}{2}$ in. headspace.

Serving   Put into a covered dish in the oven in blanching liquid and heat at 350°F (Gas Mark 4) for 40 minutes. Drain and serve with butter.
High Quality Storage Life   6 months

Corn on the Cob

Preparation   (a) Use fresh tender corn. Remove leaves and threads and grade cobs for size. Blanch 4 minutes (small cobs); 6 minutes (medium cobs); 8 minutes (large cobs). Cool and dry. Pack individually in foil or freezer paper. Freeze and pack in bags for storage. (b) Blanch cobs and scrape off kernels. Pack in boxes, leaving $\frac{1}{2}$ in. headspace.

Serving   (a) Thaw before cooking. Put cobs in cold water, bring to a fast boil and simmer 5 minutes. (b) Thaw in wrappings in refrigerator. Cook 10 minutes in boiling water.
High Quality Storage Life   12 months

Cucumber

Preparation   Cut in thin slices and pack in boxes. Cover with equal quantities white vinegar and water, seasoned with $\frac{1}{2}$ teaspoon sugar and 1 teaspoon black pepper to 1 pint liquid.

Serving   Thaw in container in refrigerator. Drain and season with salt.
High Quality Storage Life   2 months

Fennel

Preparation   Use crisp young stalks. Scrub well. Blanch 3 minutes. Cool and pack in blanching water in boxes.

Serving   Simmer 30 minutes in blanching water or stock. Slip hard cores from roots when cooked.
High Quality Storage Life   6 months

Herbs (Mint, Parsley and Chives)

Preparation   (a) Wash and pack sprigs in bags. (b) Chop finely and pack into ice-cube trays. Transfer frozen cubes to bags for storage.

Serving   Thaw at room temperature for sandwich fillings. Add cubes to sauces, soups or stews. Do not use for garnish.
High Quality Storage Life   6 months

Kale

Preparation   Use young, tender kale. Remove dry or tough leaves. Strip leaves from stems and blanch 1 minute. Cool and drain. Chop leaves for convenient packing. Pack into bags.

Serving   Cook 8 minutes in boiling water.
High Quality Storage Life   6 months

Kohlrabi

Preparation   Use young and tender, not too large, and mild-flavoured. Trim, wash and peel. Small ones may be frozen whole, but large ones should be diced. Blanch 3 minutes (whole); 2 minutes (diced). Cool and pack in bags or boxes.

Serving   Cook 10 minutes in boiling water.
High Quality Storage Life   12 months

Leeks

Preparation   Trim off roots and green stems. Wash very well and remove dirty outer layers. Cut either finely or coarsely into even lengths. Blanch finely-cut leeks for 1½ minutes; coarsely-cut leeks for 3 minutes. Cool thoroughly and drain, or pack in blanching liquid.

Serving   Cook drained leeks until tender in salted water, and serve with butter or sauce, or make into a purée, or add to a soup or stew. Leeks packed in blanching liquid can be used to make soup.
High Quality Storage Life   12 months

Marrow

Preparation   (a) Cut young marrows or courgettes in $\frac{1}{2}$ in. slices without peeling. Blanch 3 minutes and pack in boxes, leaving $\frac{1}{2}$ in. headspace. (b) Peel and seed large marrows. Cook until soft, mash and pack in boxes.

Serving   (a) Fry in oil, and season well. (b) Reheat in double boiler with butter and seasoning.
High Quality Storage Life   6 months

Mushrooms

Preparation   (a) Wipe but do not peel. Cut large mushrooms in slices. Stalks may be frozen separately. Blanch $1\frac{1}{2}$ minutes in 6 pints water with 1 tablespoon lemon juice. Pack cups down in boxes, leaving $1\frac{1}{2}$ in. headspace. (b) Grade and cook in butter for 5 minutes. Allow 6 tablespoons butter to 1 lb. mushrooms. Cool quickly, take off excess fat, and pack in boxes.

Serving   (a) Thaw in container in refrigerator, and cook in butter. (b) Add while frozen to soups, stews or other dishes.
High Quality Storage Life   (a) 3 months, (b) 2 months

Onions

Preparation   (a) Peel, chop and pack in small boxes. Overwrap. (b) Cut in slices and wrap in foil or freezer paper, dividing layers with paper. Overwrap. (c) Chop or slice, blanch 2 minutes. Cool and drain. Pack in boxes. Overwrap. (d) Leave tiny onions whole. Blanch 4 minutes. Pack in boxes. Overwrap.

Serving   Thaw raw onions in refrigerator. Add to salads while frosty. Add frozen onions to dishes according to recipe.
High Quality Storage Life   2 months

Parsnips

Preparation Use young parsnips. Trim and peel. Cut into narrow strips or dice. Blanch 2 minutes. Pack in bags or boxes.

Serving Cook 15 minutes in boiling water.
High Quality Storage Life 12 months

Peas, Green

Preparation Use young sweet peas. Shell. Blanch 1 minute, shaking basket to distribute heat. Cool and drain. Pack in boxes or bags.

Serving Cook 7 minutes in boiling water.
High Quality Storage Life 12 months

Peas (Edible Pods)

Preparation Use flat tender pods. Wash well. Remove ends and strings. Blanch $\frac{1}{2}$ minute in small quantities.

Serving Cook 7 minutes in boiling water.
High Quality Storage Life 12 months

Peppers (Green and Red)

Preparation (a) Wash well. Cut off stems and caps, and remove seeds and membranes. Blanch 2 minutes (slices); 3 minutes (halves). Pack in boxes or bags. (b) Grill on high heat until skin is charred. Plunge into cold water and rub off skins. Remove caps and seeds. Pack tightly in boxes in salt solution (1 tablespoon salt to 1 pint water), leaving 1 in. headspace.

Serving (a) Thaw $1\frac{1}{2}$ hours at room temperature. (b) Thaw in liquid and drain. Dress with oil and seasoning.
High Quality Storage Life 12 months

Potatoes

Preparation (a) Scrape and wash new potatoes. Blanch 4 minutes. Cool and pack in bags. (b) Slightly undercook new potatoes. Drain, toss in butter, cool and pack in bags. (c) Mash potatoes with butter and hot milk. Pack in boxes or bags. (d) Form potatoes into croquettes or Duchesse Potatoes.

Cook, cool and pack in boxes. (e) Fry chips in clean fat for 4 minutes. Do not brown. Cool and pack in bags.

Serving (a) Cook 15 minutes in boiling water. (b) Plunge bag in boiling water. Take off heat and leave 10 minutes. (c) Reheat in double boiler. (d) Thaw 2 hours. Heat at 350°F, 180°C (Gas Mark 4) for 20 minutes. (e) Fry in deep fat.
High Quality Storage Life (a) 12 months, (b) 3 months, (c) 3 months, (d) 3 months, (e) 3 months

Pumpkin

Preparation Peel and seed. Cook until soft. Mash and pack in boxes.

Serving (a) Reheat in double boiler with butter and seasoning. (b) Thaw 2 hours at room temperature and use as a pie filling.
High Quality Storage Life 6 months

Spinach

Preparation Use young tender spinach. Remove stems. Wash very well. Blanch 2 minutes, shaking basket so the leaves separate. Cool and press out moisture. Pack in boxes or bags.

Serving Melt a little butter and cook frozen spinach 7 minutes.
High Quality Storage Life 12 months

Tomatoes

Preparation (a) Wipe tomatoes and remove stems. Grade and pack in small quantities in bags. (b) Skin and core tomatoes. Simmer in own juice for 5 minutes until soft. Sieve, cool and pack in boxes. (c) Core tomatoes and cut in quarters. Simmer with lid on for 10 minutes. Put through muslin. Cool juice and pack in boxes, leaving 1 in. headspace.

Serving (a) Thaw 2 hours at room temperature, skins slip off when thawed. Grill, or use in recipes. Do not use raw. (b) Thaw 2 hours at room temperature. Use for soups or stews. (c) Thaw in refrigerator. Serve frosty. Add seasoning.
High Quality Storage Life 12 months

Turnips

Preparation (a) Use small, young mild turnips. Peel and cut in dice. Blanch $2\frac{1}{2}$ minutes. Cool and pack in boxes. (b) Cook turnips until tender. Drain and mash. Pack in boxes, leaving $\frac{1}{2}$ in. headspace.

Serving (a) Cook 10 minutes in boiling water. (b) Reheat in double boiler with butter and seasoning.
High Quality Storage Life   (a) 12 months, (b) 3 months

Vegetables (Mixed)

Preparation Prepare and blanch vegetables separately. Mix and pack in boxes.

Serving Cook 7 minutes in boiling water.
High Quality Storage Life   12 months

Vegetable Purée

Preparation Cook and sieve vegetables. Pack in boxes. Small quantities can be frozen in ice-cube trays, and the cubes transferred to bags for easy storage.

Serving Add to soups. Purée may be reheated in a double boiler.
High Quality Storage Life   3 months

Vegetables in Sauce

Preparation Slightly undercook vegetables. Cool and fold into sauce. Pack into boxes.

Serving Reheat in double boiler.
High Quality Storage Life   2 months

FREEZING FRUIT

The best results are obtained from fully-flavoured fruits, particularly berries. The blander fruits such as pears are satisfactory, but have little flavour. In general, fruit for freezing should be of top quality; over-ripe fruit will be mushy (though it may be possible to store as purée); unripe fruit will be tasteless and poorly-coloured.
It is important to work quickly when preparing fruit; home-picked fruit

should be frozen on the same day, while fruit from shop or market should only be bought in manageable quantities which can be handled in a short space of time.

Whichever method of packing is to be used, wash the fruit in plenty of water containing ice cubes as this will prevent the fruit becoming soggy and losing juice. Fruit should be drained immediately in an enamel, aluminium, stainless steel or earthenware container (avoid copper, iron and galvanised ware which produce off-flavours), and may be further drained on absorbent paper. It is important to be gentle in removing stems of stones from fruit to be frozen; this should be done with the tips of the fingers, without squeezing.

Fruit Freezing Methods

UNSWEETENED DRY PACK

Unsweetened Dry Pack. This pack can be used for fruit for use in pies, puddings and jams, or for people on a sugar-free diet. It should not be used for fruit which discolours badly during preparation, as sugar helps to retard the action of the enzymes which cause darkening.

To pack fruit by this method, wash and drain and pack into cartons. Do not use excess water in cleaning the fruit. Seal and freeze and label carefully. For an unsweetened pack, it is better to open-freeze fruit. Spread it out on metal or plastic trays for fast-freezing. When frozen, pour into polythene bags or boxes for storage. Small quantities can easily be shaken out for use.

UNSWEETENED WET PACK

This method is little used, but is acceptable for very sweet fruit or for puddings to be made for people on a diet. The fruit should be packed in liquid-proof containers, either gently crushed in its own juice, or covered with water to which lemon juice has been added to prevent discolouration (juice of 1 lemon to 1½ pints water). If the fruit is tart but no sugar is to be used, it may be frozen in water sweetened with a sugar substitute, or with a sugar-free carbonated beverage. Seal, freeze and label carefully.

DRY SUGAR PACK

This is a good method for crushed or sliced fruit, or for soft juicy fruit from which the juice draws easily such as berries. The fruit should be washed and drained and may be packed by two methods: (a) mix fruit and sugar in a bowl with a silver spoon, adjusting sweetening to tartness of fruit (average 3 lb. fruit to 1 lb. sugar). Pack fruit into containers, leaving ½ in. headspace, seal and freeze, and label carefully: (b) pack fruit in layers, using the same proportion of fruit and sugar; start with a layer of fruit, sprinkle with sugar, then more fruit and sugar, leaving ½ in. headspace. Seal and freeze, labelling carefully.

SYRUP PACK

This method is best for non-juicy fruits and those which discolour easily. Syrup is normally made from white sugar and water. (For those who dislike white sugar for dietary reasons, honey may be used, but it flavours the fruit strongly. Brown sugar may likewise be used, but affects the colour of the fruit.)

63

The syrup is referred to as a percentage, according to the amount of sugar and water used. A medium syrup or 40% syrup is best for most purposes as a heavier syrup tends to make the fruit flabby. The sugar must be completely dissolved in boiling water, then cooled. It must be completely cold before adding it to the fruit, and it is best stored in a refrigerator for a day before using. The fruit should be packed into containers and covered with syrup, leaving ½–1 in. headspace. To prevent discolouration, a piece of Cellophane should be pressed down over the fruit into the syrup before sealing, freezing and labelling.

Syrup

Sugar	Water	Type of Syrup
4 oz	1 pint	20% very light syrup
7 oz	1 pint	30% light syrup
11 oz	1 pint	40% medium syrup
16 oz	1 pint	50% heavy syrup
25 oz	1 pint	60% very heavy syrup

HEADSPACE

Headspace must be allowed for all fruit in sugar or syrup, for juice or purée: ½ in. should be allowed for all dry packs; ½–1 in. per pint for wide-topped wet packs and ¾–1 in. per pint for narrow-topped wet packs. Double headspace is needed for quart containers.

DIS-COLOURATION

Discolouration is the greatest problem in fruit packing for freezing. Apples, peaches and pears are particularly subject to this during preparation, storage and thawing. In general, fruit which has a lot of Vitamin C darkens less easily, so adding lemon juice or citric acid to the sugar pack will help to arrest darkening. Use the juice of 1 lemon to 1½ pints water, or 1 teaspoon citric acid to each 1 lb. of sugar in dry pack. Ascorbic acid can likewise be used; it can be bought in tablet or crystalline form from the chemist. 500 milligrammes or 1 tablet of ascorbic acid should be used for 1 pint of water (1 teaspoon of the acid equals 6 tablets). The tablets should be crushed to a powder and mixed in a teaspoon of cold water before being added to the sugar syrup. Fruit purée in particular is subject to darkening since large amounts of air are forced through a sieve during preparation. Air reacts on the cells of fruit to produce darkening; and for this reason fruit should be prepared quickly for freezing once the natural protection of skin or rind is broken. For the same reason, the fruit should be eaten immediately on thawing, or while a few ice crystals remain. Fruit which discolours badly is better for rapid thawing, and unsweetened frozen fruit should immediately be put into hot syrup or other liquid.

JAM FRUIT

Any fruit can be packed for use in jam-making later. Pack without sweetening, and allow 10% extra fruit in the recipe when making the jam, as there is a slight pectin loss in frozen fruit.

TOP A frozen flan case filled with redcurrants frozen separately in a deep sugar pack (see p. 63).

ABOVE Freezer-stored raw fish, fresh and smoked, and a 'starter' course using a smoked fish pâté (p. 111).

A frozen baked meat loaf (p. 157) with salad added after thawing.

FRUIT PURÉE   It is useful to freeze purée for certain kinds of puddings and cakes, and when there is a lot of ripe fruit. The fruit should not be over-ripe or bruised. Raw fruit such as raspberries or strawberries should be sieved, to remove all the pips. Other fruit can be put in a covered dish in the oven to start the juice running before the fruit is sieved. Purée can be made from cooked fruit but must be well cooled before freezing (it will keep less than 4 months). This purée should be sweetened, as if for immediate use. Ways of preparing purée from individual fruits are given under the individual fruits below.

FRUIT SYRUPS   Fruit syrups can be frozen; blackcurrant is thought best, and it is far easier to freeze than to bottle. Any standard syrup recipe can be used, and fruit syrup is best frozen in small quantities in ice-cube trays. Each cube should be wrapped in foil; then, a useful number of cubes are packed into a bag for storage. One syrup cube gives one individual serving to use with puddings or ice cream, or to dissolve in water as a drink.

FRUIT JUICES   Ripe fruit can be turned into juice, and frozen in this form. Citrus fruit juice can also be frozen. Non-citrus fruit should be carefully checked for any bruising or insects, then mashed with a silver fork. For every 4 cups of fruit, allow 1 cup of water and simmer gently for 10 minutes. Strain through a jelly bag or cloth, and cool completely before freezing. These juices can be frozen unsweetened, or sweetened to taste, and are useful for drinks, jellies and fruit pies. Freeze them in a rigid container, leaving $\frac{1}{2}$ in. headspace, or in ice-cube trays, wrapping each cube in foil and storing in quantities in polythene bags. Apple juice can be made, using $\frac{1}{2}$ pint water to each 2 lb. apples, or it can be made by simmering leftover peelings in water; it should *not* be sweetened before freezing since fermentation sets in quickly.

Citrus fruit juices can easily be prepared from good-quality fruit which is heavy in the hand for its size. The unpeeled fruit should be chilled in iced water or in the refrigerator before the juice is extracted; the juice can be strained, but the fine pulp can be left in if preferred. Freeze in rigid containers, leaving 1 in. headspace. Lemon and lime juice can usefully be frozen in ice-cube trays for drinks, the cubes being wrapped in foil and stored in useful quantities in polythene bags.

CATERING PACKS OF FRUIT AND JUICE   Large tins of fruit in syrup and of fruit juices are often economical to buy. They can be opened and divided into normal family portions, and then be frozen in smaller containers.

THAWING FROZEN FRUIT   Unsweetened fruit packs take longer to thaw than sweetened ones; fruit in dry sugar thaws most quickly of all. All fruit should be thawed in its container unopened; and all fruit is at its best when just thawed, with a few ice crystals left if it is to be eaten raw. Fruit to use with ice cream should only be partly defrosted. To cook frozen fruit, thaw until pieces

65

can just be separated and put into a pie; if fruit is to be cooked in a sauce-pan, it can be put into the pan in its frozen state, keeping in mind the amount of sugar or syrup used earlier in freezing if a pudding is being made. Frozen fruits are likely to have a lot of juice after thawing; to avoid leaky pies or damp cake fillings, add a little thickening for pies (such as cornflour, arrowroot or flake tapioca), or drain off excess juice. For every 1 lb. fruit packed in syrup, allow 6–8 hours thawing time in the refrigerator, 2–4 hours thawing at room temperature, or $\frac{1}{2}$–1 hour if the pack is placed in a bowl of cold water.

Fruit will lose quality and flavour if left to stand for any length of time after thawing, so do not thaw more than you need immediately. However, if leftover fruit is cooked, it will last for several days in a refrigerator.

Here are notes on preparing, packing, storing and cooking various fruits:

Apples

Preparation   Peel, core and drop in cold water. Cut in twelfths or sixteenths. Pack in bags or boxes. (a) Dry sugar pack (8 oz sugar to 2 lb. fruit). (b) 40% syrup pack. (c) Sweetened purée.

Serving   (a) Use for pies and puddings. (c) Use for sauce, fools and ices.
High Quality Storage Life   (a) 8–12 months, (c) 4–8 months

Apricots

Preparation   (a) Peeled and halved in dry sugar pack (4 oz sugar to 1 lb. fruit) or 40% syrup pack. (b) Peeled and sliced in 40% syrup pack. (c) Sweetened purée (very ripe fruit).

Serving   (a) Thaw $3\frac{1}{2}$ hours at room temperature. (b) Use for sauce, and ices.
High Quality Storage Life   (a) 12 months, (c) 4 months

Avocado Pears

Preparation   (a) Rub halves in lemon juice, wrap in foil and pack in polythene bags. (b) Dip slices in lemon juice and freeze in boxes. (c) Mash pulp with lemon juice (1 tablespoon to 1 avocado) and pack in small containers.

Serving   (a) Thaw $2\frac{1}{2}$ to 3 hours at room temperature and use at once. (b) Season pulp with onion, garlic or herbs as a spread.
High Quality Storage Life   2 months

Bananas

Preparation   Mash with sugar and lemon juice (8 oz sugar to 3 tablespoons lemon juice to 3 breakfastcups banana pulp). Pack in small containers.

Serving   Thaw 6 hours in unopened container in refrigerator. Use in sandwiches or cakes.
High Quality Storage Life   2 months

Blackberries

Preparation   Wash dark glossy ripe berries and dry well. (a) Fast-freeze unsweetened berries on trays and pack in bags. (b) Dry sugar pack (8 oz sugar to 2 lb. fruit). (c) Sweetened purée (raw or cooked fruit).

Serving   Thaw 3 hours at room temperature. Use raw, cooked or in pies and puddings.
High Quality Storage Life   12 months

Blueberries

Preparation   Wash in chilled water and drain thoroughly. Crush fruit slightly as skins toughen on freezing. (a) Fast-freeze unsweetened berries on trays and pack in bags. (b) Dry sugar pack (4 oz sugar to 4 breakfastcups crushed berries). (c) 50% syrup pack.

Serving   Use raw, cooked or in pies and puddings.
High Quality Storage Life   12 months

Cherries

Preparation   Put in chilled water for 1 hour; remove stones. Pack in glass or plastic containers, as cherry juice remains liquid and leaks through waxed containers. (a) Dry sugar pack (8 oz sugar to 2 lb. stoned cherries). (b) 40% syrup pack for sweet cherries. (c) 50% or 60% syrup pack for sour cherries.

Serving   Thaw 3 hours at room temperature. Serve cold, or use for pies.
High Quality Storage Life   12 months

Coconut

Preparation   Grate or shred, moisten with coconut milk, and pack into bags or boxes; 4 oz sugar to 4 breakfastcups shredded coconut may be added if liked.

Serving   Thaw 2 hours at room temperature. Drain off milk. Use for fruit salads, icings or curries.
High Quality Storage Life   2 months

Cranberries

Preparation   Wash firm glossy berries and drain. (a) Dry unsweetened pack. (b) Sweetened purée.

Serving   Cook in water and sugar while still frozen. Can be thawed $3\frac{1}{2}$ hours at room temperature.
High Quality Storage Life   12 months

Currants, Black, Red and White

Preparation   Prepare black, red or white currants by the same methods. Strip fruit from stems with a fork, wash in chilled water and dry gently. Currants can be fast-frozen on trays and the stalks stripped off before packing. This makes the job easier. (a) Dry unsweetened pack. (b) Dry sugar pack (8 oz sugar to 1 lb. currants). (c) 40% syrup pack. (d) Sweetened purée (particularly blackcurrants).

Serving   (a) Thaw 45 minutes at room temperature. Use for jam, pies and puddings. (c) and (d) Use as sauce, or for drinks, ices or puddings.
High Quality Storage Life   12 months

Damsons

Preparation   Wash in chilled water; cut in half and remove stones. (a) 50% syrup pack. (b) Sweetened purée.

Serving   Thaw at room temperature for $2\frac{1}{2}$ hours. Use cold, or for pies or puddings.
High Quality Storage Life   12 months

Dates

Preparation (a) Wrap block dates in foil or polythene bags. (b) Remove stones from dessert dates; pack in bags or boxes.

Serving Thaw 30 minutes at room temperature. Serve as dessert, or use for cakes or puddings.
High Quality Storage Life 12 months

Figs

Preparation Wash fresh sweet ripe figs in chilled water; remove stems. Do not bruise. (a) Peeled or unpeeled in dry unsweetened pack. (b) 30% syrup pack for peeled figs. (c) Wrap dried dessert figs in foil or polythene bags.

Serving Thaw $1\frac{1}{2}$ hours at room temperature. Eat raw or cooked in syrup.
High Quality Storage Life 12 months

Gooseberries

Preparation Wash in chilled water and dry. For pies, freeze fully ripe fruit; for jam, fruit may be slightly under-ripe. (a) Dry unsweetened pack. (b) 40% syrup pack. (c) Sweetened purée.

Serving (a) and (b) Thaw $2\frac{1}{2}$ hours at room temperature. Fruit may be put into pies or cooked while still frozen. (c) Thaw $2\frac{1}{2}$ hours at room temperature and use for fools, mousses or ices.
High Quality Storage Life 12 months

Grapefruit

Preparation Peel; remove pith; cut into segments. (a) Dry sugar pack (8 oz sugar to 2 breakfastcups segments). (b) 50% syrup pack.

Serving Thaw $2\frac{1}{2}$ hours at room temperature.
High Quality Storage Life 12 months

Grapes

Preparation Pack seedless varieties whole. Skin, seed other types. Pack in 30% syrup.

Serving Thaw $2\frac{1}{2}$ hours at room temperature.
High Quality Storage Life 12 months

Greengages

Preparation Wash in chilled water and dry. Cut in half and remove stones. Pack in 40% syrup.

Serving Thaw 2½ hours at room temperature.
High Quality Storage Life 12 months

Guavas

Preparation (a) Wash fruit, cook in a little water, and purée. Pineapple juice gives better flavour than water. (b) Peel, halve and cook until tender, then pack in 30% syrup.

Serving Thaw 1½ hours at room temperature.
High Quality Storage Life 12 months·

Kumquats

Preparation (a) Wrap whole fruit in foil. (b) 50% syrup pack.

Serving Thaw 2 hours at room temperature.
High Quality Storage Life (a) 2 months, (b) 12 months

Lemons and Limes

Preparation Peel fruit, cut in slices, and pack in 20% syrup.

Serving Thaw 1 hour at toom temperature.
High Quality Storage Life 12 months

Loganberries

Preparation Wash berries and dry well. (a) Fast-freeze unsweetened berries on trays and pack in bags. (b) Dry sugar pack (8 oz sugar to 2 lb. fruit). (c) 50% syrup pack. (d) Sweetened puree (cooked fruit).

Serving Thaw 3 hours at room temperature. Use particularly for ices and mousses.
High Quality Storage Life 12 months

Mangoes

Preparation Peel ripe fruit, and pack in slices in 50% syrup. Add 1 tablespoonful lemon juice to each quart syrup.

Serving Thaw 1½ hours at room temperature.
High Quality Storage Life 12 months

Melons

Preparation Cut into cubes or balls. Toss in lemon juice and pack in 30% syrup.

Serving Thaw unopened in refrigerator. Serve while still frosty.
High Quality Storage Life 12 months

Nectarines

Preparation Wipe fruit, and peel or not as desired. Cut in halves or slices and brush with lemon juice. (a) 40% syrup pack. (b) Sweetened purée (fresh fruit) with 1 tablespoonful lemon juice to each lb. fruit.

Serving Thaw 3 hours in refrigerator.
High Quality Storage Life 12 months

Oranges

Preparation Peel and divide into sections or cut into slices. (a) Dry sugar pack (8 oz sugar to 3 breakfastcups sections or slices). (b) 30% syrup. (c) Pack slices in slightly sweetened fresh orange juice.

Serving Thaw 2½ hours at room temperature.
High Quality Storage Life 12 months
Navel oranges become bitter in the freezer. Seville oranges may be frozen whole in their skins in polythene bags for marmalade.

Peaches

Preparation Work quickly as fruit discolours. Peel, cut in halves or slices and brush with lemon juice. (a) 40% syrup pack. (b) Sweetened purée (fresh fruit) with 1 tablespoon lemon juice to each lb. fruit.

Serving Thaw 3 hours in refrigerator.
High Quality Storage Life 12 months

Pears

Preparation   Pears should be ripe, but not over-ripe. They discolour quickly and do not retain their delicate flavour in the freezer. Peel and quarter fruit, remove cores, and dip pieces in lemon juice. Poach in 30% syrup for $1\frac{1}{2}$ minutes. Drain and cool. Pack in cold 30% syrup.

Serving   Thaw 3 hours at room temperature.
High Quality Storage Life   12 months

Persimmons

Preparation   (a) Wrap whole fruit in foil. (b) Peel and freeze in 50% syrup adding 1 dessertspoon lemon juice to each quart syrup. (c) Sweetened purée (fresh fruit).

Serving   Thaw 3 hours at room temperature. Use unpeeled raw fruit as soon as it has thawed or it will darken and lose flavour.
High Quality Storage Life   (a) 2 months, (b) 12 months

Pineapple

Preparation   Use fully-ripe and golden-yellow fruit. Peel fruit and cut into slices or chunks. (a) Dry unsweetened pack, with slices separated by paper or cellophane. (b) Dry sugar pack (4 oz sugar to 1 lb. fruit). (c) 30% syrup pack. (d) Crush fruit and mix 4 oz sugar to 2 breakfastcups fruit.

Serving   Thaw 3 hours at room temperature.
High Quality Storage Life   12 months

Plums

Preparation   Wash in chilled water and dry. Cut in half and remove stones. Pack in 40% syrup.

Serving   Thaw $2\frac{1}{2}$ hours at room temperature.
High Quality Storage Life   12 months

Pomegranates

Preparation   (a) Cut ripe fruit in half; scoop out juice sacs and pack in 50% syrup. (b) Extract juice and sweeten to taste. Freeze in ice cube trays, and wrap frozen cubes in foil for storage.

Quinces

Preparation Peel, core and slice. Simmer in boiling 20% syrup for 20 minutes. Cool and pack in cold 20% syrup.

Serving Thaw 3 hours at room temperature.
High Quality Storage Life 12 months

Raspberries

Preparation (a) Dry unsweetened pack. (b) Dry sugar pack (4 oz sugar to 1 lb. fruit). (c) 30% syrup. (d) Sweetened purée (fresh fruit).

Serving Thaw 3 hours at room temperature. Use purée as sauce, or for drinks, ices, or mousses.
High Quality Storage Life 12 months

Rhubarb

Preparation Wash sticks in cold running water, and trim to required length. (a) Blanch sticks 1 minute, then wrap in foil or polythene. (b) 40% syrup pack. (c) Sweetened purée (cooked fruit).

Serving Thaw 3 hours at room temperature. Raw fruit can be cooked while still frozen.
High Quality Storage Life 12 months

Strawberries

Preparation Use ripe, mature and firm fruit. Pick over fruit, removing hulls. (a) Grade for size in dry unsweetened pack. (b) Dry sugar pack (4 oz sugar to 1 lb. fruit). Fruit may be sliced or lightly crushed. (c) 40% syrup for whole or sliced fruit. (d) Sweetened purée (fresh fruit).

Serving Thaw 1½ hours at room temperature.
High Quality Storage Life 12 months

FREEZING MEAT

Both raw and cooked meat usually store extremely well in the freezer. But it is important to choose high-quality raw meat for storage, whether fresh or frozen, since freezing does not improve poor meat in either texture or flavour (although tender meat may become a little more tender in storage).

Many authorities feel that fresh meat should not be frozen in domestic freezers, since it is not possible to achieve the very low temperatures thought necessary for successful freezing. This point should be thought about carefully when buying in bulk for the freezer. It is also important not to overload the freezer with bulky quantities of meat at the expense of other items, and to keep a good regular turnover of supplies. One good compromise is to use the freezer for keeping special high quality cuts, or those which are not often obtainable, such as pork fillet, veal and fillet steak, together with a variety of prepared dishes made from the cheaper cuts which are useful when time is likely to be short for food preparation. Fresh meat must be hung for the required time before freezing.

CHOOSING MEAT FOR THE FREEZER — Meat should be chosen with the family needs in mind. The better cuts are bound to be more popular, but bulk buying will be a false economy if the family does not eat the cheaper cuts at all. Meat must be of good quality whatever the cut, and must be properly hung (beef 8–12 days; lamb 5–7 days; pork and veal chilled only). Before buying bulk meat, check the diagrams given and suggested uses for each part of the animal, and see if this will fit into the family eating plan.

Beef

THE BETTER CUTS	SUGGESTED USES
Sirloin	Roasting, preferably on the bone
	Grilling as Sirloin Steak
	Entrecôte Steak
	Porterhouse Steak
	T-bone Steak
Fillet	Roasting in pastry case
	Grilling as Châteaubriand
	Fillet Steak
	Tournedos (trimmed)
Rump Steak	Roasting in the piece
	Grilling
Fore Ribs, Wing Ribs, Back Ribs	Roasting preferably on the bone

Top Ribs	Grilling as Minute Steak (thin)
Topside	Roasting, if larded
	Pot Roasting

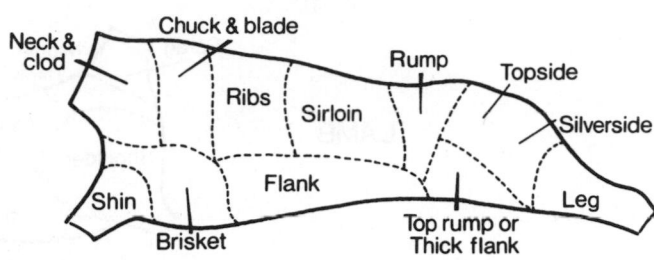

BEEF

THE ECONOMY CUTS

Top Rump or Thick Flank	Pot Roasting
Flank	Pot Roasting (if boned and rolled)
Brisket	Slow Roasting (if de-fatted and rolled)
	Pot Roasting
Silverside	Pot Roasting
Shin	Stewing
	Stock
Leg	Stewing
	Stock
Neck and Clod	Stewing
	Stock
Chuck and Blade	Stewing
	Pies and Puddings
Skirt	Stewing
	Pies and Puddings

Lamb and Mutton

THE BETTER CUTS	**SUGGESTED USES**
Saddle (Double Loin)	Roasting
Loin	Roasting (on or off bone)
	Chops

Leg (Fillet End and Knuckle End)	Roasting Boiling
Shoulder (Blade End and Knuckle End)	Roasting (on or off bone)

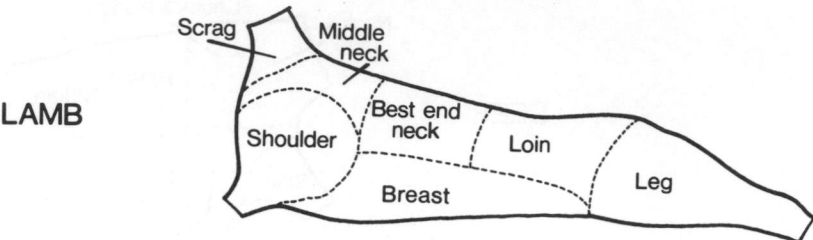

LAMB

THE ECONOMY CUTS

Best End of Neck	Roasting (chined, and as Crown of Lamb) Cutlets Stewing
Middle Neck	Stewing
Scrag End of Neck	Stewing
Breast of Lamb	Roasting (boned, stuffed and rolled) Stewing

Pork

THE BETTER CUTS	**SUGGESTED USES**
Leg	Roasting (on or off bone)
Loin	Roasting (on or off bone) Chops

THE ECONOMY CUTS	
Blade	Roasting

PORK

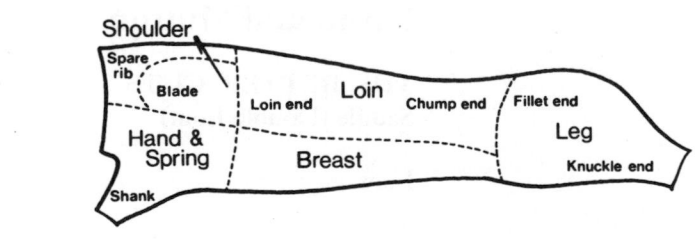

Spare Rib	Roasting
Hand and Spring	Roasting (boned, stuffed and rolled)
Belly	Roasting (boned)
	Grilling (slices)
	Pâté

Bulk supplies of meat should be packaged in quantities which can be used up on a single occasion if possible. Ideally, meat should be boned and the surplus fat removed so as not to take up unnecessary freezer space; if the bones are *not* removed, the ends should be wrapped in several layers of greaseproof paper to avoid piercing freezer wrappings. Meat must be carefully labelled for identification, as identification may be difficult otherwise. Air must be excluded from the packages so that the freezer wrap can touch the surface of the meat all over.

If a whole animal or a variety of different meats are being prepared for freezing at one time, the offal should be processed first, then pork, veal and lamb, and finally beef as this will keep best under refrigeration if delays occur. Normally, not more than 4 lb. of meat per cubic foot of freezer space should be frozen at one time for good results.

The wrapping for meat must be strong, since oxygen from the air which may penetrate wrappings affects fat and may cause rancidity (pork is the most subject to this problem). In addition to moisture-vapour-proof wrapping, an overwrap of brown paper, greaseproof paper or stockinette will protect packages and will guard against punctures from projecting bones or other packets; place the label on the outside of this wrapping. It is worth taking this precaution, since meat is likely to be the most costly item stored in the freezer.

COOKING
FROZEN MEAT

Frozen meat can be cooked when thawed or unthawed, but partial or complete thawing helps it to retain its juiciness. Thin cuts of meat and minced meat may toughen if cooked while still frozen. Offal must always be completely thawed. All meat should be thawed in its wrapping, and preferably in a refrigerator since slow thawing is required. Allow 5 hours per lb. in a refrigerator and 2 hours per lb. at room temperature. If it is really necessary to hurry thawing, this can be done in a cool oven (200°F, 100°C or Gas Mark $\frac{1}{4}$ allowing 25 minutes per lb. but the meat's flavour will not be so good. If meat must be cooked from the frozen state, unthawed large cuts will take $1\frac{1}{2}$ times as long as fresh ones; smaller thin cuts will take $1\frac{1}{4}$ times as long. When thawing offal, sausages and mince, allow $1\frac{1}{2}$ hours at room temperature or 3 hours in a refrigerator for 1 lb. of meat.

Frozen meat can be roasted, braised, grilled, fried or stewed in the same way as fresh meat. In any roasting process, however, it is best to use a slow oven method (for beef, use 300°F, 150°C or Gas Mark 2, and also for lamb; for pork use 350°F, 180°C or Gas Mark 4). Chops and steaks will cook while still frozen if put into a thick frying pan just rubbed with fat and cooked very gently for the first 5 minutes on each side, then browned more quickly. Meat should be cooked as soon as it is thawed, and still cold, to prevent loss of juices.

Here are notes on preparing, packing, storing and cooking various kinds of meat:

Cubed Meat

Preparation Package in usable quantities. Trim fat and cut meat into neat pieces. Press tightly into bags or boxes, removing air.

Serving Thaw in wrappings in refrigerator for 3 hours (1½ hours at room temperature).
High Quality Storage Life 2 months

Ham

Preparation Package in the piece rather than sliced. Pack in freezer paper, foil or polythene, and overwrap. Vacuum-packed bacon may be frozen in its packing. Storage life is limited as salt causes rancidity.

Serving Thaw in wrappings in refrigerator.
High Quality Storage Life 3 months (whole); 1 month (sliced)
Note For BACON, see page 80.

Hearts, Kidneys, Sweetbreads, Tongue

Preparation Wash and dry thoroughly. Remove blood vessels and pipes. Wrap in cellophane or polythene and pack in bags or boxes. Off-flavours may develop if offal is not packed with care.

Serving Thaw in wrappings in refrigerator for 3 hours (1½ hours at room temperature.
High Quality Storage Life 2 months

Joints

Preparation Trim surplus fat. Bone and roll if possible. Pad sharp bones. Wipe meat. Pack in polythene bag or sheeting, freezer paper or foil. Remove air. Freeze quickly.

Serving Thaw in wrappings in refrigerator, allow 5 hours per lb. Roast by slow-oven method (300°F, 150°C or Gas Mark 2 for beef and lamb; 350°F, 130°C or Gas Mark 4 for pork).
High Quality Storage Life Beef 12 months; Lamb 9 months; Pork 6 months; Veal 9 months.

Liver

Preparation Package whole or in slices. Separate slices with greaseproof paper or cellophane.

Serving Thaw in wrappings in refrigerator for 3 hours ($1\frac{1}{2}$ hours at room temperature).
High Quality Storage Life 2 months

Minced Meat

Preparation (a) Use good quality mince without fat. Pack in bags or boxes. Do not add salt. Remove air. Freeze quickly. (b) Shape mince into patties, separated, and pack in bags or boxes. Remove air. Freeze quickly.

Serving Thaw in wrappings in refrigerator for 3 hours ($1\frac{1}{2}$ hours at room temperature). Can be used while frozen, but may be tough.
High Quality Storage Life 2 months

Sausages and Sausage Meat

Preparation Omit salt in preparation. Pack in usable quantities. Wrap tightly in freezer paper, foil or polythene.

Serving Thaw in wrappings in refrigerator for 2 hours. Sausages can be cooked while frozen.
High Quality Storage Life 1 month

Steaks and Chops

Preparation Package in usable quantities. Separate pieces of meat with greaseproof paper or cellophane. Pack in polythene bag or sheeting, freezer paper or foil. Remove air. Freeze quickly.

Serving Thaw in wrappings in refrigerator or use while frozen. Cook gently on both sides in a lightly-oiled thick pan. Brown to serve.
High Quality Storage Life 6–12 months (according to type of meat)

Tripe

Preparation Cut in 1 in. squares and pack tightly in bags or boxes.

Serving Thaw in wrappings in refrigerator for 3 hours (1½ hours at room temperature).
High Quality Storage Life 2 months

Bacon

BUYING BACON
FOR FREEZING **Buying Bacon for Freezing.** (a) Freshness of the bacon is the first vital step to successful freezing. Try and get the bacon the day that the retailer gets delivery from his supplier.
(b) Determine storage period in relation to freshness, and reduce the recommended period if in doubt.
(c) Smoked bacon can be stored for longer than unsmoked bacon.
(d) The quicker bacon is frozen right through, the better it will be. It is therefore inadvisable to freeze pieces weighing more than 5 lb.

PREPARING
BACON FOR
FREEZING **(a) Freshly-cut bacon joints** (i) Determine the size of joint to be required for each meal and cut to this size; (ii) wrap each piece in foil, allowing ample coverage; (iii) exclude as much air as possible; (iv) place each parcel of bacon into a polythene bag. The thicker the bag the better; (v) again exclude as much air as possible. Clip or tie the bag immediately; (vi) mark date and content on each packet.
(b) Bacon rashers, chops and steaks. It may be necessary to freeze these small pieces of bacon but storage time is much less than for joints, only 2 to 4 weeks. This is because so much of the meat and fat surface has been exposed to air with risk of rancidity developing. It is more practical to buy vacuum packed bacon which can be stored in a refrigerator for the same periods. ½ lb. packets which can be thawed and eaten promptly are recommended. If freezing, say before going away on holiday, follow packing instructions for bacon joints.

FREEZING
VACUUM PACKED
BACON Vacuum packing of bacon is the ideal preparation for storage in the freezer because air has already been withdrawn from the packet. Vacuum packing is a commercial process and cannot be undertaken at home. Vacuum packed rashers and joints are almost always available in all shops.
A lot of vacuum packed bacon is so marked; but as vacuum-packing can be confused with other types of wrappings, it is advisable to check this if one is in doubt.
To prepare these packets for the freezer, inspect each one to ensure the vacuum is not damaged, i.e. the bacon should not be loose in the packet. Wrap the packets in foil, and label.

Freezer-stored bacon chops (p. 80) after thawing and cooking.

Sausages, cooked while still frozen (p. 79) and used to top a thawed fruit puree (p. 65).

High quality and economy cuts chosen for the freezer: the roasted joints (in the foreground and at the back) and steaks and breaded chops come from the top quality range, while the chopped meats are from economy cuts (pp. 74–6).

(a) Joints. Allow bacon plenty of time to thaw slowly, preferably in a refrigerator. Bacon can be thawed at room temperature before cooking. Time required depends on the thickness of the piece and the temperature. The wrapping should be removed as soon as possible during thawing.

(b) Bacon rashers and small pieces may be thawed overnight in the refrigerator or dipped in hot water for a few minutes until soft. Dry on kitchen paper before cooking.

(c) Vacuum packed joints. These should be thawed in the bag, in the refrigerator or at room temperature. Cook immediately following instructions on packet. Note: If time is short, joints may be thawed in running water, but should be wrapped in a plastic bag to prevent them getting wet.

COOKING
FROZEN BACON

All frozen bacon should be cooked immediately it has thawed. The usual cooking methods – boiling, grilling, frying and baking are suitable. Once cooked, the bacon will keep 1–2 days in a refrigerator.

Do not re-freeze after thawing either in the raw or cooked state

Cooked fresh bacon joints should not be frozen as this may result in poor appearance with keeping and flavour problems. Small pieces can be used for flavouring stews or such dishes as Quiche Lorraine which are to be put in the freezer for short periods. The dishes should be well wrapped before freezing.

HIGH QUALITY
STORAGE LIFE

1. Bacon joints wrapped as recommended:
   (a) Smoked bacon up to 8 weeks
   (b) Unsmoked bacon up to 5 weeks
2. Vacuum packed bacon joints up to 10 weeks.
3. Vacuum packed rashers or steaks up to 10 weeks.
4. Foil-wrapped rashers, chops or steaks, smoked, 2–4 weeks only.

FREEZING POULTRY AND GAME

PREPARATION
FOR FREEZING
POULTRY

Birds to be frozen should be in perfect condition. They should be starved for 24 hours before killing, then hung and bled well. When the bird is plucked, it is important to avoid skin damage; if scalding, beware of over-scalding which may increase the chance of freezer-burn (grey spots occurring during storage). The bird should be cooled in a refrigerator or cold larder for 12 hours, drawn and completely cleaned. With geese and ducks, it is particularly important to see the oil glands are removed as these will cause tainting.

PACKING

A whole bird should be carefully trussed to make a neat shape for packing. Birds can be frozen as halves or joints. When packing pieces, it is not always ideal to pack a complete bird in each package; it may be more useful ultimately if all drumsticks are packaged together, all breasts or all wings, according to the way in which the flesh will be cooked. Giblets have only a storage life of 2 months, so unless a whole bird is to be used within that time, it is not advisable to pack them inside the bird. Giblets should be cleaned, washed, dried and chilled, then wrapped in moisture-vapour-proof paper or a bag, excluding air; frozen in batches, they can be used for soup, stews or pies. Livers should be treated in the same way, and packaged in batches for use in omelettes, risotto or pâté.

Bones of poultry joints should be padded with paper or foil to avoid tearing the freezer wrappings. Joints should be divided by two layers of Cellophane. Bones of young birds may turn brown in storage, but this does not affect flavour or quality.

STUFFINGS

Stuffing can, if necessary, be put into a bird before freezing, but it is not advisable as the storage life of stuffing is only about 1 month. Pork sausage stuffing should not be used; if a bird must be stuffed, a bread-crumb stuffing is best. It is better to package stuffing separately if some is available when the bird is put into freezer storage; otherwise, it is not worth making specially, as it can easily be prepared while the bird is thawing.

COOKED POULTRY

Old birds such as boiling fowls are best frozen after being cooked; the meat should be stripped from the bones, and frozen; or it can be made at once into pies or casseroles, while the carcass is simmered in the cooking liquid to make strong stock for freezing. Slices of cooked poultry can be frozen on their own, or in sauce (the latter method is preferable to prevent drying out). If the meat is frozen without sauce, slices should be divided by two sheets of Cellophane and then closely packed together excluding air. Roast and fried poultry frozen to be eaten cold are not particularly successful; on thawing they tend to exude moisture and become flabby.

THAWING

Uncooked poultry must thaw completely before cooking. Thawing in the refrigerator will allow slow, even thawing; thawing at room temperature will be twice as fast but the product will be much less satisfactory. A 4–5 lb. chicken will thaw overnight in a refrigerator and will take 6 hours at room temperature. A turkey weighing 9 lb. will take 36 hours; as much as 3 days should be allowed for a very large bird. A thawed bird can be stored for up to 24 hours in a refrigerator, but no more.

All poultry should be thawed in the unopened freezer wrappings. In an emergency, poultry can be thawed quickly by leaving the bag immersed in running cold water, allowing 30 minutes per lb. thawing time; but this is not advisable in the usual way.

PREPARATION FOR FREEZING GAME

Freeze raw birds or animals which are young and well shot. Roast game is usefully frozen in its season, to eat cold later; but on thawing it exudes moisture so that the flesh may be flabby. Old or badly shot game is usually best converted immediately into made-up dishes such as casseroles.

All game intended for freezing should be hung to its required state *before* freezing, as hanging after thawing will result in the flesh going bad. Grouse, pheasant and partridge should be plucked and drawn before freezing. So should any waterfowl fed on fish. Plover, quail, snipe and woodcock should be plucked but not drawn. Hare and rabbit are handled like poultry. Venison is treated like beef; it is best if aged for 5 to 6 days before freezing if the carcass is in good condition and should be chilled soon after shooting, in a cold larder.

All game should be kept cool between shooting and freezing; care should be taken to remove as much shot as possible, and to make sure the shot wounds are thoroughly clean. Birds should be bled as soon as shot, and then hung to individual taste. After plucking and drawing, the cavity should be thoroughly washed and drained and the body wiped with a damp cloth. The birds should then be packed, cooled and frozen like poultry.

THAWING GAME   All game should be thawed in its sealed freezer package; thawing in a refrigerator is more uniform, but of course takes longer. In a refrigerator, allow 5 hours per lb. thawing time; at room temperature, allow 2 hours per lb. Start cooking as soon as game is thawed and still cold, to prevent loss of juices.

Here are notes on the preparation, packing, storage and cooking of the various types of poultry and game:

Chicken

Preparation   Hang and cool. Pluck and draw and pack giblets separately. Truss whole bird or cut in joints. Chill 12 hours. Pack in bag, removing air.

Serving   Thaw in bag in refrigerator. Allow 4–5 lb. bird to thaw overnight (6 hours at room temperature).
High Quality Storage Life   12 months

Duck

Preparation   Hang and cool. Remove oil glands. Pluck and draw and pack giblets separately. Chill 12 hours. Pack in bag, removing air.

Serving   Thaw in bag in refrigerator. Allow 4–5 lb. bird to thaw overnight (6 hours at room temperature).
High Quality Storage Life   6 months

Giblets

Preparation   (a) Clean, wash, dry and chill. Pack in bag, removing air. (b) Cook and pack in cooking liquid in box.

Serving   (a) Thaw in bag in refrigerator for 2 hours. (b) Heat gently and use for soups, stews or pies.
High Quality Storage Life   (a) 2 months, (b) 1 month

Goose

Preparation   Hang and cool. Remove oil glands. Pluck and draw and pack giblets separately. Chill 12 hours. Pack in bag, removing air.

Serving   Thaw in bag in refrigerator. Allow small bird to thaw overnight; large bird will need 24 hours.
High Quality Storage Life   6 months

Guinea Fowl

Preparation   Hang and cool. Pluck and draw and pack giblets separately. Truss and chill 12 hours. Pack in bag, removing air.

Serving   Thaw in bag in refrigerator for 8 hours. As this is a dry bird, lard before roasting.
High Quality Storage Life   12 months

Grouse (12th Aug.–10th Dec.) Partridge (1st Sept.–1st Feb.)

Pheasant (1st Oct.–1st Feb.)

Preparation   Remove shot and clean wounds. Bleed as soon as shot, keep cool and hang to taste. Pluck, draw and truss. Pad bones. Pack in bag, removing air. If birds are old or badly shot, prepare as casseroles, soups, pies.

Serving   Thaw in bag in refrigerator for 5 hours per lb. (2 hours per lb. at room temperature). Cook as soon as thawed.
High Quality Storage Life   6 months

Hares and Rabbits

Preparation   Clean shot wounds. Behead and bleed as soon as possible, collecting hare's blood if needed for cooking. Hang for 24 hours in a cool place. Skin, clean and wipe. Cut into joints and wrap each piece in cellophane. Pack in usable quantities in bags. Pack blood in box.

Serving Thaw in bag in refrigerator for 5 hours per lb. (2 hours per lb. at room temperature).
High Quality Storage Life 6 months

Livers

Preparation Clean, wash, dry and chill. Pack in bag, removing air.

Serving Thaw in bag in refrigerator for 2 hours.
High Quality Storage Life 2 months

Pigeons

Preparation Remove shot and clean wounds. Prepare and pack as feathered game. Pigeons are usefully prepared as casseroles or pies for freezing.

Serving Thaw in bag in refrigerator for 5 hours per lb. (2 hours per lb. at room temperature).
High Quality Storage Life 6 months

Plover, Quail, Snipe, Woodcock

Preparation Remove shot and clean wounds. Prepare as other feathered game but do not draw. Pad bones. Pack in bag, removing air.

Serving Thaw in bag in refrigerator for 5 hours per lb. (2 hours per lb. at room temperature). Cook as soon as thawed.
High Quality Storage Life 6 months

Stuffing

Preparation (a) Prepare stuffing to standard recipe. Pack in box or bag. (b) Prepare stuffing and form into balls. Deep-fry, cool and pack into box or bag.

Serving (a) Thaw in bag in refrigerator for 2 hours. (b) Thaw in bag in refrigerator for 2 hours. Put into roasting tin or casserole 10 minutes before serving.
High Quality Storage Life 1 month

Turkey

Preparation Hang and cool. Pluck and draw, and pack giblets separately. Truss whole or cut in joints. Chill for 12 hours. Pack in bag, removing air.

Serving Thaw in bag in refrigerator for 2 days (small birds); 3 days (large birds).
High Quality Storage Life 12 months

Venison

Preparation Clean shot wounds. Keep the carcase cold until butchered. Behead, bleed, skin and clean, wash and wipe flesh. Hang in a cool place for 5 days. Joint and pack in bags, removing air. Freeze the good joints, but prepare other cuts as cooked dishes for freezing.

Serving Thaw in wrappings in refrigerator for 4 hours. Remove from wrappings and put into marinade. Continue thawing, allowing 5 hours per lb. Lard meat for roasting. Use the marinade for gravy or casseroles. For the marinade, which will prevent the meat from being dry when cooked, mix $\frac{1}{2}$ pint red wine, $\frac{1}{2}$ pint vinegar, 1 large sliced onion, parsley, thyme and bayleaf. Turn the venison frequently while marinading.
High Quality Storage Life 8 months

FREEZING FISH AND SHELLFISH

Only really fresh fish can be frozen, since it must be processed within 24 hours. Therefore it is not advisable to freeze shop-purchased fish.
Cooked fish can be frozen in sauces or pies, or ready-fried, but it is rarely worth the trouble to cook fish specially for freezing. Fish should never be overcooked and the time taken to reheat will not only spoil flavour and rob the fish of any nutritive value, but will also take as long as the original cooking.
Fatty fish (i.e. haddock, halibut, herring, mackerel, salmon, trout, turbot) will keep for 4 months at most. White fish (i.e. cod, plaice, sole, whiting) will keep for 6 months. Shellfish are best stored no longer than 1 month. It is wise to keep fish for only the shortest possible time in the freezer.
It is interesting to freeze smoked fish such as bloaters, kippers and haddock.

PREPARATION FOR FREEZING Since the fish must be fresh, one must clean home-caught fish ready for freezing as soon as it is caught. The fish should be killed at once, scaled if necessary and fins removed. Small fish can be left whole; large fish should have heads and tails removed, or can be divided into steaks. Flat fish and herrings are best gutted, and flat fish skinned and filleted. White fish should be washed well in salted water during cleaning to remove blood and membranes, but fatty fish should be washed in fresh water.

FREEZING METHODS

There are four ways of preparing fish for freezing, the first two being the most common.

(a) Dry Pack. Separate pieces of fish with double thickness of Cellophane, wrap in moisture-vapour-proof paper, carton or bag, seal and freeze. Be sure the paper is in close contact with the fish to exclude air which will dry the fish and make it tasteless. Freeze quickly on the floor of the freezer.

(b) Brine Pack. (This is *not* suitable for fatty fish, as salt tends to oxidise and lead to rancidity.) Dip fish into cold salted water (1 tablespoon salt to 1 quart water), drain, wrap and seal. Do not keep brine-dipped fish longer than 3 months.

(c) Acid Pack. Citric acid preserves the colour and flavour of fish; ascorbic acid is an anti-oxidant which stops the development of rancidity in fish which can cause off-flavours and smells. A chemist can provide an ascorbic-citric acid powder, to be diluted in a proportion of 1 part powder to 100 parts of water. Dip fish into this solution, drain, wrap and seal.

(d) Solid Ice Pack. Small fish, steaks or fillets can be covered with water in refrigerator trays or loaf tins and frozen into solid blocks. The fish should be separated by double paper as usual. Remove ice blocks from pan, wrap in freezer paper and store. The fish can also be frozen in a solid ice pack in large waxed tubs; cover the fish completely to within $\frac{1}{2}$ in. of container top and crumple a piece of Cellophane over the top of the fish before closing the lid. The only advantage in this solid ice method is a saving of containers and wrapping material.

FREEZING LARGE WHOLE FISH

Sometimes a large whole fish may be wanted; if so, it can be frozen whole, but is best protected by 'glazing'. Salmon and salmon trout are obvious examples, or perhaps a haddock or halibut to serve stuffed for a party.

To Glaze a Large Fish

First clean the fish. Then place the unwrapped fish against the freezer wall in the coldest possible part of the freezer. When the fish is frozen solid, dip it very quickly into very cold water so a thin coating of ice will form. Return fish to freezer for an hour, and repeat process. Continue until ice has built up to $\frac{1}{4}$ in. thickness. The fish can be stored without wrappings for 2 weeks, but is better wrapped in freezer paper for longer storage.

SMOKED FISH

Bloaters, kippers and haddock can be wrapped and frozen and will keep for 2 months. No special preparation is necessary.

87

Freshly caught shellfish can be frozen immediately after cooking. Scallops and oysters are frozen raw. Shrimps can be frozen when cooked, or after being potted in butter.

THAWING AND COOKING All fish should be thawed slowly in unopened wrappings. A 1-lb. or 1-pint package takes about 3 hours at room temperature, or 6 hours in a refrigerator. Frozen fish may be used for boiling, steaming, grilling or frying; except for frying, complete thawing is not necessary.

Here are notes on preparing, freezing, storing and cooking fish:

Crab

Preparation Cook, drain and cool. Clean crab and remove edible meat. Pack into boxes or bags.

Serving Thaw in container in refrigerator. Serve cold, or add to hot dishes.
High Quality Storage Life 1 month

Fatty Fish (Haddock, Halibut, Mackerel, Salmon, Trout, Turbot)

Preparation Clean. Fillet or cut in steaks if liked, or leave whole. Separate pieces of fish with double thickness of cellophane. Wrap in freezer paper, or put in box or bag. Be sure air is excluded, or fish will be dry and tasteless. Keep pack shallow. Freeze quickly. Large fish may be prepared in solid ice pack. Do not use brine pack.

Serving Thaw large fish in unopened container in refrigerator. Cook small pieces of fish while frozen.
High Quality Storage Life 1 month

Lobster and Crayfish

Preparation Cook, cool and split. Remove flesh and pack into boxes or bags.

Serving Thaw in container in refrigerator. Serve cold, or add to hot dishes.
High Quality Storage Life 1 month

Mussels

Preparation Scrub very thoroughly and remove any fibrous matter sticking out from the shell. Put in a large saucepan and cover with a damp cloth. Put over medium heat about 3 minutes until they open. Cool in the pan. Remove from shells and pack in boxes, covering with their own juice.

Serving Thaw in container in refrigerator and cook, using as fresh fish.
High Quality Storage Life   1 month

Oysters

Preparation Open oysters and save liquid. Wash fish in salt water (1 teaspoon salt to 1 pint water). Pack in boxes, covering with own liquid.

Serving Thaw in container in refrigerator. Serve raw or cooked.
High Quality Storage Life   1 month

Prawns

Preparation Cook and cool in cooking water. Remove shells. Pack tightly in boxes or bags.

Serving Thaw in container in refrigerator. Serve cold, or use for cooking.
High Quality Storage Life   1 month

Scallops

Preparation Open shells. Wash fish in salt water (1 teaspoon salt to 1 pint water). Pack in boxes covering with salt water, and leaving $\frac{1}{2}$ in. headspace.

Serving Thaw in container in refrigerator. Drain and cook, using as fresh fish.
High Quality Storage Life   1 month

Shrimps

Preparation (a) Cook and cool in cooking water. Remove shells. Pack in boxes or bags. (b) Cook and shell shrimps. Pack in waxed boxes and cover with melted spiced butter.

Serving (a) Thaw in container in refrigerator to eat cold. Add frozen shrimps to hot dishes. (b) Thaw in container in refrigerator.
High Quality Storage Life   1 month

Smoked Fish (Bloaters, Eel, Haddock, Kippers, Mackerel, Salmon, Sprats, Trout)

Preparation   Pack fish in layers with Cellophane between. Keep pack shallow.

Serving   To eat cold, thaw in refrigerator. Haddock and kippers may be cooked while frozen.
High Quality Storage Life   2 months

White Fish (Cod, Plaice, Sole, Whiting)

Preparation   Clean. Fillet or cut in steaks if liked, or leave whole. Separate pieces of fish with double thickness of Cellophane. Wrap in freezer paper, or put in box or bag. Be sure air is excluded, or fish will be dry and tasteless. Keep pack shallow. Freeze quickly.

Serving   Thaw large fish in unopened container in refrigerator. Cook small pieces of fish while frozen.
High Quality Storage Life   3 months

FREEZING DAIRY PRODUCE

Dairy produce should not be allowed to take up much freezer space. But it can be useful to freeze quantities of cheap fat or eggs when available; cheese left after large parties; leftover egg yolks or whites or cracked eggs bought cheaply, or thick cream brought back from a country holiday.

Butter or Margarine

Preparation   Overwrap blocks in foil or polythene.

Serving   Thaw enough for one week's use.
High Quality Storage Life   6 months (unsalted); 3 months (salted)

Cheese

Preparation   (a) Freeze hard cheese such as Cheddar in small portions (8 oz or less). Divide slices with double Cellophane and wrap in foil or freezer paper.
(b) Freeze grated cheese in polythene bags; the pieces remain separated.
(c) Freeze Camembert, Port Salut, Stilton, Danish Blue and Roquefort with careful sealing to avoid drying out and cross-contamination.

(a) Thaw in open wrappings at room temperature for 2 hours. Cut while slightly frozen to avoid crumbling. (b) Sprinkle on dishes or thaw for 1 hour before adding to sauces. (c) Thaw 1 day in refrigerator and 1 day at room temperature for full flavour.
High Quality Storage Life (a) 3 months, (b) 3 months, (c) 6 months

Cottage Cheese

Preparation Freeze in waxed tubs or rigid plastic containers. Freeze quickly to avoid water separation.

Serving Thaw in container in refrigerator overnight.
High Quality Storage Life 3 months

Cream

Preparation Use pasteurised cream, over 40% butterfat. Freeze in cartons (1 in. headspace).

Serving Thaw in container at room temperature. Beat lightly with a fork to make smooth. Note that in hot drinks, oil will rise to the surface.
High Quality Storage Life 6 months

Cream Cheese

Preparation Best blended with heavy cream and frozen as a cocktail dip in waxed tubs or rigid plastic containers.

Serving Thaw in container in refrigerator overnight. Blend with a fork to make smooth.
High Quality Storage Life 3 months

Eggs

Preparation Do not freeze eggs in shell. Blend lightly with a fork. Add $\frac{1}{2}$ teaspoon salt or $\frac{1}{2}$ teaspoon sugar to 5 eggs. Pack in waxed or rigid plastic containers. Label with number of eggs and 'salt' or 'sugar'.

Serving Thaw in unopened container in refrigerator. Use as fresh eggs as soon as thawed. 3 tablespoons whole egg = 1 fresh egg.
High Quality Storage Life 12 months

Egg Whites

Preparation   Freeze in waxed or rigid plastic containers or in ice-cube trays. Label with number of whites.

Serving   Thaw in refrigerator, but bring to room temperature before use. Can be whipped successfully.
High Quality Storage Life   12 months

Egg Yolks

Preparation   Mix lightly with a fork. Add $\frac{1}{2}$ teaspoon salt or $\frac{1}{2}$ tablespoon sugar to 6 yolks. Label with number of yolks and 'salt' or 'sugar'. Can be frozen in waxed or rigid plastic containers or in ice-cube trays. Transfer cubes to polythene bags for storage.

Serving   Thaw in refrigerator. Use alone or mix with whites.
High Quality Storage Life   12 months

Milk

Preparation   Freeze homogenised milk in cartons (1 in. headspace).

Serving   Thaw at room temperature and use quickly.
High Quality Storage Life   1 month

Whipped Cream

Preparation   Use 1 tablespoon sugar to 1 pint cream. (a) Freeze in cartons (1 in. head-space). (b) Pipe in rosettes, freeze on open trays and pack in boxes.

Serving   Thaw in container at room temperature. Rosettes will thaw in 15 minutes at room temperature.
High Quality Storage Life   6 months

ICE CREAM

Home-made ice cream can be stored in the freezer for 3 months. Bought ice cream is best stored no longer than 1 month. If large containers of bought ice cream are stored, and not repackaged into serving sizes before storage, they should be used sooner than this after opening. When portions have been taken out of a large container, a piece of foil over the unused portion will help to retain flavour and texture.

Home-made ice cream for the freezer is best made with pure cream and gelatine or egg yolks. For immediate use, evaporated milk may be used, but the flavour is less good (before using the unopened tin of milk should be boiled for 10 minutes, cooled and left in a refrigerator overnight). A smooth commercial product cannot be produced from a home freezer. The ingredients are different and so is the equipment which gives a smooth ice cream. Crank attachments can now be bought for freezers, however, which work on the principle of the old dasher-churn, giving a constant beating which produces a relatively smooth product.

All home-made ice cream should be frozen quickly, or it will be 'grainy'. The correct emulsifying agent will help to make a smooth product. Egg, gelatine, cream or sugar syrup will stop large ice crystals forming; gelatine gives a particularly smooth ice. Whipped egg whites give lightness. Freezing diminishes sweetness, but too much sugar will prevent freezing. The correct proportion is one part sugar to four parts liquid.

PREPARATION
FOR FREEZING
ICE CREAM

Whatever emulsifying agent is used, the preparation is similar. The mixture should be packed into trays and frozen until just solid about $\frac{1}{2}$ in. from the edge. The mixture should then be beaten quickly in a chilled bowl, and then frozen again for a further hour. This 'freezing and beating' technique should be repeated for up to three hours. Some freezer owners save time by packing the ice cream into storage containers and freezing after the first beating, but results are less smooth, and it is preferable to complete the ice cream before packing for storage. To remove portions of ice cream from a large container, dip a scoop into boiling water before cutting into the ice cream.

To make moulds of ice cream, press the finished ice into metal moulds (if double-sided moulds are not available, use metal jelly moulds, cover tops with foil, wrap and seal). To turn out, invert mould on plate and cover metal with cloth wrung out in hot water. Two-flavoured moulds can be made by lining mould with one flavour and filling with another (chopped fruit or nuts may be added to the inner ice cream).

Basic Ice Cream

Preparation
Prepare standard recipe and freeze in trays. When completed, pack in rigid plastic boxes, filling air space with crumpled foil or Cellophane. Seal tightly.

Serving
Scoop out into dishes. Fill remaining airspace in container with crumpled foil or Cellophane.
High Quality Storage Life   3 months

Fresh Fruit Ices

Preparation   Prepare standard recipe and freeze in trays. Add pieces of fresh fruit before final freezing. Pack in rigid plastic boxes, filling air space with crumpled foil or Cellophane. Seal tightly.

Serving   Scoop out into dishes. Fill remaining air space in container with crumpled foil or Cellophane.
High Quality Storage Life   3 months

Ice Cream Cakes

Preparation   Alternate round or square layers of sponge cake with layers of ice cream in a freezer container. Decorate the top if wished. If cake is decorated, freeze unwrapped before packing.

Serving   Unwrap and thaw at room temperature for 15 minutes.
High Quality Storage Life   3 months

Moulds or Bombes

Preparation   Use double-sided moulds, jelly moulds or pudding basins. Soften ice cream slightly and line the mould. Freeze for 1 hour, then put in the next layer of ice cream. Freeze again then add another ice cream, or a filling of fruit and/or liqueur. Wrap in foil, seal and freeze.

Serving   Turn out on chilled plate, using cloth wrung out in hot water. Wrap in foil and freeze 1 hour before serving.
High Quality Storage Life   3 months

Sorbets

Preparation   (a) Pack in leakproof rigid plastic or waxed containers and seal tightly, as these water ices do not freeze completely hard during storage. (b) Pack into clean orange or lemon skins and wrap in foil, sealing tightly.

Serving   (a) Scoop on to plates or fill fresh fruit skins. (b) Remove foil and return to freezer for 1 hour to frost the skins.
High Quality Storage Life   3 months

FREEZING BREAD, CAKES, PASTRY AND SANDWICHES

PREPARATION FOR FREEZING BREAD AND CAKES

Small cakes, buns and rolls are most easily frozen in polythene bags; small iced cakes are better packed in boxes. Large quantities of small iced cakes can be frozen in single layers, then packed in larger boxes with Cellophane or greaseproof paper between the layers. Bread and large cakes can both be frozen in polythene bags. While it is usually most convenient to pack cakes whole, some families may need meal-size wedges or individual pieces for lunch-boxes. These pieces can be frozen individually in bags or boxes, but it is easier to slice the whole cake in wedges before freezing, and take slices as needed without thawing the whole cake. When making cakes for freezing, it is most important to use good ingredients. Stale flour deteriorates quickly after freezing, so it is important to use fresh flour. Butter cakes retain a good flavour, but margarine is more suitable for strongly-flavoured cakes such as chocolate, and it always gives a good light texture. Eggs should be fresh and very well beaten, as whites and yolks freeze at different speeds and this can affect the texture of the cake. Icings for freezing are best made with butter and icing sugar; cakes should *not* be filled with boiled icing or with cream as these will crumble on thawing; so will icings made with egg whites. Fruit fillings and jams will make a cake soggy, and are best added after thawing. Flavourings must always be pure, as synthetics develop off-flavours in storage (this is particularly important with vanilla, and only pure extract or vanilla sugar made with a pod should be used). If the freezer user is not an enthusiastic bread or cake cook, there is no reason why bought cakes should not be frozen for emergencies. Buns, Dundee cakes, unfilled sponges and sponge flan cases all freeze well and are very useful, but the same limitations concerning icings and fillings will apply to bought cakes as to home-baked ones. Crumpets and muffins are bought seasonal delicacies which can be frozen for future use.

UNCOOKED YEAST MIXTURES

It is possible to freeze unbaked bread and buns for up to 2 weeks, but proving after freezing takes a long time, and the final texture may be heavier. If unbaked dough is frozen, it should be allowed to prove once, and either shaped for baking or kept in bulk if storage in this form is easier. Brush the surface with a little olive oil or unsalted melted butter to prevent toughening of the crust, and add a little extra sugar to sweet mixtures.

Single loaves or a quantity of dough can be packed in freezer paper or polythene, and rolls can be packed in layers separated by Cellophane before wrapping in freezer paper or polythene.

The dough should be thawed in a moist warm place, quickly. Speed will help to give a light-textured loaf. After thawing the dough can be shaped and proved again before baking. Shaped bread and rolls should only be proved once, in a warm place, before baking.

BISCUITS   Biscuits are the exception to the rule that cooked frozen goods are better than uncooked ones. Baked biscuits do freeze very well, but they store equally well in tins, so there is no advantage in using valuable freezer space for them. The most useful and time-saving way of preparing biscuits is to freeze batches of any favourite recipe in cylinder shapes, wrapped in freezer paper, polythene or.foil. Overwrapping is advisable to avoid dents in the freezer from other packages. The dough will be all the better for having been frozen, giving light crisp biscuits. To use, leave in freezer wrappings in the refrigerator for 45 minutes until just beginning to soften, then cut in slices and bake; if the dough gets too soft it will be difficult to cut. If baked biscuits are to be stored, they must be carefully packed in layers in cartons with Cellophane or greaseproof paper between layers and with crumpled up paper in air spaces to safeguard freshness and stop breakages.

ICINGS AND FILLINGS   Cakes for storage should not be filled with cream, jam or fruit. Butter icings are best, but an iced cake must be absolutely firm before wrapping and freezing. Brief chilling in the refrigerator will achieve this in hot weather. Wrappings must be removed before thawing to allow moisture to escape and to avoid smudging the icing. If sponge or flavoured cakes are to be packed for future icing later on, the layers can be stacked with Cellophane, foil or greaseproof paper between them, and can be separated easily for filling when thawed.

FLAVOURINGS AND DECORATIONS   Flavourings must be pure for all icings and fillings, and vanilla extract or vanilla sugar should be used when vanilla is needed. Highly spiced foods may develop off-flavours, so spice cakes should not usually be frozen, though an ordinary gingerbread is perfectly satisfactory. Chocolate, coffee, and fruit-flavoured cakes freeze very well. There is no particular advantage in decorating cakes before they are frozen, and nuts, coloured balls, grated chocolate etc. should be put on when the cake is fully thawed, just before serving; otherwise moisture may be absorbed and colour changes affect the appearance of the cake.

PREPARATION FOR FREEZING PASTRY   Short pastry and flaky pastry freeze equally well either cooked or uncooked, but a standard balanced recipe should be used for best results. Commercially-frozen pastry is one of the most useful and successful freezer stand-bys. Pastry can be stored unbaked or baked; baked pastry keeps longer (baked: 6 months; unbaked: 4 months), but unbaked pastry has a better flavour and scent, and is crisper and flakier.

UNBAKED PASTRY   Pastry can be rolled, formed into a square, wrapped in greaseproof paper, then in foil or polythene for freezing. This pastry takes time to thaw, and may crumble when rolled. It should be thawed slowly, then cooked as fresh pastry and eaten fresh-baked, *not* returned to the freezer in cooked form.

96

TOP Frozen vols-au-vent (p. 97) and ice cream (p. 93) make this party dessert.
ABOVE Pastry made into turnovers or pasties and frozen when baked (p. 97).

Danish pastries (p. 204).

BAKED PASTRY	Flan cases, patty cases and vol-au-vent cases are all useful to keep ready-baked. For storage, it is best to keep them in the cases in which they are baked or in foil cases. Small cases can be packed in boxes in layers with paper between. Baked cases should be thawed in their wrappings at room temperature before filling. They can be heated in a low oven if a hot filling is to be used.
PREPARATION FOR FREEZING PIES	Frozen pies provide useful meals, and are a neat way of storing surplus fruit, meat and poultry. Large pies can be stored, also turnovers, pasties and individual fruit pies. Both pies and flans can be stored baked or unbaked. A baked pie usually keeps longer (depending on the filling), but an unbaked pie has a better flavour and scent, and the pastry is crisper and flakier. Almost all fillings can be used, except those with custard which separates. Meringue toppings should not be used as they toughen and dry during storage.
BAKED PIES	Pies can be baked in the normal way, then cooled quickly before freezing. A pie is best prepared and frozen in foil, but can be stored in a rust-proof and crack-proof container. The container should be put into freezer paper or polythene for freezing. A cooked pie should be heated at 375°F, 190°C, Gas Mark 5, for 40–50 minutes for a double-crust pie and for 30–50 minutes for a one-crust pie, depending on size. Cooked pies can also be thawed in their wrappings at room temperature and eaten without reheating.
UNBAKED PIES	Pies can be prepared with or without a bottom crust. To prevent sogginess, it is better to freeze unbaked pies before wrapping them. Air vents should be cut in the top crust after freezing, not before. To bake pies, cut slits in the frozen top crust and bake unthawed like fresh pies, allowing about 10 minutes longer than the normal cooking time.
FRUIT FILLINGS	If the surface of the bottom crust of fruit pies is brushed with egg white, it will not get soggy. Fruit pies can be made with cooked or uncooked fillings. Apples tend to brown if stored in a pie for more than 4 weeks, even if treated with lemon juice, so it is better to combine frozen pastry and frozen apples to make a pie.
	If time is likely to be short, it is often convenient to freeze ready-made fruit pie fillings ahead, ready to fit into fresh pastry when needed; this is also a good way of freezing surplus fruit in a handy form. The mixture is best frozen in a sponge-cake tin or an oven-glass pie plate lined with foil, then removed from container and wrapped in foil for storage; the same container can then be used for making the pie later on. A little cornflour or flaked tapioca added to fruit when cooking it gives a firm pie filling which cuts well and does not seep through the pastry.
MEAT FILLINGS	Meat pies can be completely cooked so that they need only be reheated for serving. Preparation time is saved however if the meat filling is

cooked and cooled, then topped with pastry. If the pie is made in this form, the time taken to cook the pastry is enough to heat the meat filling, and the process takes only a little longer than heating the whole pie.

Pies are most easily frozen in foil containers which can be used in the oven for final cooking. If a bottom crust is used, sogginess will be prevented if the bottom pastry is brushed with melted butter or lard just before filling. Pies should be reheated at 400°F, 200°C, Gas Mark 6, for the required time, according to size; they should not be stored longer than 2 months.

HOT WATER CRUST PIES
These are normally eaten cold, and can be frozen baked or unbaked; but there are obvious risks attached to freezing them. The pastry is made with hot water, and the pie must be completely baked *and cooled* before freezing; and the jelly must only be added just before the pie is to be served. The easiest way to do this is to freeze the stock separately at the time of making the pie, and when the pie is thawing (which takes about 4 hours) the partially-thawed pie can be filled with boiling stock through the hole in the crust (which will speed up the thawing process). Another method involves freezing the pie unbaked, partially thawing it and then baking it. However, this means that the uncooked meat is in contact with the warm uncooked pastry during the making process, and unless the pie is very carefully handled while cooling, there is every risk of dangerous organisms entering the meat.

It seems better therefore to avoid freezing game or pork pies made with this type of pastry.

OPEN TARTS
Tarts with only a bottom crust can be filled and frozen very successfully. They are better frozen before wrapping to avoid spoiling the surface of the filling during packing.

PIZZA
Bought or home-made pizza can be frozen, and are useful for entertaining and for snack meals. The pizza is best frozen on a flat foil plate on which it can be baked, wrapped in foil for storage. Anchovies should be omitted from the topping if possible as their saltiness may cause rancidity in the fatty cheese during storage; they can be added at the reheating stage. Fresh herbs should be used rather than dried. To serve, unwrap and thaw at room temperature for 1 hour, then bake at 375°F, 190°C, Gas Mark 5, for 25 minutes, and serve very hot.

QUICHES
Open savoury flans or quiches made with short pastry are best completed and baked before freezing. They should be frozen without wrapping to avoid spoiling the surface, then wrapped in foil or polythene for storage, or packed in boxes to avoid damage. It is easier to bake and freeze these flans in foil cases, but this does not give much depth of filling, so that it is preferable to prepare them in flan rings, freeze unwrapped, and pack in boxes to avoid breaking the sides. They should be thawed in loose wrappings at room temperature to serve cold, but taste

better if reheated. The traditional Quiche Lorraine freezes well, and spinach, shellfish and mushroom flans are also good. Leftover meat, fish or vegetables can also be bound with a savoury sauce and frozen in a pastry case.

FLAN CASES   Unfilled flan cases can be frozen baked or unbaked. Unbaked cases should be frozen in flan rings. Baked cases are fragile, and are best packed in boxes to avoid crushing. Baked cases are the most useful to keep in the freezer as a meal can be produced more quickly with them. Baked cases should be thawed in their wrappings at room temperature before filling (about 1 hour should be enough); but a hot filling can be used when the case is taken from the freezer and the whole flan then heated in a slow oven.

FLANS   Filled flans with open tops are best completed and baked before freezing, whether they are savoury or sweet. They should be frozen without wrapping to avoid spoiling the surface, then wrapped in foil or polythene for storage, or packed in boxes to avoid damage. Custard fillings should be avoided; so should meringue toppings which toughen and dry during storage. A meringue topping can be added just before serving. Thaw flans in loose wrappings at room temperature for 2 hours to serve cold, or reheat if required. Storage time: 2 months with fresh fillings; 1 month if made with leftover meat or vegetables.

PREPARATION FOR FREEZING SANDWICHES   Every filling keeps for a different length of time; so the best general rule is not to store any sandwiches in the freezer for longer than 4 weeks. Sandwiches should be packaged in groups of six or eight rather than individually; an extra slice or crust of bread at each end of the package will help to prevent them drying out.

Avoid fillings which contain cooked egg whites, which become dry and tough with freezing. Also avoid raw vegetables such as celery, lettuce, tomatoes and carrots, and salad cream or mayonnaise which will curdle and separate when frozen and soak into the bread when thawed. To prevent fillings seeping through, butter the bread liberally; this is easier to do if the bread is one day old.

Give variety to sandwiches by using a number of breads. Whole wheat, rye, pumpernickel and fruit breads are all excellent (the brown breads are particularly good for fish fillings, and the fruit bread for cheese and sweet fillings).

Sandwiches should not be frozen against the freezer wall as it will result in uneven thawing. Put the packages a few inches from the wall of the freezer, and see that the crusty edges of the sandwiches are towards the wall. Sandwiches should be defrosted in their wrappings at room temperature for four hours.

When quantities of sandwiches must be prepared, an assembly-line technique will speed up matters. Try doing them this way:

(a) Soften butter or margarine (but do not melt).

(b) Prepare fillings and refrigerate ready for use.

(c) Assemble wrapping materials.

(d) Assemble breads and cut (or split rolls or baps).

(e) Spread bread slices, going right to the edge to prevent fillings soaking in.

(f) Spread fillings evenly on bread to ensure even thawing time.

(g) Close and stack sandwiches.

(h) Cut with a sharp knife (sandwiches are best left in rather large portions, such as half slices) and leave crusts on.

(i) Wrap sandwiches tightly in Cellophane, then in foil or other moisture-vapour-proof wrap. With an inner wrapping, the other covering may be removed and retained at home and the neat inner package taken in a lunch box for thawing.

(j) Label and freeze.

These fillings are very satisfactory:

Cheese Cream cheese with olives and peanuts
Cream cheese with chutney
Cream cheese with chopped dates, figs or prunes
Cottage cheese with orange marmalade or apricot jam
Blue cheese with roast beef
Blue cheese with chopped cooked bacon
Cheddar cheese and chopped olives or chutney

Fish Mashed sardines, hard-boiled egg yolk and a squeeze of lemon juice
Minced shrimps, crab or lobster with cream cheese and lemon juice
Tuna with chutney
Canned salmon with cream cheese and lemon juice

Meat and Poultry Sliced meat such as tongue, corned beef, luncheon meat and chutney
Sliced roast beef with horseradish sauce
Sliced roast lamb with mint jelly
Sliced chicken or turkey with ham and chutney
Minced ham with chopped pickled cucumber and cream cheese

OPEN FREEZING BAKED GOODS It is preferable to freeze iced cakes and delicate pies before packaging them. They can be frozen on metal or plastic trays, and then packed in polythene or foil, or in a rigid box to prevent crushing.

Here are notes on preparing, packing, storing and cooking various baked goods:

Babas and Savarins

Preparation (a) If syrup has been poured on to cake, pack in leakproof container.

(b) Pack cake without syrup in foil or polythene.

Serving   (a) Thaw (without wrappings) at room temperature. (b) Thaw without wrappings at room temperature, and pour on warm syrup.
High Quality Storage Life   3 months

Biscuits

Preparation   (a) Make dough and form into cylinder about 2 in. diameter. Wrap in foil or polythene. (b) Bake biscuits. Pack carefully in boxes to avoid crushing. Biscuits keep well in tins, so freezer space need not be wasted.

Serving   (a) Thaw in wrappings in refrigerator for 45 minutes. Cut in slices and bake at 375°F, 190°C, Gas Mark 5, for 10 minutes. (b) Thaw in wrappings at room temperature for 1 hour. Baked biscuits may be rather soft when thawed.
High Quality Storage Life   (a) 2 months, (b) 4 months

Bread (Baked)

Preparation   Wrap in foil or polythene bags.

Serving   (a) Thaw in wrappings at room temperature for 3–6 hours, or in refrigerator overnight. (b) Put frozen loaf in foil in moderate oven (400°F, 200°C or Gas Mark 6) for 45 minutes.
High Quality Storage Life   4 weeks (plain bread); 6 weeks (enriched bread); 1 week (crisp-crusted bread).

Bread Dough

Preparation   (a) Form kneaded dough into a ball. Put in lightly greased polythene bag. Seal tightly and freeze at once. (b) Put dough in a large lightly greased polythene bag; tie loosely at top and leave to rise. Turn on to floured surface, knock back and knead until firm. Replace in polythene bag, seal tightly and freeze at once.

Serving   Unseal bag, and tie loosely at the top to allow space for rising. Thaw 6 hours at room temperature or overnight in refrigerator. Knock back, shape, rise and bake.
High Quality Storage Life   (a) 8 weeks (plain dough); 5 weeks (enriched dough); (b) 3 weeks.

Bread (Fruit and Nut)

Preparation   Do not overbake. Cool quickly. Pack in polythene bags.

Serving   Thaw in wrappings at room temperature. Slice while partly frozen to prevent crumbling.
High Quality Storage Life   2 months

Bread (Part-baked)

Preparation   Leave in wrapper and put into polythene bag. Seal and freeze at once.

Serving   Put frozen loaf in hot oven (425°F, 220°C or Gas Mark 7) for 30 minutes. Cool 2 hours before cutting.
High Quality Storage Life   4 months

Bread (Sliced)

Preparation   Leave in wrapper and put in polythene bags. Seal and freeze at once.

Serving   (a) Thaw in wrappings at room temperature for 3–6 hours, or in refrigerator overnight. (b) Separate frozen slices with a knife and toast at once.
High Quality Storage Life   4 weeks

Brioche

Preparation   Pack immediately after baking and cooling in polythene bags.

Serving   Thaw in wrappings at room temperature for 30 minutes, and heat in oven or under grill, with or without filling.
High Quality Storage Life   2 months

Cake (Butter-iced)

Preparation   Put together cake layers with butter icing, and ice top with butter icing. Do not add decorations. Fast-freeze on a tray without wrappings. When frozen, pack in box, or in foil or polythene bag.

Serving   Remove wrappings and thaw at room temperature for $1\frac{1}{2}$ hours. Add decorations.
High Quality Storage Life   4 months

Cake (Light Fruit)

Preparation   A light fruit cake, such as Dundee or sultana cake, will freeze well. Wrap in foil or polythene bag.

Serving   Thaw in wrappings at room temperature for 2 hours.
High Quality Storage Life   4 months

Cake (Sponge)

Preparation   Sponges made with and without fat freeze equally well. Pack in layers with greaseproof paper or Cellophane between. Pack in foil or polythene bag.

Serving   Thaw in wrappings at room temperature for 1½ hours.
High Quality Storage Life   4 months (with fat); 10 months (fatless).

Cakes (Slab)

Preparation   Light fruit cakes, flavoured cakes (e.g. chocolate), gingerbread and spicecakes may be frozen in their baking tins, wrapped in foil or polythene.

Serving   Thaw in wrappings at room temperature for 1½ hours. Ice if required and cut in pieces.
High Quality Storage Life   4 months (fruit and flavoured); 2 months (ginger and spice).

Cakes (Small)

Preparation   Cakes made in bun tins, paper or foil cases can be frozen plain or iced. (a) Pack plain cakes in usable quantities in polythene bags. (b) Pack iced cakes in boxes layered with greaseproof paper or Cellophane. Iced cakes are best fast-frozen on tray before packing.

Serving   (a) Thaw in wrappings at room temperature for 1 hour. (b) Remove wrappings and thaw at room temperature for 1 hour.
High Quality Storage Life   4 months

Cake (Rich Fruit)

Preparation This type of cake will keep well in a tin, so freezer space should not be wasted. If a rich fruit cake is to be frozen, wrap in foil or polythene bag.

Serving Thaw in wrappings at room temperature for 2 hours.
High Quality Storage Life 10 months

Choux Pastry, Éclairs and Cream Buns

Preparation (a) Bake éclairs or cream buns. Freeze without filling or icing. Pack in boxes or bags. (b) Fill cases with ice cream. Freeze unwrapped on trays. Pack in boxes.

Serving (a) Thaw in wrappings at room temperature for 2 hours. Fill and ice. (b) Thaw at room temperature for 10 minutes. Pour over chocolate or toffee sauce.
High Quality Storage Life 1 month

Croissants

Preparation Pack immediately after baking and cooling. Pack in bags, or in boxes to avoid crushing and flaking.

Serving Thaw in wrappings at room temperature for 30 minutes, and heat in oven or under grill.
High Quality Storage Life 2 months

Crumpets

Preparation Pack in usable quantities in polythene bags.

Serving Thaw in wrappings at room temperature for 30 minutes, then toast.
High Quality Storage Life 10 months

Danish Pastries

Preparation Prepare un-iced or with a light water icing. Pack in foil trays with lids, or in boxes to prevent crushing.

Serving Remove wrappings and thaw at room temperature for 1 hour. Heat lightly if liked.
High Quality Storage Life 2 months

Doughnuts

Preparation   Ring doughnuts freeze better than jam doughnuts which may become soggy. Drain well from fat, and do not roll in sugar. Pack in polythene bags.

Serving   Heat frozen doughnuts at 400°F, 200°C, Gas Mark 6 for 8 minutes, then roll in sugar.
High Quality Storage Life   1 month

Drop Scones

Preparation   Cool thoroughly before packing. Pack in boxes, foil or bags.

Serving   Thaw in wrappings at room temperature for 1 hour.
High Quality Storage Life   2 months

Muffins

Preparation   Pack in usable quantities in polythene bags.

Serving   Thaw in wrappings at room temperature for 30 minutes, then toast.
High Quality Storage Life   10 months

Pancakes

Preparation   Cool thoroughly before packing. Put layers of greaseproof paper or Cellophane between large thin pancakes. Wrap in foil or polythene.

Serving   Thaw in wrappings at room temperature and separate. Heat in low oven, or on a plate over steam, covered with a cloth.
High Quality Storage Life   2 months

Pastry Cases

Preparation   Make up flan cases, patty cases and vol-au-vent cases. Use foil containers if possible. (a) Freeze unbaked cases packed in foil or polythene. (b) Bake cases and pack in boxes to prevent crushing.

Serving   Thaw unbaked cases at room temperature for 1 hour before baking. (a) Thaw baked cases at room temperature before filling. (b) Put hot filling into frozen cases and heat in oven.
High Quality Storage Life   4 months

Pastry (Slab)

Preparation   Roll pastry, form into a square and in greaseproof paper. Overwrap in foil or polythene. Pack in usable quantities (i.e. 8 oz or 1 lb.).

Serving   Thaw at room temperature for 2 hours. Eat freshly baked.
High Quality Storage Life   4 months

Rolls and Buns

Preparation   Pack in polythene bags in usable quantities. Seal and freeze at once.

Serving   (a) Thaw in wrappings at room temperature for $1\frac{1}{2}$ hours. (b) Put frozen rolls or buns in foil in a hot oven (450°F, 230°C or Gas Mark 8) for 15 minutes.
High Quality Storage Life   4 weeks

Rolls (Part-baked)

Preparation   Leave in wrapper and put into polythene bag. Seal and freeze at once.

Serving   Put frozen rolls in moderate oven (400°F, 200°C or Gas Mark 6) for 15 minutes.
High Quality Storage Life   4 months

Sandwiches

Preparation   Avoid fillings of cooked egg whites, salad dressings, mayonnaise, raw vegetables or jam. Spread bread with butter. Pack in groups of six or eight sandwiches, with an extra crust at each end to prevent drying out. Keep crusts on, and do not cut sandwiches in pieces. Wrap in foil or polythene and seal tightly.

Serving   (a) Thaw in wrappings in refrigerator for 12 hours, or at room temperature for 4 hours. Trim crusts and cut in pieces. (b) Put frozen sandwiches under grill to thaw while toasting.
High Quality Storage Life   1 month

Sandwiches (Open)

Preparation   Butter bread thickly. Make up without salad garnishes, open freeze and pack in single layer in rigid plastic box.

| Serving | Thaw at room temperature for 2 hours. Garnish with salad and dressings.
High Quality Storage Life   1 week |

Sandwiches (Pinwheel, Club and Ribbon)

| Preparation | Prepare but do not cut in pieces. Wrap tightly in foil. |

| Serving | Thaw in wrappings in refrigerator for 12 hours, or at room temperature for 4 hours. Cut in pieces.
High Quality Storage Life   1 month |

Sandwiches (Rolled)

| Preparation | Flatten bread with rolling pin to ease rolling. Butter well and wrap around filling. Pack closely together in box to prevent unrolling. |

| Serving | Thaw in wrappings in refrigerator for 12 hours, or at room temperature for 4 hours.
High Quality Storage Life   1 month |

Scones

| Preparation | Pack in usable quantities in polythene bags. |

| Serving | (a) Thaw in wrappings at room temperature for 1 hour. (b) Heat frozen scones (with a covering of foil) at 350°F, 180°C, Gas Mark 4 for 10 minutes.
High Quality Storage Life   2 months |

Yeast

| Preparation | Weigh into ¼ oz, ½ oz or 1 oz cubes. Wrap cubes in polythene and label carefully. Pack in box. |

| Serving | Thaw 30 minutes at room temperature. Frozen yeast may be grated coarsely for immediate use.
High Quality Storage Life   12 months |

Waffles

Preparation Do not brown too much. Cool and pack in usable quantities.

Serving Heat frozen waffles under grill or in oven until crisp.
High Quality Storage Life 2 months

FREEZING COOKED DISHES

Cooked meals, and items which can be used straight from the freezer without further cooking are very useful. Strict hygiene must be observed in preparing cooked food for the freezer, and only fresh good-quality raw materials should be used. Cooked food must be cooled promptly and quickly by standing the container in cold water and ice cubes. Surplus fat should be removed after cooling and before freezing. Fried foods must be well drained on absorbent paper, and must be very cold before packing to avoid sogginess. Dishes such as pies, piped potatoes and decorated puddings should be frozen before wrapping to avoid damage to the surface of the food.

PREPARATION FOR FREEZING SOUP

Besides completed soups, meat, chicken and fish stock can all be frozen to use as a basis for fresh soups. These stocks should be strained, cooled and defatted, and packed into cartons with headspace. They are best thawed in a saucepan over low heat.

Soup which is thickened with ordinary flour tends to curdle on reheating, so cornflour is best as a thickening agent; it gives a creamy result. Rice flour can be used, but makes the soup glutinous. Porridge oats can be used for thicker meat soups. Starchy foods such as rice, pasta, barley and potatoes become slushy when frozen in liquid, and should only be added during the final reheating after freezing. It is also better to omit milk or cream from frozen soups, as results with these ingredients are variable; they, too, can be added when reheating.

Soup to be frozen should be cooled, and surplus fat removed as this will separate in storage and may cause off-flavours. Soup should be frozen in leak-proof containers, allowing $\frac{1}{2}$ in. headspace for wide-topped containers and $\frac{3}{4}$ in. headspace for narrow-topped containers. Rigid plastic containers are useful for storage; a very large quantity of soup can be frozen in a bread tin or in freezer boxes lined with foil; the solid block can then be wrapped in foil and stored like a brick.

Soup should not be stored for longer than 2 months. It will thicken during freezing, and allowance should be made for this in the recipe so that additional liquid can be added on reheating without spoiling the soup. Seasoning can cause off-flavours, so it is best to season after thawing. Clear soups can be heated in a saucepan over low heat, but cream soups should be heated in a double boiler and beaten well to keep them smooth.

Herbs and croûtons can be frozen to give an attractive finish to soups, even when time is limited.

Herb Cubes

Herbs such as parsley and chives should be chopped and packed in ice cube trays with a little water, then each frozen cube wrapped in foil. The herb cubes can be reheated in the soup.

Croûtons and Cheese Croûtons

Croûtons can be prepared from lightly-toasted $\frac{1}{2}$ in. slices of bread which are then cut in cubes and dried out in an oven set at 350°F, 180°C, Gas Mark 4. They are best packed in small polythene bags and thawed in their wrappings at room temperature, but they can be reheated if preferred. As a variation, the bread can be toasted on one side only and the other side can be spread with grated cheese mixed with a little melted butter, egg yolk and seasoning; this is then toasted and the bread cut in cubes before packing.

PREPARATION FOR FREEZING OF COOKED MEAT

Time can be saved by preparing meat dishes which can be frozen, then eaten cold or reheated after thawing. Pre-cooked joints, steaks and chops do not freeze successfully, since the outer surface sometimes develops an off-flavour, and reheating dries out the meat. Fried meats also tend to toughness, dryness and rancidity when frozen. Cold meat can however be frozen in slices, with or without sauce. Any combination dishes of meat and vegetables should include the vegetables when they are slightly undercooked, to avoid softness on reheating. In addition to casseroles and stews, good cooked dishes for freezing include cottage pie, galantines and meat loaves, meat balls, meat sauces, and meat pies. It is very important that all cooked meats should be cooled quickly before freezing. Where ingredients such as meat and gravy are to be combined, they should be thoroughly chilled separately before mixing; for instance hot gravy should not be poured over cold meat.

PREPARATION FOR FREEZING OF COOKED POULTRY

Old birds such as boiling chickens are best if frozen when cooked, with the meat stripped from the bones. This meat can then be frozen or made at once into pies or casseroles, while the carcass can be simmered in the cooking liquid to make strong stock for freezing. Slices of cooked poultry can be frozen on their own or in a sauce (the latter is preferable to prevent drying out). If the meat is frozen without sauce, slices should be divided by sheets of Cellophane and then closely packed together to exclude air. Roast and fried poultry frozen to be eaten cold are not particularly successful; on thawing they tend to exude moisture and be flabby.

SLICED MEAT AND POULTRY

Cold poached, boiled or steamed meat and poultry can well be frozen in slices to serve cold. Slices should be at least $\frac{1}{4}$ in. thick, separated by Cellophane or greaseproof paper, and must be packed tightly to avoid surfaces drying. They can then be put into cartons or bags. They should be thawed for 3 hours in a refrigerator in their container, then separated and placed on absorbent paper to remove any moisture. They are good; only ham and pork will lose colour when frozen like this.

It is preferable to freeze meat and poultry slices in gravy or sauce to make them keep their juiciness. The liquid may be thickened with corn-flour, and both the meat and the gravy or sauce should be cooled quickly, separately, before packing. These slices are best packaged in foil containers, covered with a lid, and this can save time in reheating as the container can go straight into the oven, keeping the meat moist. These frozen slices in gravy should be heated for 30 minutes at 350°F, 180°C, Gas Mark 4.

CASSEROLES

Casseroled meat and poultry is very useful to keep in the freezer. It is good sense to double the quantity of a casserole, using half when fresh and freezing the second half. For freezing, vegetables should be slightly undercooked in the casserole; pasta, rice, barley or potatoes should not be included or they will go slushy; onions, garlic and herbs should only be used sparingly, or should be added during reheating; sauces should be thickened with tomato purée, vegetable purée or cornflour, to avoid curdling on reheating. Oven-to-freezer casseroles can well be used if they are of the type advertised for the purpose, and they can be returned straight to the oven for reheating. Other oven-glass containers should be allowed to cool before placing in the freezer, and should be thawed before returning to the oven for serving. Casseroles and stews are very successful when frozen in foil containers which can be used in the oven, or in foil-lined containers so that the foil can be formed into a parcel for freezing, and the contents returned to the original container for heating and serving. If frozen in cartons, the dishes can be transferred to oven-ware, or reheated in a double boiler, or even over direct heat if curdling is not likely to occur.

GALANTINES AND MEAT LOAVES

Galantines are most easily used if cooked before freezing, ready to serve cold. They can be prepared directly in loaf tins, then turned out, wrapped and frozen. Meat loaves can be frozen uncooked. This is made easy if the mixture is packed into loaf tins lined with foil, the foil then being formed into a parcel for freezing; the frozen meat loaf can be returned to the original tin for baking.

For cold serving, any of these compact meats can be packed in slices, divided by Cellophane or greaseproof paper, and re-formed into a loaf shape for freezing. Slices can be separated while still frozen and thawed quickly on absorbent paper.

PÂTÉS

Pâtés made from liver, game or poultry, freeze extremely well. They can be packed in individual pots ready for serving, or cooked in loaf tins or terrines, then turned out and wrapped in foil for easy storage. Pâtés containing strong seasoning, herbs or garlic should be carefully over-wrapped.

Any pâté which has exuded fat or excess juices during cooking must be carefully cooled and the excess fat or jelly scraped off before freezing. To serve, thaw small individual containers at room temperature for 1 hour. Thaw large pâtés in their wrappings in the refrigerator for 6 hours, or at room temperature for 3 hours, and use immediately after thawing. High quality storage life: 1 month. Pâtés can also be made with smoked fish, such as kippers or cod's roe. These are best prepared in small containers, well over-wrapped. Any fish pâté should be thawed in a refrigerator for 3 hours, stirring occasionally to blend ingredients.

COOKED FISH Fish should never be overcooked, and the time taken to reheat a cooked fish dish will not only spoil flavour and rob the fish of any nutritive value, but will also take as long as the original cooking. Leftover cooked fish can however be frozen in the form of a fish pie, fish cakes, or a ready-to-eat dish in sauce. Raw fish can be frozen, coated in batter or egg and breadcrumbs and fried; but it tends to go rancid, and will take about 15 minutes to reheat, so there is little advantage in freezing it.

PASTA Pasta such as spaghetti and macaroni can be frozen successfully to be used with a variety of sauces. Composite meals such as macaroni cheese can also be frozen when cooked. Pasta shapes can be frozen to use with soup; but they should not be frozen in liquid as they become slushy, so are most conveniently added to the soup during the reheating period. Pasta should be slightly undercooked, in boiling salted water. After thorough draining, it should be cooled under cold running water in a sieve, then shaken as dry as possible, packed into polythene bags, and frozen. To serve, the pasta is put into a pan of boiling water and brought back to the boil, then simmered until just tender, the time depending on the state in which it has been frozen. Composite dishes can be reheated in a double boiler or in the oven under a foil lid. High quality storage life: 1 month.

While it may not save much time to prepare pasta specially for the freezer, it is useful to be able to save excess quantities prepared for a meal, or to turn them into a composite dish for the freezer.

SAUCES Sweet and savoury sauces can well be frozen, and are useful for emergency meals. They can be in the form of complete sauces such as a meat sauce to use with spaghetti or rice, or you can freeze a basic white or brown sauce to be used with other ingredients when reheated. Sauces for freezing are best thickened by reduction or with cornflour, as flour-thickened sauces are likely to curdle when reheated. Only mayonnaise and custard sauces cannot be frozen, since the ingredients freeze at different temperatures and give unsatisfactory results.

Sauces can be stored in large quantities in cartons, or in 'brick' form using loaf tins. Small quantities can be frozen in ice cube trays, then wrapped individually in foil and packed in quantities in bags for easy storage.

FREEZING PUDDINGS

PREPARATION
FOR FREEZING
OF PUDDINGS

A wide variety of puddings can be frozen and are useful for emergency use; this can also be a way of storing surplus fruit in a convenient form. Puddings which can be frozen include obvious items such as ice cream and pies, and pancakes and sponge-cakes which can be combined quickly with fruit, cream or sauces to make complete puddings. Steamed puddings can also be frozen, together with fruit crumbles, gelatine sweets, cold soufflés and mousses and cheesecakes. Milk puddings do not freeze well, however, since they become mushy or curdle.

BAKED AND
STEAMED
PUDDINGS

These can be made from almost all standard cake and pudding recipes, and are most easily made in foil containers which can be used for freezing and for heating. It is better not to put jam or syrup in the bottom of these puddings before cooking, as they become soggy on thawing, but dried fruit, fresh fruit and nuts can be added. Highly-spiced puddings may develop off-flavours.

Suet puddings containing fresh fruit can be frozen raw or cooked. It is more useful, however, to cook them before freezing, since only a short time need then be allowed for reheating before serving. Puddings made from cake mixtures, or any traditional sponge or suet puddings, can also be frozen raw or cooked. Cake mixtures can be used to top such fruits as apples, plums, gooseberries and apricots; these are just as easily frozen raw since the complete cooking time in the oven is only a little longer than reheating time. This also applies to fruit puddings with a crumble topping.

FRUIT PUDDINGS

It is useful to use some fruit to make prepared puddings for the freezer. Fruit in syrup can be flavoured with wine or liqueurs and needs no further cooking; this is particularly useful for such fruits as pears and peaches which are difficult to freeze well in their raw state.

GELATINE
PUDDINGS

Many cold puddings involve the use of gelatine. When gelatine is frozen in a creamy mixture, it is entirely successful, although clear jellies are not recommended for the freezer. The ice crystals formed in freezing break up the structure of the jelly, and while it retains its setting quality, the jelly becomes granular and uneven and loses clarity. This granular effect is masked in such puddings as mousses.

PUDDING SAUCES

A supply of sweet sauces such as fruit sauce or chocolate sauce can be

Fruit crumble (p. 188).

TOP Pancakes (p. 186).
ABOVE Frozen salmon in triple-decker sandwiches (p. 100) toasted after thawing.

usefully frozen for use with puddings or ices. These are best prepared and frozen in small containers, and reheated in a double boiler.

FREEZING SNACKS AND APPETISERS

Appetisers

Preparation   Wrap rindless bacon round chicken livers, cocktail sausages, seafood or cooked prunes. Secure with cocktail sticks. Fast-freeze on trays. Transfer to polythene bags for storage.

Serving   Cook frozen appetisers under grill or in hot oven until bacon is crisp.
High Quality Storage Life   2 weeks

Canapés

Preparation   Cut day-old bread into shapes, but do not use toast or fried bread. Spread butter to edge of bread. Add toppings, but avoid hard-boiled egg whites or mayonnaise. Aspic becomes cloudy on thawing. Fast-freeze unwrapped on trays. Pack in boxes for storage.

Serving   Thaw on dish 1 hour before serving. Garnish if necessary.
High Quality Storage Life   2 weeks

Dips

Preparation   Make dips with a base of cottage or cream cheese. Avoid mayonnaise, hard-boiled egg whites or crisp vegetables. Pack in waxed or rigid plastic containers. Overwrap if dips contain garlic or onion.

Serving   Thaw in containers at room temperature for 5 hours. Blend in mayonnaise, egg whites or vegetables if necessary.
High Quality Storage Life   1 month

Flavoured Butters

Preparation   (a) Fast-freeze butter balls or curls on trays. Transfer to polythene bags for storage. (b) Cream butter with herbs, lemon juice, or shellfish. Form into cylinders and wrap in greaseproof paper and polythene.

Serving   (a) Thaw in serving dishes at room temperature for 1 hour. (b) Cut in slices to put on hot meat or fish.
High Quality Storage Life   6 months (unsalted); 3 months (salted)

PREPARATION, PACKING, STORING AND COOKING SPECIFIC ITEMS

Casseroles and Stews

Preparation   Use a standard recipe, but slightly undercook vegetables. Do not add potatoes, rice or pasta. Thicken with cornflour if necessary. Cool completely and remove surplus fat. Pack in boxes or in foil-lined casserole, making sure meat is covered with liquid. When frozen, remove foil package from casserole for storage.

Serving   Heat in double boiler or in oven at 350°F, 180°C, Gas Mark 4 for 45 minutes.
High Quality Storage Life   2 months

Cheesecake

Preparation   Make baked or gelatine-set cheesecake in cake tin with removable base. Cool. Freeze without wrappings on a tray. Pack in box to prevent damage.

Serving   Thaw in refrigerator for 8 hours.
High Quality Storage Life   1 month

Flans (Savoury and Sweet)

Preparation   Prepare and bake flan, and finish completely. Freeze on a tray without wrappings. Wrap in foil or polythene, or pack in box to prevent damage.

Serving   Thaw in loose wrappings at room temperature for 2 hours. Reheat if required.
High Quality Storage Life   2 months (fresh filling); 1 month (leftover meat or vegetables)

Fruit Crumble

Preparation   Prepare fresh fruit with sugar in a foil basin. Cover with crumble topping. Cover with foil lid or pack in polythene bag.

Serving   Put frozen pudding in oven and bake at 400°F, 200°C, Gas Mark 6 for 30 minutes; then at 375°F, 190°C, Gas Mark 5 for 30 minutes.
High Quality Storage Life   2 months

Fruit Garnishes

Preparation Fast-freeze strawberries with hulls, or cherries on stalks on trays. Transfer to polythene bags for storage.

Serving Put on puddings or into drinks while still frozen.
High Quality Storage Life 9 months

Fruit Pies

Preparation Avoid using apples, which tend to discolour. Brush bottom crust with egg white to prevent sogginess. (a) Bake pie. Cool and cover with foil or pack in polythene bag. (b) Cover uncooked fruit and sugar with pastry. Pack in foil or polythene bag.

Serving (a) Thaw at room temperature for 2 hours to serve cold, or heat at 400°F, 200°C, Gas Mark 6 for 30 minutes to serve hot. (b) Bake at 400°F, 200°C, Gas Mark 6 for 1 hour.
High Quality Storage Life (a) 4 months, (b) 2 months

Fruit Puddings (Suet)

Preparation Use plums, gooseberries or rhubarb fillings with suet crust. Apples tend to discolour. Prepare in foil or polythene basin and steam. Cool and cover with foil.

Serving Thaw at room temperature for 2 hours. Steam for 45 minutes.
High Quality Storage Life 2 months

Ice

Preparation (a) Freeze extra supplies of ice cubes and pack in polythene bags for storage. (b) Freeze large blocks of ice in baking tins or foil containers. (c) Freeze cubes of fruit squash or syrup. (d) Add sprigs of mint, orange or lemon peel, or cocktail cherries to water in ice-cube trays. Transfer cubes to polythene bags for storage.

Serving (a) Add immediately to drinks. (b) Add to punches and cups in bowls, or put round wine bottles. (c) Add to fruit drinks, punches or cups. (d) Add to individual drinks, or to bowls of punch or cups.
High Quality Storage Life 12 months

Herb Garnishes

Preparation   Freeze sprigs of parsley and mint in foil or polythene.

Serving   Put frozen herbs on to sandwiches and cooked dishes just before serving, as they become limp on thawing.
High Quality Storage Life   12 months

Glacé Fruit

Preparation   Pack tightly in foil or polythene. It is useful to freeze a few pieces of fruit from Christmas for later parties, as glacé fruit is difficult to buy at other times of the year.

Serving   Thaw in wrappings at room temperature for 3 hours.
High Quality Storage Life   12 months

Jelly

Preparation   Jelly does not freeze very well. Although it remains set, it becomes granular, uneven and cloudy. If wanted, prepare in foil cases or serving dishes, if these are freezer-tested.

Serving   Thaw in refrigerator for 8 hours.
High Quality Storage Life   1 month

Meat Balls

Preparation   Use standard recipe. Pack in polythene bags, or in boxes, or in foil dishes with lids.

Serving   Fry frozen meat balls quickly in hot fat, or heat in savoury sauce.
High Quality Storage Life   2 months

Meat (Cooked)

Preparation   Avoid freezing whole cooked joints, steaks or chops, and fried meats, which tend to toughness, dryness and rancidity when frozen. (a) Slice cooked meat in $\frac{1}{4}$ in. slices and separate with greaseproof paper or Cellophane. Pack tightly in boxes or foil dishes with lids. (b) Slice meat and pack in gravy or sauce, which should be thickened with cornflour rather than flour. Pack in foil dishes with lids.

Serving   (a) Thaw in wrappings in refrigerator for 3 hours. Separate slices and dry

on absorbent paper. (b) Heat in container at 350°F, 120°C, Gas Mark 4 for 30 minutes.
High Quality Storage Life 2 months

Meat Loaf

Preparation (a) Use standard recipe, and prepare in a loaf tin. Cool completely and wrap in foil or polythene. (b) Prepare but do not cook. Pack into loaf tin lined with foil. Freeze, and then form foil into a parcel for storage.

Serving (a) Thaw in wrappings in refrigerator overnight. Reheat without thawing at 350°F, 180°C, Gas Mark 4 for 45 minutes to serve hot. (b) Cook without thawing at 350°F, 180°C, Gas Mark 4 for 1 hour 40 minutes.
High Quality Storage Life 2 months

Meat Pies

Preparation (a) Prepare and cook pie in foil container. Before filling, brush bottom crust with melted fat to prevent sogginess. Cool and wrap in foil or in polythene bag. (b) Prepare and cook meat filling. Put into foil container and cover with fresh pastry. Wrap in foil or in polythene bag.

Serving (a) Thaw in refrigerator for 6 hours to serve cold. Heat at 375°F, 190°C, Gas Mark 5 for 1 hour to serve hot. (b) Remove wrappings. Bake at 400°F, 200°C, Gas Mark 6 for 1 hour.
High Quality Storage Life 2 months

Meat Pudding

Preparation (a) Prepare pudding with suet crust to standard recipe. Cook in foil or polythene basin and cool quickly. Wrap tightly in foil. (b) Cook meat filling and pack in foil or polythene basins for freezing.

Serving Remove wrapping. Cover pastry with foil and cook frozen pudding for 3 hours. (b) Remove lids. Cover with fresh suet pastry, cook 3 hours.
High Quality Storage Life 2 months

Mousses and Cold Soufflés

Preparation Prepare in serving dishes if these are freezer-tested.

Serving Thaw in refrigerator for 8 hours.
High Quality Storage Life 1 month

Pasta

Preparation Slightly undercook macaroni, spaghetti or other pasta. Drain thoroughly and cool. Pack in polythene bags in usable quantities.

Serving Plunge into boiling water. Bring water to the boil and cook pasta until just tender.
High Quality Storage Life 1 month

Pasta Dishes

Preparation Pack pasta and sauce (e.g. macaroni cheese) in foil container with lid.

Serving Remove lid and bake at 400°F, 200°C, Gas Mark 6 for 45 minutes.
High Quality Storage Life 1 month

Pasties and Sausage Rolls

Preparation Make with short, flaky or puff pastry. (a) Freeze unbaked on trays, and pack in boxes or bags. (b) Bake and pack in boxes or foil trays to avoid damage.

Serving (a) Brush with egg and bake at 450°F, 230°C, Gas Mark 8 for 20 minutes; then at 375°F, 190°C, Gas Mark 5 for 10 minutes. (b) Thaw in wrappings in refrigerator for 6 hours. Heat frozen baked items at 400°F, 200°C, Gas Mark 6 for 25 minutes to serve hot.
High Quality Storage Life 1 month

Pâtés

Preparation (a) Cool meat pâtés completely, and remove excess fat and jelly. Pack in individual pots and cover with foil lids, or wrap a large pâté in foil. Overwrap carefully, since garlic and herbs may cross-flavour other food in the freezer. (b) Pack fish pâté in serving dish or small pots if they are freezer-proof. Pâté may also be packed into small plastic boxes.

Serving (a) Thaw in wrappings in refrigerator for 6 hours; at room temperature 3 hours. Serve at once. (b) Thaw in refrigerator for 3 hours, stirring occasionally.
High Quality Storage Life 1 month

Pizza

Preparation   Prepare on flat foil plate and bake. Anchovies may cause rancidity, so can be added at reheating stage. Use fresh herbs rather than dried ones. Wrap in foil or polythene bag.

Serving   Unwrap and thaw at room temperature for 1 hour, then bake at 375°F, 190°C, Gas Mark 5 for 25 minutes. Serve very hot.
High Quality Storage Life   1 month

Rice

Preparation   Slightly undercook rice. Drain thoroughly and pack in polythene bags in usable quantities.

Serving   (a) Plunge into boiling water. Bring water to boil and cook rice until just tender. (b) Reheat in melted butter in a thick pan. (c) Reheat in a shallow pan in a low oven.
High Quality Storage Life   1 month

Rice Dishes

Preparation   Cook rice dishes completely (e.g. risotto, kedgeree). Do not season, or add hard-boiled eggs. Pack into boxes.

Serving   Reheat in double boiler, stirring well. Season and add additional ingredients.
High Quality Storage Life   1 month

Sauce (Brown)

Preparation   Use standard recipe, but thicken by reduction as much as possible. Use cornflour rather than flour if needed in recipe. Season sparingly. Pack in boxes in ½ pint and 1 pint quantities, leaving headspace.

Serving   Heat in double boiler, stirring well. Add additional flavourings and seasoning.
High Quality Storage Life   1 month

Sauces (Meat)

Preparation   Use standard recipe for sauce to serve with spaghetti or rice. Cool completely and remove surplus fat. Pack in boxes in usable portions, leaving headspace.

Serving   Heat in double boiler. Adjust seasoning.
High Quality Storage Life   1 month

Sauce (White)

Preparation   Use standard recipe, with cornflour rather than flour. Season sparingly. Pack in boxes in $\frac{1}{2}$ pint or 1 pint quantities, leaving headspace.

Serving   Heat in double boiler, stirring well. Add additional flavourings and seasoning.
High Quality Storage Life   1 month

Sauces (Sweet)

Preparation   (a) Sauces made from sieved fresh or stewed fruit freeze well. Pack in boxes in usable portions, leaving headspace. (b) Pudding sauces made from fruit juice, chocolate, etc. can be frozen. They should be thickened with cornflour. Pack in boxes in usable portions, leaving headspace.

Serving   (a) Heat in double boiler *or* Thaw in container in refrigerator for 2 hours and serve cold. (b) Heat in double boiler, stirring well.
High Quality Storage Life   (a) 12 months, (b) 1 month

Shepherd's Pie

Preparation   Make from fresh or cooked meat, using plenty of stock or gravy to keep moist. Cool meat completely and put into foil container. Prepare mashed potatoes and cool completely. Spread on meat. Cover with foil or pack in polythene bag.

Serving   Bake at 400°F, 200°C, Gas Mark 6 for 45 minutes until potatoes are golden.
High Quality Storage Life   2 months

Soup

Preparation Use standard recipes, but avoid flour thickening. Do not add rice, pasta, barley or potatoes; nor milk or cream. Pack in cartons, leaving headspace. Soup may also be frozen in loaf tins, and the frozen blocks transferred to polythene bags for storage.

Serving Heat in double boiler, stirring well. Add rice, pasta, barley or potatoes, and milk or cream if required. Season to taste.
High Quality Storage Life 2 months

Steamed and Baked Puddings

Preparation Prepare standard sponge pudding or cake mixture recipes. Use with jam, fresh or dried fruit. Steam or bake in foil containers. Cool completely. Cover with foil or pack in polythene bag.

Serving Thaw at room temperature for 2 hours. Steam for 45 minutes.
High Quality Storage Life 4 months

Stock

Preparation Prepare from meat, poultry, bones or vegetables. Strain and cool, and remove fat. Reduce liquid by half to save freezer space. Pack in cartons, leaving headspace. Stock may also be frozen in loaf tins or ice-cube trays, and the frozen blocks transferred to polythene bags for storage.

Serving Heat gently and use as required.
High Quality Storage Life 1 month

FREEZING LEFTOVERS AND SPARE INGREDIENTS

Bacon

Preparation Crumble cooked bacon and freeze in small containers.

Serving Add to casseroles or use on potatoes, cheese or fish dishes. Thaw in refrigerator for 2 hours to use in sandwich spreads.
High Quality Storage Life 2 weeks

Bread

Preparation (a) Freeze crumbs in polythene bags. Can be mixed with butter or grated cheese. (b) Freeze slices divided with greaseproof paper in polythene bags. (c) Fry or toast bread cubes and pack in boxes or polythene bags.

Serving (a) Sprinkle on savoury dishes for browning and serving. (b) Toast while frozen or thaw at room temperature for sandwiches. (c) Use as croûtons for soup.
High Quality Storage Life 1 month

Cake

Preparation (a) Freeze cake wedges wrapped in foil or polythene and packed in boxes or bags. (b) Freeze cake crumbs in polythene bags.

Serving (a) Thaw in wrappings in refrigerator for 3 hours. (b) Thaw at room temperature to use for puddings.
High Quality Storage Life 1 month

Cheese

Preparation (a) Freeze grated cheese, with or without breadcrumbs in small containers. (b) Mix with white sauce to freeze in small containers, or to bind vegetables or poultry to make complete freezer dishes.

Serving Sprinkle on to savoury dishes for browning and serving, or thaw to add to sauces and stuffings.
High Quality Storage Life 1 month

Coffee

Preparation Freeze strong coffee in ice-cube trays. Transfer cubes to polythene bags for storage.

Serving Add coffee cubes to iced coffee.
High Quality Storage Life 1 month

Complete Meals

Preparation Freeze individual portions of meat or poultry in sauce or gravy, vegetables and potatoes in compartmented foil trays. Mash potatoes, or make croquettes. All items used should have same thawing or reheating times. Cover tray with foil lid.

Serving   Heat with lid on at 375°F, 190°C, Gas Mark 5 for 30 to 45 minutes.
High Quality Storage Life 1 month

Cream

Preparation   Whip cream with sugar (1 tablespoon sugar to 1 pint cream). Pipe rosettes or put spoonfuls on to baking sheets and fast-freeze. Pack in boxes or bags.

Serving   Thaw 15 minutes at room temperature.
High Quality Storage Life 6 months

Egg Whites

Preparation   Freeze in waxed or rigid plastic containers, or in ice-cube trays. Label with number of whites.

Serving   Thaw in refrigerator but bring to room temperature before use. Can be whipped successfully.
High Quality Storage Life 12 months

Egg Yolks

Preparation   Mix lightly with a fork. Add $\frac{1}{2}$ teaspoon salt or $\frac{1}{2}$ tablespoon sugar to 6 yolks. Label with number of yolks and 'salt' or 'sugar'. Can be frozen in waxed or rigid plastic containers, or in ice-cube trays. Transfer cubes to polythene bags for storage.

Serving   Thaw in refrigerator. Use alone or mix with whites.
High Quality Storage Life 12 months

Fish

Preparation   (a) Freeze in the form of fish cakes or fish pie. (b) Mash with butter, anchovy essence and chopped parsley and freeze as a spread.

Serving   (a) Heat fish cakes in fat or in a moderate oven. Heat fish pie at 350°F, 180°C, Gas Mark 4 for 35 minutes. (b) Thaw spread in the refrigerator for 3 hours.
High Quality Storage Life 1 month

Fruit Juice

Preparation Freeze in ice-cube trays. Transfer cubes to polythene bags for storage.

Serving Add juice cubes to fruit drinks or punch.
High Quality Storage Life 6 months

Fruit Syrup

Preparation Freeze in ice-cube trays. Transfer cubes to polythene bags for storage.

Serving Add juice cubes to fruit drinks or punch.
High Quality Storage Life 6 months

Gravy

Preparation (a) Add to pies or casseroles, or pour over cold meat or poultry slices for freezing. (b) Freeze in ice-cube trays. Transfer cubes to polythene bags for storage.

Serving (a) Reheat according to directions for serving cooked dishes. (b) Add to soups or casseroles, or heat in a double boiler to serve with meat or poultry.
High Quality Storage Life 1 month

Ham

Preparation (a) Mince or chop cooked ham and pack tightly in small containers. (b) Mash with butter and pack in small containers.

Serving Thaw in refrigerator for 2 hours to use in casseroles, stuffings or spreads.
High Quality Storage Life 2 weeks

Lemon Peel

Preparation (a) Grate peel and pack in small containers. (b) Pack scooped-out halved lemons in polythene bags.

Serving (a) Thaw at room temperature for cakes and puddings. (b) Fill with ice cream while still frozen, or thaw in refrigerator and fill with mousse or fruit salad.
High Quality Storage Life 2 months

Meat

Preparation (a) Slice $\frac{1}{4}$ in. thick and freeze with gravy or sauce in a lidded foil dish, or as part of a complete meal. (b) Slice $\frac{1}{4}$ in. thick and pack in layers separated by paper into boxes. (c) Mince or cube meat and mix with gravy or sauce, then pack in rigid containers. (d) Make into cottage pie, rissoles or meat loaf and freeze in foil containers. (e) Mash with butter and pack into small containers as a spread.

Serving (a) Reheat with lid on at 350°F, 180°C, Gas Mark 4, for 35 minutes. (b) Thaw in wrappings in refrigerator for 3 hours, and drain on absorbent paper. (c) Reheat in double boiler. (d) Reheat according to directions for serving cooked dishes. (e) Thaw spread in the refrigerator for 3 hours.
High Quality Storage Life   1 month

Orange Peel

Preparation (a) Grate peel and pack in small containers. (b) Pack scooped-out halved oranges in polythene bags.

Serving (a) Thaw at room temperature for cakes and puddings. (b) Fill with ice cream while still frozen, or thaw in refrigerator and fill with mousse or fruit salad.
High Quality Storage Life   2 months

Poultry

Preparation (a) Slice $\frac{1}{4}$ in. thick and freeze with gravy or sauce in a lidded foil dish, or as part of a complete meal. (b) Slice $\frac{1}{4}$ in. thick and pack in layers separated by paper into boxes. (c) Mash with butter and pack into small containers as a paste.

Serving (a) Reheat with lid on at 350°F, 180°C, Gas Mark 4, for 35 minutes. (b) Thaw in wrappings in refrigerator for 3 hours, and drain on absorbent paper. (c) Thaw spread in the refrigerator for 3 hours.
High Quality Storage Life   1 month

Poultry Stuffing

Preparation Freeze cooked stuffing separately from poultry meat in polythene bags.

Serving Thaw in refrigerator and use in poultry sandwiches or made-up dishes.
High Quality Storage Life   1 week

Sauces

Preparation   (a) Add to pies or casseroles, pour over cold meat or poultry slices or fish for freezing. (b) Freeze in ice-cube trays. Transfer cubes to polythene bags for storage.

Serving   (a) Reheat according to directions for serving cooked dishes. (b) Add to soups or casseroles, or heat in a double boiler to serve with meat, poultry or fish.
High Quality Storage Life   1 month

Tea

Preparation   Freeze strong tea in ice-cube trays. Transfer cubes to polythene bags for storage.

Serving   Add tea cubes to iced tea or punch.
High Quality Storage Life   1 month

Vegetables

Preparation   (a) Add to casseroles, pies or flans, with sauce if necessary. (b) Make into a purée with stock and pack into small containers or ice-cube trays. Transfer cubes to polythene bags for storage.

Serving   (a) Reheat according to directions for serving cooked dishes. (b) Add frozen cubes to soups, stews or sauces.
High Quality Storage Life   1 month

Part V FOOD IN SEASON

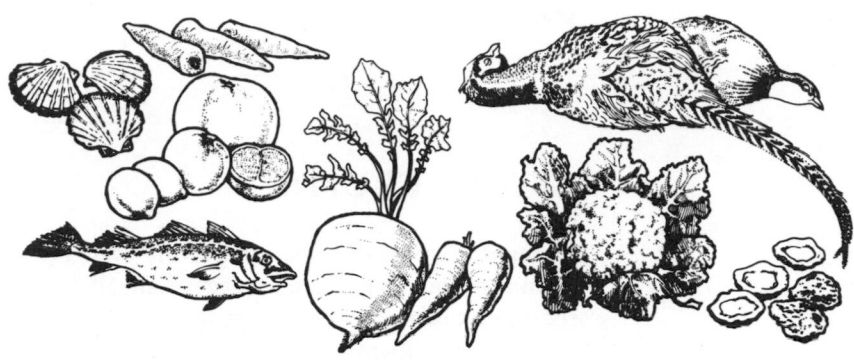

ALL YEAR ROUND FOODS

Many raw materials can be bought all through the year, so freezer space need not be wasted on them unless the family has special needs. They can be bought whenever the quality is high and prices are really low.
Crops of course rely on the weather, and meat prices reflect supply and demand, so it is a good idea to be prepared to get bargains when they appear, and to seize opportunities to obtain special items for the freezer. Buy fresh fish at the end of a holiday or on a day visit to the sea. A day trip to the country can yield fresh produce from gardens or markets, and gardening friends may have glut produce or herbs to spare.
It is practical to strike a balance between price and quality when home-freezing food, so the seasons should be considered rather than individual months. At the beginning of the season, for instance, soft fruit is a luxury and cannot be bought in quantity; towards the end of the season, there will be plenty of cheap fruit, but it may be poor quality. If the freezer programme is considered in three-monthly cycles, seasonal foods will not be missed and appropriate cooked dishes can be included and will have a regular turnover.

Freeze at any time of year when in good supply, and when quality is high and prices are low:—
Fruit   Melons, oranges, pineapples
Vegetables   Aubergines, broccoli, cabbage, courgettes, mushrooms, peppers, spinach, tomatoes
Fish (quality drops when spawning)   Cod, halibut, herrings, plaice, shrimps, sole, trout, turbot
Poultry and Game   Capons, chicken, duck, pigeon, rabbit, turkey
Meat   Beef, pork

SEASONAL FOODS

On the following pages there are recipes and suggestions for freezing foods which are economical and in good supply at certain times of the year.

CITRUS FRUITS

Oranges, lemons, limes, grapefruit, tangerines, clementines, persimmons and marmalade oranges can all be frozen whole to use as required, but are better (except for marmalade oranges) when prepared in slices or segments, or as juice.

CITRUS FRUIT JUICE
Use oranges, grapefruit, lemons or limes, making sure fruit is of good quality, heavy in the hand for its size. Chill unpeeled fruit in ice water or in the refrigerator until ready to extract juice. Squeeze juice and strain. Pack in waxed or rigid plastic containers, leaving $\frac{1}{2}$ in. headspace. Lemon and lime juice may be frozen in ice-cube trays, each cube being wrapped in foil when frozen.

Serving
Thaw at room temperature for 1 hour and sweeten to taste. Small cubes of lemon or lime juice are very useful for individual drinks.
High Quality Storage Life 1 year

GRAPEFRUIT
Peel the fruit, removing all pith, and cut segments away from pith. Pack dry with sugar (8 oz sugar to 2 breakfastcups of segments) in cartons, or pack in 50% syrup (16 oz sugar to 1 pint water).

Serving
Thaw at room temperature for $2\frac{1}{2}$ hours.
High Quality Storage Life 1 year

LEMONS
Lemon slices can be stored in the freezer, and also lemon juice and lemon peel.
Lemon slices or wedges can be frozen peeled or unpeeled to be used as a garnish, or in drinks. If unpeeled, they can be frozen dry in bags, and used as soon as thawed. If peeled, freeze in 20% syrup (4 oz sugar to 1 pint water).

Serving
Thaw at room temperature for 1 hour.
High Quality Storage Life 1 year

Lemon juice is most easily frozen in ice-cube trays, and each cube then wrapped in foil and packaged in quantity in polythene, to be used for drinks or for cooking.
High Quality Storage Life 1 year

Lamb chops cooked while still frozen (p. 79).

Full cream fudge (p. 200) in a selection of sweetmeats.

Lemon peel can be grated finely and packed in small waxed or rigid plastic containers. It should be thawed in container at room temperature to use for cakes and puddings.
High Quality Storage Life 1 year

ORANGES Sweet oranges can be frozen in sections, but pack better if frozen in slices. Peel fruit and remove all pith, and cut flesh in $\frac{1}{4}$ in. slices, then proceed by one of these methods:
(a) Use a dry sugar pack, allowing 8 oz sugar to 3 breakfastcups of orange pieces, and pack in containers or polythene bags.
(b) Use 30% syrup (7 oz sugar to 1 pint water) and pack oranges in waxed or rigid plastic containers, covering with Cellophane and leaving $\frac{1}{2}$ in. headspace.
(c) Pack slices in slightly sweetened fresh orange juice in cartons. It is worth noting that navel oranges develop a bitter flavour when frozen.

Serving Thaw $2\frac{1}{2}$ hours at room temperature.
High Quality Storage Life 1 year
Orange peel can be grated and frozen in small waxed or plastic containers to use for flavouring cakes, puddings and preserves.
High Quality Storage Life 2 months

PERSIMMONS These fruit may be frozen whole and raw, or packed in syrup, or as purée. Whole unpeeled fruit should be wrapped in foil for freezing, and will take 3 hours to thaw at room temperature. Fruit should be used when barely thawed, as it darkens and loses flavour if it stands after freezing.
High Quality Storage Life 2 months

Fully ripe fruit should be peeled and frozen whole in 50% syrup (16 oz sugar to 1 pint water), with the addition of 1 dessertspoon lemon juice to 1 quart syrup. Purée may be sweetened, allowing 8 oz sugar to 4 breakfastcups of purée.
High Quality Storage Life 1 year.

SEVILLE ORANGES Bitter oranges for marmalade may be frozen whole in their skins in polythene bags, to use later for marmalade. Pack in half-dozens or dozens according to recipe quantities likely to be used.

TANGERINES Divide tangerines into sections, removing all pith. Pack in dry sugar, allowing 8 oz sugar to 3 breakfastcups of tangerine segments, and pack in containers or polythene bags. Sections can also be packed in 30% syrup (7 oz sugar to 1 pint water) in waxed or rigid plastic containers, covering with Cellophane and leaving $\frac{1}{2}$ in. headspace.

Serving Thaw $2\frac{1}{2}$ hours at room temperature.
High Quality Storage Life 1 year

129

(a) Citrus Fruit Skins Freeze clean half-skins and use them as containers for water ices, jelly or fruit cocktail.

(b) Butter Icing Freeze orange and lemon butter icings in portions which are enough to decorate one cake or a batch of small cakes.

(c) Orange Sauce Freeze orange juice in portions which will be enough to make one meal-serving of sauce. Thicken with arrowroot after defrosting and serve with puddings, ice cream and pancakes.

(d) Lemon Meringue Pie Freeze the filling in a pastry shell. After defrosting, top with meringue and bake as usual.

(e) Lemon Curd This has a short storage life in a store-cupboard and is worth keeping in the freezer as it keeps its colour and flavour well.

(f) Lemonade This is worth making in concentrated form for freezer storage, since it will not ferment. It is far cheaper than any bought squash.

Seville Orange Sauce (for duck or pork)

Wash the oranges and peel them very thinly. Cut the peel into matchstick strips, and boil it in a little water for 10 minutes until soft. Cool and mix with the strained juice of the oranges. Pack in small cartons to freeze. The juice and peel of 3 oranges will be enough for one joint or bird.

To serve

Thaw the juice, and take out and reserve the strips of peel. Baste the pork or duck with the juice. When the meat is done, pour off the surplus fat. Add a little white wine or stock to the pan juices and stir while heating. Stir in the peel strips just before serving.

High Quality Storage Life 1 year

Lemon Curd

*3 lemons or ¼ pint
lemon juice
2 oz butter
12 oz caster sugar
3 eggs*

Grate the rind of the lemons and squeeze out the juice. There should be about ¼ pint juice. Put the rind, juice, butter and sugar into the top of a double saucepan, or into a bowl over hot water. Heat gently until the butter melts and the sugar has dissolved. Add the lightly beaten eggs and stir constantly over low heat until the mixture becomes thick. Do not boil. Cool and put into small freezer cartons.

To serve

Thaw at room temperature for 3 hours.

High Quality Storage Life 6 months

Lemonade

2 lb caster sugar
4 large lemons
1 teaspoon citric acid
1 teaspoon tartaric acid
2 pints boiling water

Put the sugar into a bowl and squeeze on the juice of the lemons. Stir well and add the acids and the boiling water. Stir until the sugar has dissolved. Cool and strain into freezer cartons. It is best to pack this in ½ pint quantities.

To serve
Thaw at room temperature and dilute to taste. This also makes a good cold weather drink if diluted with boiling water, and there is then no need to thaw the lemonade concentrate first. Individual portions of lemonade may be frozen in ice cube trays.
High Quality Storage Life   3 months

DRIED FRUIT, GLACÉ FRUIT AND SWEETS

After Christmas, there is usually a surplus of dried and glacé fruit, and bargains in these lines can often be found in supermarkets when the seasonal demand has been fulfilled. They keep very well in the freezer, and so do most kinds of sweets and candies.

DRIED FRUIT   Dates and dried figs freeze very well. If dates are frozen in the boxes in which they are packed they tend to dry out and acquire off-flavours. When good quality fruit is available, remove stones and freeze fruit in polythene bags or in waxed cartons. Block dates may be wrapped in foil or put into polythene bags (to avoid stickiness, they may be left in their original wrappings before being put into freezer packaging). Frozen dates may be eaten raw, or used for cakes and puddings. Dried dessert figs may be wrapped in foil or polythene bags, and are useful in the freezer since they have only a short season.
High Quality Storage Life   1 year

GLACÉ FRUIT   Keep glacé fruit in its original box and overwrap with a polythene bag. Separate pieces of fruit can be wrapped in foil and packaged in polythene.

Serving   Thaw in wrappings at room temperature for 3 hours before using.
High Quality Storage Life   1 year

SWEETS   Chocolate covered nuts and chocolates with hard centres may chip. Marshmallows, fudges, chocolates and caramels keep well for about 6 months. Wrappings should not be removed from any sweet until it has thawed, except for marshmallows which may be cut while still frozen (they are very useful for puddings and cake icings).

SUNSHINE PUDDINGS

Ready-made puddings are useful in the freezer, and they are delicious if made from dried or canned fruit. These sweet fruit puddings are excellent after simple first courses of cold meat and salad, or after grills or roasts.

Pear and Gingerbread Upside-Down Pudding

3 oz butter
3 oz honey
1 × 15 oz can pears
2 oz golden syrup
2 level tablespoons sugar
1 egg
5 oz flour
½ level teaspoon
  bicarbonate of soda
3 level teaspoons
  ginger
¼ pint milk
Pinch of salt
Glacé cherries

Grease the sides of a 7-in. cake tin. Melt 1 oz butter and the honey in the base of the tin and stir to mix. Cut the pears lengthways and arrange in the tin with a cherry in the centre of each. Cream the rest of the butter with the syrup and sugar and beat in the egg. Sift the dry ingredients into the mixture, and stir well, adding enough milk to make a thick batter. Pour over the pears. Bake at 350°F, 180°C, Gas Mark 4 for 40 minutes until the centre feels firm. Cool and wrap in foil for freezing.

To serve
Thaw at room temperature for 3 hours.
High Quality Storage Life   2 months

Ambrosia

8 oz dried apricots
4 oz honey
2 large oranges
4 oz desiccated
  coconut
1 oz sugar

Soak the apricots overnight in ½ pint water. Cook in the soaking liquid until tender. Add the honey and then cool the fruit. Grate the rind from the oranges and mix with the sugar. Peel the oranges with a sharp knife and remove all pith. Cut the flesh into thin slices. Arrange the oranges, apricots and coconut in layers with the apricot and honey juice. Top with coconut and sprinkle with orange rind and sugar. Cover and freeze.

To serve
Thaw at room temperature for 3 hours and serve with cream or ice cream.
High Quality Storage Life   3 months

Fruity Cheesecake

6 oz gingernut
  biscuits
2 teaspoons
  ground ginger
2 oz sugar
4 oz melted butter
8 oz cream cheese
Grated rind and
  juice of 1 lemon
3 eggs
1 oz gelatine
2 tablespoons water
2 tablespoons
  double cream
Raisins and sultanas
Chopped candied
  peel

Grease and line a loose-bottomed 7-in. cake tin. Crush the biscuits and mix the crumbs with ginger, sugar and butter. Spoon the mixture into the base of the cake tin, press down lightly, and set in the refrigerator. Beat the cream cheese, rind and juice of the lemon and the egg yolks until soft and creamy. Whisk the egg whites until stiff, but not dry. Melt the gelatine in 2 tablespoons water and stand the bowl in hot water until the gelatine is syrupy. Stir into the egg mixture, and then fold in the lightly whipped cream and the egg white. Pour into the cake tin, covering the biscuit base. Set for 2 hours in the refrigerator. Cover the top thickly with raisins, sultanas and candied peel, wrap in foil and freeze.

To serve
Thaw at room temperature for 3 hours.
High Quality Storage Life   2 months

GROCERIES

A large number of freezer centres and supermarkets sell bulk quantities of other groceries. Tea, ground coffee, brown sugar, raisins and sultanas, and coconut keep particularly well in the freezer, remaining fresh and full of flavour. This is worth considering if other storage space is limited.

SALADS

Traditional salad vegetables such as lettuce, raw cabbage, radishes and tomatoes do not freeze well because of their high moisture content (tomatoes, of course, are excellent for cooking after freezing). This does not mean that a freezer cannot be a useful aid in providing delicious salads throughout the year, either using only raw materials from the freezer, or combining them with fresh seasonal vegetables or fruit.
In addition to the basic salad ingredients, a variety of protein foods can be stored ready to complete the meal. It is always worth keeping a supply of sliced cooked meat and poultry; grated cheese; meat and fish pies and pasties; shrimps and prawns; crab and lobster; and smoked fish. Quickly cooked items such as chicken joints, lamb cutlets and salmon steaks can be taken from the freezer, cooked and cooled ready to accompany salads. Try some of these freezer combinations to make unusual first courses, or main course salads.

French beans and tomatoes make a refreshing salad to eat with cold meat, poultry or fish. Cook the French beans from the freezer and when they are just cool, combine with sliced fresh tomatoes. Pour over an oil and vinegar dressing just before serving, and sprinkle with chopped herbs, either fresh or frozen.

Mixed vegetables in a variety of combinations can be made into a filling salad. Combine peas, baby carrots, corn kernels and French or broad beans when cooked and cooled. Toss in mayonnaise.

Cauliflower, broccoli or spinach can be cooked and when just cooled they should be tossed in oil and vinegar dressing. Put the dressed vegetable into a serving bowl and sprinkle with crumbled crisply cooked bacon. Sprigs of cauliflower or broccoli also combine well with freshly sliced tomatoes.

New potatoes from the freezer can be cooked and while still just warm tossed in an oil and vinegar dressing with plenty of fresh or frozen parsley, and some chopped green or red pepper, or olives.

Fruit salads are unusual and very refreshing, particularly served as a first course, or with poultry. Try melon balls and orange or grapefruit segments mixed together, or try cherries or plums tossed in oil and vinegar. These are particularly good with cold chicken, duck, or cottage cheese.

FRUIT PURÉES

Fruit purées are invaluable standbys to keep in the freezer, since they take up little space, and can be quickly used for the preparation of fruit fools and other puddings, and for sorbets. Two different types of purée are needed for these recipes.

Basic Fruit Purées

Purée fresh or cooked fruit and mix with sugar to store. If the fruit is cooked, a better flavour is obtained by cooking without water in a low oven in a covered casserole. A little lemon juice will prevent the fruit discolouring. *Raspberries, strawberries, cultivated blackberries* and *peaches* may be made into purée without cooking. *Apricots, damsons, plums, currants, rhubarb* and *cherries* are better cooked. Use approximately 4 oz sugar to each lb. fruit for sweetening. Sweetening can be adjusted when the purée is mixed with other ingredients in recipes.

Fruit Sorbet Purées

For fresh fruit sorbets, the purée is mixed with a sugar syrup, and can be flavoured with an appropriate liqueur. The addition of a little lemon juice is also advisable. The sugar syrup should be made up over low heat and chilled before mixing with the fruit purée and lemon juice.

For *raspberry*, *strawberry*, *apricot* and *peach* purées, allow $\frac{1}{2}$ pint purée to syrup made from $1\frac{1}{2}$ pints water and 1 lb. sugar (add the juice of $1\frac{1}{2}$ lemons to *apricot and peach* purées). For *redcurrant or blackcurrant* purées or *fresh pineapple* purée, allow only 8 fl. oz fruit purée to the same amount of syrup, and add lemon juice as for apricot and peach purées.

HERBS

It is not generally a good idea to freeze herbs for garnishing, since they become limp on thawing. Their flavour is useful for sauces, soups, sandwich fillings and butters, and their colour remains good in the freezer. Herbs smell strongly in the freezer, particularly mint, so it is worth overwrapping them, or storing them in glass jars which have been tested for freezing, or in rigid freezer boxes. Parsley, mint, chives, fennel, basil and thyme are useful herbs to freeze, and they can be prepared in three ways:

(a) Pick sprigs of herbs, wash, drain and dry well. Pack whole in polythene bags. These can be crumbled while still frozen to add to dishes, but the leaves tend to be a bit leathery and difficult to rub into small pieces.

(b) Wash herbs well and remove from stems. Cut finely and pack into ice-cube trays, adding a little water. Freeze until solid, then wrap each cube in foil, and package quantities in polythene bags, labelling carefully. A cube can be put into casseroles or sauces while still frozen and just before serving time.

(c) *Make a bouquet garni*, a useful aid to good cooking, which can be frozen. Tie together with cotton, small bunches of parsley, thyme and bayleaves (allow 2 sprigs of parsley to 1 sprig of thyme and 1 bayleaf). Pack in quantities in a polythene bag.

FROZEN ROSES

Roses can be cut for freezing when the flowers are in full bud, and they can also be frozen when in full bloom.

IN BUD Cut the roses and immerse them up to their necks in cold water for a few hours. Use a rigid freezer container which is 1 in. longer than the roses and at least 3 in. deep. Put the roses in the box head to tail and put in enough water just to hold them on the bottom of the box. Cover and freeze. When ice has formed, cover completely with water, leaving 1 in. headspace. Cover and return to the freezer. To use the roses, allow a few hours for thawing at room temperature; they will last about 36 hours. Choose varieties with strong heads, or they will have to be wired after freezing.

IN FULL BLOOM Use half a plastic ball and immerse a fully blown flower in water to freeze. To use, put into a rather flat bowl and allow to thaw out during the meal.

CREAM

Cream is not just a useful topping for fruit or puddings, but a basic ingredient of cakes, sweets and puddings. Fresh double cream can be used if sweetened and whipped and the dishes can be frozen. Frozen whipping cream can be used in recipes, either added to pastries when they are taken from the freezer, or thawed and incorporated in a recipe which is cooked and frozen.

Raspberry Cream Palmiers

12 oz puff pastry
3 oz caster sugar
½ pint double cream
4 oz raspberries

These may be made from ingredients which have been stored in the freezer. Alternatively the palmiers may be made from frozen puff pastry, and then they can be frozen again ready for assembly with fruit and cream at a later date. Roll out the pastry to a piece 24 × 12 in. and very thin. Sprinkle the top with 1 oz sugar. Fold the sides in to the centre, press and sprinkle with 1 oz sugar. Fold again to the centre and sprinkle with remaining sugar. Cut the pastry into ¼ in. slices. Place the cut side down on a baking sheet and press lightly. Repeat with all the slices, ensuring that 2 in. is allowed in between each palmier during cooking. Leave to rest for 1 hour. Bake at 425°F, 220°C, Gas Mark 7 for 5 minutes, turn and cook the other side for 4 minutes until the palmiers are lightly brown with a caramelised surface. Cool and pack in layers interleaved with waxed paper to freeze.

To serve
Thaw the palmiers at room temperature for 2 hours. Spread half of them with whipped cream and raspberries and top with remaining palmiers.
High Quality Storage Life   3 months

136

Foil-wrapped salmon steaks can be cooked in the same foil. Here are raw and cooked steaks from the same catch (p. 88).
OVERLEAF Types of food to freeze.

Variety breads baked and frozen (p. 95) then thawed for a special occasion.

Chocolate Mint Truffles

4 oz stale cake
   crumbs
¼ pint double cream
½ oz cocoa powder
¼ teaspoon
   peppermint essence
2 oz chocolate
   vermicelli

Sieve the cake crumbs or blend them in a liquidiser. Mix together the crumbs, cocoa, cream and essence until the mixture is a smooth but manageable paste. Cool in the refrigerator for 1 hour. Shape into 12 balls of equal size and roll in chocolate vermicelli. If the vermicelli does not coat the truffles neatly, brush them with a little warm apricot jam before rolling in the chocolate. Pack into a shallow airtight container lined with greaseproof paper for freezing.

To serve
Thaw at room temperature for 2 hours.
High Quality Storage Life 2 months

Orange Creams

¾ pint double cream
2 fl. oz orange juice
3 eggs
6 oz sugar
Grated rind of
   3 oranges
1 tablespoon
   gelatine

Soften the gelatine in the orange juice and stir until dissolved over hot water. Beat the eggs until frothy, mix in the sugar and continue to beat until the mixture is very thick. Stir in the grated orange rind. Whip the cream into soft peaks, and fold two-thirds of it into the egg mixture together with the gelatine. When thoroughly mixed, put into six individual freezer dishes. Pipe a whirl of cream on to each one. Cover and freeze.

To serve
Thaw at room temperature for 3 hours.
High Quality Storage Life 2 months

FREEZER JAMS

Uncooked jams are particularly suitable for freezing. They are quickly and easily made, with no tedious boiling and testing, and will store for up to six months. The colour and flavour of these jams is particularly good.

These jams should be packed in small containers to be used at one serving. If they are stiff, or if 'weeping' has occurred at the time of serving, they can be lightly stirred, to soften and blend them.

Apricot or Peach Jam

1½ lb ripe fresh apricots
  or peaches
2 lb caster sugar
4 fl. oz liquid pectin
1 teaspoon powdered
  citric acid

Skin apricots or peaches and remove stones. Mash fruit and stir in sugar and acid. Leave for 20 minutes, stirring occasionally, then add pectin and stir for 3 minutes. Pack in small waxed or rigid plastic containers, cover tightly and seal. Leave at room temperature for 24–48 hours until jelled before freezing.

To serve
Thaw at room temperature for 1 hour.
High Quality Storage Life   1 year

Raspberry Jam

1½ lb raspberries
3 lb caster sugar
4 fl. oz liquid pectin

Mash or sieve raspberries and stir with sugar. Leave for 20 minutes, stirring occasionally, then add pectin and stir for 3 minutes. Pack in small waxed or rigid plastic containers, cover tightly and seal. Leave at room temperature for 24–48 hours until jelled before freezing.

To serve
Thaw at room temperature for 1 hour.
High Quality Storage Life   1 year

Strawberry Jam

1½ lb strawberries
2 lb caster sugar
4 fl. oz liquid pectin

Mash or sieve strawberries and stir with sugar in a bowl. Leave for 20 minutes, stirring occasionally, then add pectin and stir for 3 minutes. Pack in small waxed or rigid plastic containers, cover tightly and seal. Leave at room temperature for 24–48 hours until jelled before freezing.

To serve
Thaw at room temperature for 1 hour.
High Quality Storage Life   6 months

FRESH FRUIT SYRUPS

Any standard syrup recipe can be used for fresh fruit syrups, which may be frozen in small waxed or rigid plastic containers. They can also be frozen in ice-cube trays, then each cube wrapped in foil and packed in quantities in bags for easy storage; one cube will give an individual serving to use with pudding or ice cream, or to dissolve as a drink.
The rules for making fruit syrups are similar to those for jelly-making.

Gentle heat should be used to extract the juice, with a little water added to the fruit. A jelly bag should be used to let the juice drip through; this juice is then measured and the appropriate quantity of sugar added and dissolved by stirring, before freezing in the preferred containers. A little colouring can be added to deepen the colour of pale syrups.

Soft Fruit Syrups

Raspberries, or *Blackcurrants*, or *Strawberries*, or *Redcurrants*; *Sugar*.

The fruit can be used singly, or combined, e.g. raspberries and red-currants. Use fresh clean ripe fruit and avoid washing if possible; discard mouldy or damaged fruit. Add ¼ pint water for each lb. of raspberries or strawberries; ½ pint for each lb. of currants. Cook very gently (this can be done in the oven in a covered jar) for about 1 hour, crushing fruit at intervals. Turn into jelly bag or clean cloth, and leave to drip overnight. Measure cold juice, and add ¾ lb. sugar to each pint of juice. Stir well until dissolved. Pack into small waxed or rigid plastic containers, leaving ½ in. headspace. Syrup can also be poured into ice-cube trays, and each cube wrapped in foil after freezing.

To serve
Thaw at room temperature for 1 hour, and use for sauces, mousses and drinks.
High Quality Storage Life   1 year

Rose Hip Syrup

2½ lb ripe red rose hips
3 pints water
1¼ lb sugar

Wash rose hips well and remove calyces. Put through mincer and pour on boiling water. Bring to the boil, then remove from heat and leave for 15 minutes. Strain through jelly bag or cloth overnight. Measure juice and reduce to 1½ pints by boiling. Add sugar, stir well to dissolve and boil hard for 5 minutes. Leave until cold. Pack by pouring into ice cube trays and wrapping cubes in foil when frozen.

To serve
Thaw at room temperature for 1 hour.
High Quality Storage Life   1 year

FRUIT PIE FILLINGS

A variety of fruit pie fillings can be prepared in advance and kept in the freezer, ready to fit into fresh pastry when needed; this is a good way of freezing surplus fruit in a handy form. Using the recipe method given here, try such combinations as rhubarb and orange, apricot and pineapple, or single fruits like cherries or blackberries. The mixture is best frozen in a sponge-cake tin or an ovenglass pie plate. A little cornflour or flaked tapioca will give a firm filling which cuts well and does not seep through the pastry.

Raspberry and Apple Pie

8 oz thinly sliced
    cooking apples
1 lb raspberries
1 tablespoon lemon juice
8 oz sugar
2 tablespoons tapioca
    flakes
Pinch of salt

Mix all ingredients well in a bowl and leave to stand for 15 minutes. Line a pie plate with foil, leaving 6 in. rim. Put filling into foil, fold over, and freeze. Remove frozen filling from pie plate and store in freezer. *Storage time:* 6 months. *To use,* line pie plate with pastry, put in frozen filling, dot with butter, cover with pastry lid, make slits in top crust, and bake at 425°F, 220°C, Gas Mark 7, for 45 minutes.

PRESERVES

Sweet and spicy preserves can perk up a plain meal and save space when freezing glut quantities of apples and tomatoes. The spicy preserves do not have a long storage life but are attractive for people who do not want to make large quantities of pickles, chutneys or relishes.

Blackberry Jam

1½ lb blackberries
2¾ lb caster sugar
4 fl. oz liquid pectin

This is best made with large cultivated blackberries, as the small hard wild ones are difficult to mash without liquid and are rather 'pippy'. Mash berries and stir into sugar. Leave for 20 minutes, stirring occasionally, then add pectin and stir for 3 minutes. Pack in small waxed or rigid plastic containers, cover tightly and seal. Leave at room temperature for 24–48 hours until jelled before freezing.

To serve
Thaw at room temperature for 1 hour.
High Quality Storage Life   1 year

Apple Sauce

Cook apples to a pulp with a minimum of water. For the best flavour, this should be done in a casserole in the oven, using sliced but unpeeled apples. Sieve the sauce and sweeten to taste, adding a squeeze of lemon juice. Cool and pack into rigid containers, leaving $\frac{1}{2}$ in. headspace.

To serve
Thaw for 3 hours at room temperature.
High Quality Storage Life   1 year

Apple Juice

Apple juice can be frozen, but should not be sweetened as fermentation sets in quickly. It is best made in the proportion of $\frac{1}{2}$ pint water to 2 lb. apples, or it can be made by simmering leftover peelings in water. The juice should be strained through a jelly bag or cloth, and cooled completely before freezing. It may be frozen in a rigid container, leaving $\frac{1}{2}$ in. headspace, or in a loaf tin or ice-cube trays, the frozen blocks then being wrapped in foil or polythene for easy storage.

Tomato Juice

Use ripe tomatoes, core and quarter them, and simmer them with a lid on, but with no liquid, for 10 minutes. Put through muslin, cool and pack into cartons, leaving 1 in. headspace.

To serve
Thaw juice for 1 hour in container in the refrigerator, and season with salt, pepper and a squeeze of lemon juice.
High Quality Storage Life   1 year

Cranberry Orange Relish

1 lb fresh cranberries
2 large oranges
1 lb sugar

Mince together cranberries and orange flesh, and stir in sugar until well mixed. Pack in small containers for one-meal servings.

To serve
Thaw at room temperature for 2 hours. Very good with pork, ham or poultry.
High Quality Storage Life   1 year

Cranberry Sauce

1 lb cranberries
¾ pint water
¾ lb sugar

Rinse the cranberries. Dissolve sugar in water over gentle heat. Add cranberries and cook gently for 15 minutes until cranberries pop. Cool. Pack in small waxed containers.

To serve
Thaw at room temperature for 3 hours.
High Quality Storage Life 1 year

Spiced Apples

8 oz sugar
¾ pint water
4 in. cinnamon stick
6 firm eating apples
Pink colouring

Put the sugar, water and cinnamon stick into a saucepan and heat until the sugar dissolves. Peel and core the apples and cut into ¼ in. rings. Simmer a few apple rings at a time until just tender, adding a little colouring to syrup for a better appearance. Take the slices from the syrup, drain and cool. Arrange slices on a baking sheet and freeze. Pack the slices in freezer foil or small containers. Remove the cinnamon from the syrup and freeze in small containers.

To serve
Thaw at room temperature for 1 hour, and serve round pork, ham or goose. Use the syrup for making apple sauce, or for adding to pies.
High Quality Storage Life 2 months

FOOD FOR SPECIAL OCCASIONS

Food for Easter Duckling and lamb are traditional Easter foods; buy fresh ducklings and early lamb for freezing, or ready-frozen for storage.

DUCK Freeze stuffings separately. A mixture of onions, apple, raisins, grated orange rind and seasoning, bound with an egg, is good. Orange sauce is a traditional accompaniment. Duck is also good served with cherries or with apple sauce. Duck livers make excellent pâté, and so do the remains of roast duck.

LAMB Convert the cheaper cuts such as scrag end and breast of lamb into casseroles for the holiday period. Individual lamb pies are good for picnics. Cut some of the lean meat into cubes and thread on skewers with onions, peppers, mushrooms and kidneys to make kebabs. Wrap each skewer-load in foil and then pack a quantity into a rigid container for freezing. Service with ready-cooked rice from the freezer.

Several kinds of home baking are also important at this season. Hot Cross Buns, for instance, can be fully cooked beforehand or can be prepared, ready for final baking on Good Friday morning. To do this, put the shaped and risen buns in a low oven 300°F, 150°C, Gas Mark 2 for 30 minutes until they are set but pale in colour. Cool and pack very carefully as the buns will still be slightly soft. To finish baking, put the buns on a baking sheet in a pre-heated oven set at 400°F, 200°C, Gas Mark 6 for 20 minutes.

Hot Cross Buns

1 lb plain flour
Pinch of salt
*½ pint milk and water
  mixed*
½ oz yeast
2 oz caster sugar
2 oz butter
3 oz currants
*1 oz chopped candied
  peel*
1 teaspoon cinnamon
1 teaspoon nutmeg
1 egg

Put half the flour in a bowl. Mix yeast with a little of the milk and water which should be just warm, and whisk in remaining liquid. Pour into flour and mix well. Cover with a damp cloth and leave in a warm place for 40 minutes. Mix together remaining flour, salt, cinnamon, nutmeg and sugar and stir in fruit. Melt butter and beat up the egg. Add all the dry ingredients to the yeast mixture, and pour in butter and egg, then mix thoroughly with the hands. Return to bowl, cover with damp cloth, and leave for 1 hour in a warm place. Divide dough into 16 pieces and shape each piece into a round. Put on a greased and floured baking tray, leaving room for buns to spread. Make a cross using a knife on each bun, or put on a cross made from narrow strips of pastry. Leave in a warm place for 40 minutes, then bake at 425°F, 220°C, Gas Mark 7 for 20 minutes. Five minutes before removing from the oven, brush over with milk and sugar. Cool on a rack and pack in polythene bags.

To serve
Thaw at room temperature for 1 hour. Reheat in a low oven to serve warm.
High Quality Storage Life 2 months

Easter Biscuits

8 oz plain flour ·
Pinch of salt
½ teaspoon mixed spice
3 oz butter or margarine
3 oz caster sugar
1 small beaten egg
3 oz currants

Sieve flour, salt and spice. Cream fat and sugar until light and fluffy. Beat in a little egg and flour, then stir in currants and remaining flour, adding a little more egg if necessary to make a firm paste. Roll out thinly, cut into large rounds (with a top of a tumbler) and put on greased tray. Prick with a fork, brush over with milk and sprinkle with caster sugar. Bake at 325°F, 170°C, Gas Mark 3, for 20 minutes. Cool on a rack. Pack in container to prevent crushing.

To serve
Thaw at room temperature for 1 hour.
High Quality Storage Life 2 months

Easter Bread

12 oz plain flour
1 teaspoon sugar
*6 oz currants and
    sultanas*
*1 level teaspoon mixed
    spice*
½ oz yeast
½ pint milk
1 oz melted butter
*1 oz chopped candied
    peel*

Almond Paste
3 oz ground almonds
1 egg yolk
3 oz caster sugar
1 teaspoon lemon juice

Cream yeast and sugar together and add the warmed milk. Mix into warmed sieved flour and spice from a well in the centre. Knead together and cover bowl with a damp cloth, put to rise in a warm place for approximately 30 minutes. Knock back the dough, work in dried fruit and melted butter. Shape into an oblong 10 × 5 in. and place a 9½ in. long sausage shape of almond paste on top of the dough. Press the dough round the almond paste tucking the join underneath the loaf. Place on a baking sheet and prove until double its bulk. Glaze with milk and bake in a hot oven, 425°F, 220°C, Gas Mark 7 for 10 minutes and then bake for a further 45 minutes at 350°F, 180°C, Gas Mark 4 or until loaf is evenly brown and a hollow sound is obtained when it is tapped on the underside. Allow to cool and wrap in foil.

To serve
Leave at room temperature for 2–3 hours. Slice and serve with plenty of butter.
High Quality Storage Life   2 months

Food for Picnics   Almost all freezable types of food can be pre-prepared for picnics and then frozen, including sandwiches or separate sandwich fillings, all kinds of pies, pâtés, cakes and biscuits, and individual portions of fruit or other sweet courses.

Many of these can be packed straight from the freezer and will be thawed and ready to eat at the end of any reasonable journey. The only additions need be salad vegetables, since even rolls and baps can be taken straight from the freezer and so can chunks of cheese, and individual puddings or sugared fruit. For colder weather, soup from the freezer can be quickly thawed in a double boiler and put into a Thermos flask for carrying; in the summer, frozen juices will thaw during the journey, yet will still be refreshingly chilled for drinking.

Sandwiches can be frozen in small packets of individual varieties so that a good selection can be taken for a large picnic. Individual pies can also be made; or larger pies can be made and frozen in wedges for single servings. Meat and chicken pies, meat balls and fried chicken all freeze well.

Small batches of cakes and baked biscuits are useful for quick packed meals, or larger cakes can be cut in wedges before freezing. Individual helpings of puddings, or small packs of sugared raspberries or strawberries, fruit salad in syrup or sweetened fruit purée will give variety to packed meals.

Food for Holidays   Special food prepared for the holidays obviously includes eatables for packed meals and picnics. It should also include basic items around which adaptable, good-tempered family meals may

Cranberry sauce (p. 216) with duck roasted when completely thawed (p. 83).

If you freeze scallops (p. 89) keep the shells for made-up dish like these scallops with Dutch sauce (p. 155).

be planned at any time; for instance pies, shepherd's pie, casseroles, meat loaves, fish dishes and pasta.

On the whole, these dishes are inexpensive to prepare, and can be made in sufficiently large quantities to cope with unexpected numbers at holiday time. To supplement them, bulk stocks of peas, carrots and chips will be useful. Commercially-prepared beefburgers, fish fingers and ice cream are popular with children, and can be very useful for preparing a quick high tea or light supper. The corners of the freezer shelves or baskets can also be stocked with baps for making hamburgers, and with buns and doughnuts.

Getting Ready for Christmas Christmas preparations can begin early, with poultry, meat and vegetables chosen and in store from October onwards. Cooking can continue through October and November, leaving December free for last-minute shopping, parcel packing and entertainment.

POULTRY Turkeys and chickens frozen whole will store 8–12 months; geese and ducks 6–8 months. They should be frozen without giblets or stuffing. Roast birds to be served cold are not very successful, as the flesh exudes moisture and becomes flabby on thawing; also, very little time is saved in preparation.

STUFFING The storage life of stuffing is only 1 month, and it is best packed alone. In the normal way, freezing stuffing is unnecessary as it can be prepared while the poultry is thawing, but at busy times or to use up materials, frozen stuffing can be useful. If it is vital to stuff the bird in advance, a breadcrumb stuffing can be used for a fresh bird, and the stuffed bird frozen for up to 4 weeks; a sausage stuffing should not be used.

GIBLETS Giblets only have a storage life of 2 months, and are best packed separately and frozen rather than packed in the bird. Livers can be packed separately for use in pâtés or omelettes. Giblets can be cooked and the stock frozen for gravy and soup; the chopped giblets can be frozen covered in stock and stored for up to 4 weeks for inclusion in soup or pies.

VEGETABLES Peas, beans, carrots, sweetcorn and sprouts are particularly useful for Christmas. Potatoes mashed with butter and hot milk can be frozen in bags or cartons and reheated in a double boiler. Croquettes can be made from the mixture and fried before freezing (thaw for 2 hours before heating in a moderate oven for 20 minutes).

CHRISTMAS PUDDINGS These are normally stored in bowls in a dry place, but modern homes are often deficient in storage space. Rich fruit puddings can be made to traditional recipes, in foil bowls, covered with foil lids, and stored up to 1 year in the freezer.

145

MINCE PIES — Mincemeat is highly spiced, and spices tend to develop 'off flavours' in the freezer, so storage life is no longer than 1 month. Pies can be baked and packed in cartons for freezing. If there is more space, pies can be frozen unbaked in their baking tins. Unbaked mince pies have a better flavour and scent, crisper and flakier pastry, than pies baked before freezing.

SWEET AND SAVOURY SAUCES — All kinds of sauces freeze well. Particularly useful as Christmas approaches are apple sauce, cranberry sauce, brandy butter, fruit sauces for sweet puddings and ice cream, and bread sauce for poultry.

CHRISTMAS BREADS — Special fruit breads are delicious for teatime entertaining, for serving with coffee or hot chocolate, or with glasses of festive wine.

Christmas Candle Ring

½ oz fresh yeast
¼ pint warm milk
4 tablespoons water
1 lb plain flour
1 level teaspoon salt
2 oz butter
3 oz crystallised orange slices
2 oz crystallised pineapple
1 oz blanched almonds
1 oz soft brown sugar
½ teaspoon ground cinnamon

Egg Wash
1 egg
1 teaspoon sugar
1 tablespoon water

Mix the yeast with milk and water. Mix the flour and salt and rub in the butter. Add the yeast liquid and work to a firm dough until the sides of the bowl are clean. Turn the dough out on to a lightly floured surface and knead thoroughly until firm and elastic and no longer sticky, which will take about 10 minutes. Shape the dough into a ball and place in a large, lightly oiled polythene bag, loosely tied at the top. Leave to rise until the dough has doubled in size and springs back when pressed gently with a floured finger, about 1 hour in a warm place, 2 hours at average room temperature.

Turn the dough on to a lighly floured surface and knead until the dough is firm, about 2 minutes. Divide the dough into two pieces and roll them both out to long rectangles about 12 × 5 in. Chop the orange, pineapple and almonds and mix with brown sugar and cinnamon. Spread the filling on both pieces of dough, roll up lengthways and seal edges of dough. Twist both pieces of dough together, shape into a circle and seal ends. Put on a greased baking tray, with a dariole mould in the centre, brush with egg wash and cover with oiled polythene. Leave to rise until double in size, about 30–45 minutes in a warm place.

Remove the polythene and bake the ring at 400°F, 200°C, Gas Mark 6 for 40–45 minutes until golden brown, and the loaf sounds hollow when tapped underneath. Cool, wrap and freeze.

To serve
Wrap in foil and put the frozen loaf in a hot oven set at 400°F, 200°C, Gas Mark 6, for 30 minutes. Cool in foil. Ice with a mixture of 4 oz icing sugar and 1 tablespoon water. Decorate with extra slices of crystallised orange if liked and put a candle decorated with holly in the centre of the ring.
High Quality Storage Life 3 months

Stollen

Batter
2 oz plain flour
½ level teaspoon
  sugar
½ oz fresh yeast
4 oz warm milk

Other ingredients
2 oz butter
2 oz caster sugar
1 egg
6 oz plain flour
½ level teaspoon
  salt
3 oz raisins
2 oz glacé cherries
1 oz chopped mixed
  candied peel
1 oz chopped
  almonds
Grated rind of
  ½ lemon
½ oz melted butter

Mix the batter ingredients in a large bowl, and set aside until frothy, about 20–30 minutes in a warm place. Cream the butter and sugar, add the egg and beat well. Add to the yeast batter with all the remaining ingredients except the melted butter. Mix well together to make a soft dough. Place the bowl in a large, lightly oiled polythene bag. Leave to rise until double in size, about 1½ hours in a warm place. Turn dough on to a lightly floured board and knead well for about 10 minutes until smooth and elastic. Roll out to an oval about 10×8 in., brush with melted butter and fold over lengthwise so that the top layer is 1 in. from the edge of the bottom.

Place stollen on a greased baking sheet and cover with oiled polythene. Leave to rise until doubled in size and the dough springs back when pressed with a floured finger, about 45 minutes in a warm place. Remove the polythene and bake at 375°F, 190°C, Gas Mark 5 for 30 to 35 minutes until golden brown. Cool, wrap in foil and freeze.

To serve
Put frozen stollen wrapped in foil in a hot oven set at 400°F, 200°C, Gas Mark 6 for 30 minutes. Cool and dust with icing sugar.
High Quality Storage Life   3 months

Mincemeat Pinwheel Buns

½ oz fresh yeast
1½ fl. oz. water
8 oz plain flour
1 level teaspoon salt
1 tablespoon
  caster sugar
1 egg
Grated rind and
  juice of ½ orange
4 tablespoons
  mincemeat
4 oz apples

Mix the yeast with the water. Mix the flour, salt, sugar, egg, grated rind and orange juice, and work in the yeast liquid. Turn out and knead well on a floured surface until the dough feels smooth and elastic. Put the dough to rise in a large, lightly oiled polythene bag, loosely tied at the top, until doubled in size, about 1 hour in a warm place. Turn out the risen dough and knead lightly for 2 minutes. Roll out to an oblong 6×12 in. Mix together mincemeat and grated apple and spread on the dough. Roll up lengthwise like a Swiss roll, cut into ½ in. slices and put into greased bun tins. Place the tins inside a large oiled polythene bag and leave to rise until doubled in size, about 30 minutes in a warm place. Remove the polythene and bake at 400°F, 200°C, Gas Mark 6 for 25 minutes until golden brown. Cool, wrap in foil and freeze.

To serve
Put the buns wrapped in foil in a hot oven set at 400°F, 200°C, Gas Mark 6 for 15 minutes. Cool and dust with icing sugar.
High Quality Storage Life   3 months

Party Pieces Special casseroles or puddings are always useful for unexpected guests and impromptu supper or lunch parties. It is also good to keep the makings of a small cocktail or buffet party ready for those guests who want more than a drink but less than a meal. For the large planned party, too, preparation and freezing ahead can be invaluable, for most cocktail 'food' is fiddly and can use up a couple of days before a party in preparation time.

ICE CUBES   If space is available, freeze extra quantities and store in plastic bags (to keep cubes separate, wrap each in foil). For some drinks, such as large bowls of fruit punch, it is better to freeze large pieces of ice, using ice-trays without cube divisions; prepare a number of these and store in bags. For special drinks, freeze a sprig of mint, a twist of lemon or a cherry or strawberry into individual ice cubes.

GARNISHES   Freeze mint leaves in small packages for putting into fruit cups. Freeze parsley sprigs for decorating sandwiches or pies. Freeze strawberries with hulls on for garnishing fruit drinks or puddings (spread fruit on trays to freeze, then package).

SANDWICHES   Open sandwiches can be prepared and stored for 2 weeks. Ordinary sandwiches may be prepared up to 4 weeks ahead and left in large slices, then cut into small shapes for party serving. For special parties, rolled, ribbon or checkerboard sandwiches can be prepared but left unsliced until after thawing. Open sandwiches are best arranged on a tray, baking sheet, or Cellophane-covered cardboard, without garnish, then wrapped, sealed and frozen.

CANAPÉS   Canapés can be made on thin slices of day-old bread, spreading to edge with butter and filling. They are best arranged on trays before packaging, and should be thawed for 1 hour.

PASTRY   Miniature pies and turnovers can be made and frozen unbaked. Bake them unthawed at 400°F, 200°C, Gas Mark 6 for 15–20 minutes and serve hot. Sausage rolls may be frozen unbaked, and baked unthawed at 400°F, 200°C, Gas Mark 6, for 20 minutes. Vol-au-vent cases may be frozen when baked, with fillings packaged separately, then thawed, filled and heated.

DIPS AND SPREADS   These are usually based on full or skim milk soft cheeses which freeze extremely well. Make as usual, omitting any salad dressing, mayonnaise, hard-cooked egg whites, or crisp vegetables. Thaw 5 hours at room temperature.

BACON WRAPS   Thin slices of streaky bacon without rinds can be wrapped round stuffed prunes, olives, chicken livers or cocktail sausages. Secure with toothpicks, freeze quickly on tray. Grill or cook in hot oven until bacon is crisp.

148

Part VI EVERYDAY FREEZER RECIPES

FIRST COURSES

Carrot Soup

1 lb carrots
3 large tomatoes
1 pint water
1 oz butter
1 pint milk

Scrape the carrots and cook for 30 minutes in water. Dip in the tomatoes and skin them. Drain carrots, reserving liquid. Grate carrots. Melt the butter and lightly cook skinned tomatoes. Add the grated carrot and cook until all the butter is absorbed. In a double saucepan, bring the milk to the boil, add carrot and tomato, and liquid from carrots. Simmer for 45 minutes, seasoning lightly with salt and pepper. Cool. Pack in waxed or rigid plastic container, leaving headspace.

To serve
Reheat gently in double boiler, adjusting seasoning, and garnish with toasted croûtons and chopped parsley.
High Quality Storage Life   1 month

Cock-a-Leekie

1 boiling chicken
1 lb shin beef
6 leeks
4 oz prunes
1 small teaspoon black pepper
2 level teaspoons salt

Wipe the chicken inside and out and put into a large saucepan. Cut meat into small pieces. Clean and slice leeks thinly, using some of the green parts. Add salt and pepper and cover with cold water. Bring to simmering point and cook gently for 4 hours. Add the prunes and simmer 45 minutes. Take out the chicken and cut flesh into neat small pieces, return to saucepan and reheat. Pack into containers, leaving headspace.

To serve
Reheat gently, adjusting seasoning.
High Quality Storage Life   2 months

149

Leek Soup

4 leeks
1 oz butter
1 pint chicken stock

Clean leeks thoroughly and cut into thin rings. Melt butter, and soften leeks without colouring them. Add stock, season lightly and simmer for 30 minutes. Cool. Pack in waxed or rigid plastic container, leaving headspace.

To serve
Reheat gently, adjust seasoning, and stir in $\frac{1}{4}$ pint creamy milk. Garnish with chopped parsley or chives.
High Quality Storage Life　1 month

Onion Soup

$1\frac{1}{2}$ lb onions
2 oz butter
3 pints beef stock
Salt and pepper
2 tablespoons cornflour

Slice the onions finely and cook gently in butter until soft and golden. Add stock and seasoning, bring to the boil, and simmer for 20 minutes. Thicken with cornflour and simmer for 5 minutes. Pack after cooling and removing fat, into containers, leaving headspace.

To serve
Reheat in double boiler, stirring gently. Meanwhile, spread slices of French bread with butter and grated cheese, and toast until cheese has melted. Put slices into tureen or individual bowls and pour over soup.
High Quality Storage Life　2 months

Shrimp Soup

2 sticks celery
4 oz mushrooms
1 small onion
1 carrot
2 oz butter
2 pints chicken stock
Salt and pepper
Bay leaf
Pinch of nutmeg
2 tablespoons lemon
　juice
2 tablespoons white wine
6 oz shrimps

Cut celery, mushrooms, onion and carrot in small pieces and cook gently in butter for 10 minutes. Add stock, seasoning, bay leaf, nutmeg and lemon juice, and simmer for 20 minutes. Put through a sieve. Add wine and shrimps and simmer for 5 minutes. Cool and remove fat. Pack into containers, leaving headspace.

To serve
Reheat in double boiler, stirring gently. When thawed, stir in $\frac{1}{2}$ pint double cream and continue reheating without boiling.
High Quality Storage Life　1 month

Hare Soup

1 hare
1 lb lean ham
3 medium onions
Parsley, thyme and
    marjoram
Salt and pepper
3 blades mace
6 pints beef stock
2 rolls
½ pint port

Cut hare into joints and put into a pan with chopped ham and onions, herbs, salt and pepper, mace and stock. Simmer for 2½ hours. Remove meat from bones and put into a blender with the ham, the crumbled rolls and some of the hare liquor which has been strained. Blend until smooth, then mix with remaining hare liquor and port, and simmer for 20 minutes. Cool. Pack in waxed or rigid plastic containers, leaving headspace.

To serve
Reheat gently in double boiler.
High Quality Storage Life   2 months

Iced Tomato Soup

8 thinly-sliced tomatoes
4 thinly-sliced small
    white onions
4 peeled and finely-
    chopped cloves garlic
Strip of lemon rind
4 tablespoons water
6 tablespoons tomato
    paste
4 tablespoons flour
1 pint chicken stock
1 teaspoon Tabasco
    Sauce
1 teaspoon sugar
Salt and pepper
2 tablespoons sherry
    (optional)
1 teaspoon lemon juice
¼ pint single cream

Combine thinly sliced tomatoes and onions, chopped garlic, lemon rind and water and simmer gently for 10–15 minutes. Add tomato paste and cook a further three minutes. Stir in flour made into a paste in some of the measured stock. Add remaining stock, Tabasco sauce, sugar, salt and pepper. Bring soup to the boil stirring constantly. Sieve the soup through a fine strainer. Add sherry and lemon juice. Pack into rigid container, leaving headspace, and freeze.

To serve
Thaw in refrigerator for 3 hours. Stir in cream and serve garnished with thin cucumber slices.
High Quality Storage Life   1 month

Farmhouse Pâté

12 rashers streaky bacon (rind removed)
8 oz minced pig's liver
8 oz minced stewing veal
1 medium minced onion
1 oz fresh white breadcrumbs
¼ level teaspoon dried sage
1 tablespoon brandy or sherry
Salt and pepper
1 beaten egg

Stretch bacon rashers by drawing the blade of a knife along them. Cut each rasher in half and use to line foil pudding basins. Mix together the remaining ingredients until well-blended, then spoon into prepared basins and press down well. Cover each basin tightly with a piece of foil, then place basins in a roasting tin filled with 1 inch water. Cook at 325°F, 170°C, Gas Mark 3, for 1–1½ hours. Loosen lids, allow pâté to cool. Pour off excess liquid and cover. Label and freeze quickly.

To serve
Defrost in refrigerator for 8 hours, or overnight. Serve with Melba Toast.
High Quality Storage Life   1 month

Pigeon Pâté

3 pigeons
⅜th pint (8 fl. oz) red wine
Scant ¼ pint vinegar
1 bay leaf
1 small teaspoon thyme
Grating of nutmeg
Salt and pepper
4 onions
8 oz sausagemeat
1 slice of bread
A little milk

Joint the pigeons. Mix together wine, vinegar, bay leaf, thyme, nutmeg, salt and pepper and finely chopped onions, and pour this over the birds. Leave to soak in cool place for 3 days. Remove flesh from the birds, and mince twice. Mix with sausagemeat. Remove crusts from the bread, and soak in enough milk to moisten the bread. Beat this into the meat mixture. Press mixture into a terrine, loaf tin, or oven dish and cover with a lid or foil. Stand dish in a tin of water, and cook at 350°F, 180°C, Gas Mark 4, for 1½ hours. Cool completely under weights. Remove from baking dish. Pack in heavy-duty foil.

To serve
Thaw at room temperature for 3 hours.
High Quality Storage Life   2 months

Simple Pork Pâté

12 oz pig's liver
2 lb belly of pork
1 large onion
1 large egg
1 tablespoon plain flour
Salt, pepper and nutmeg
Parsley

Put liver and pork through coarse mincer. Chop the onion and soften in a little butter. Mix together the meat, onion, egg beaten with flour, seasoning and a little chopped parsley. Put mixture into a foil dish, or terrine or loaf tin. Cover with greaseproof paper and a lid (sheet foil will do), and stand the container in a baking tin of water. Cook at 350°F, 180°C, Gas Mark 4, for 1½ hours. Cool under weights. To pack, cover a foil container with a foil lid and seal with freezer tape; or remove from the container and wrap in freezer foil for storage.

To serve
Thaw at room temperature for 3 hours.
High Quality Storage Life   2 months

Hare Pâté

1½ lb uncooked hare
¼ lb fat bacon
3 tablespoons brandy
¾ lb minced pork and
veal
Salt, pepper and nutmeg
1 egg

A mixture of game and rabbit can also be used for this recipe. Cut the hare into small pieces and the bacon into dice and mix together in a dish with brandy. Leave for 1 hour, then put through mincer with pork and veal. Season, add egg and mix well. Press mixture into a buttered container, cover with greased paper and lid and put dish in a baking tin of water. Bake at 400°F, 200°C, Gas Mark 6, for 1 hour. Leave under weights until cold. Pack by covering containers with foil lid and sealing with freezer tape, or by repacking in heavy-duty foil. This is only advisable if a large amount of pâté is to be eaten at once. Otherwise re-pack mixture into small containers and cover before freezing (if the pâté is cooked in small containers, it will be dry).

To serve
Thaw small containers at room temperature for 1 hour. Thaw large pâté in wrappings in refrigerator for 6 hours, or at room temperature for 3 hours. Use immediately after thawing.
High Quality Storage Life 1 month

Smoked Fish Pâté

2 smoked mackerel or
8 oz kipper fillets
8 oz butter
⅜th pint (8 fl. oz) cream
Juice of 1 lemon
Salt and pepper

Smoked fish pâtés may be varied according to taste. Those who like a sharp-tasting pâté may like to increase the amount of lemon juice, but others may prefer a milder flavour and use more cream. The recipe can be used for smoked trout or smoked salmon, but any fish used should be fresh and juicy. Some people like to add a dash of whisky or Worcester sauce or Tabasco sauce to these fish pâtés. It is worth experimenting. If these pâtés are sealed with a little melted clarified butter, they will keep well for a week in the refrigerator, so it may not be necessary to freeze for an occasion only a few days ahead.
Skin and bone the fish and put it into a liquidiser. Melt the butter gently and add just enough to let the mixture turn easily in the machine. When it is smooth, put the purée into a bowl and mix with cream, lemon juice, seasoning, and any chosen added flavouring. Put into one large container or individual containers, cover and freeze.

To serve
Thaw at room temperature for 3 hours.
High Quality Storage Life 1 month

153

Duckling Pâté

4 lb duckling
Duck liver
8 oz lean pork
1 garlic clove
Pinch of ground mace
Pinch of grated nutmeg
3 tablespoons dry white
    wine
1 tablespoon dry sherry
Salt and pepper

Roast the duck lightly and then mince the duck meat with the liver and pork twice. Mix this meat with all the other ingredients and pack into a foil container, loaf tin or terrine. Cover with a lid or foil and stand container in a baking tin of water. Cook at 300°F, 150°C, Gas Mark 2, for 1¾ hours, or until the mixture shrinks from the side of the dish. Cool under weights. Pack for freezing.

To serve
Thaw at room temperature for 3 hours.
High Quality Storage Life   2 months

Turkey or Chicken Liver Pâté

2 oz butter
1 chopped onion
1 crushed clove garlic
½ lb streaky bacon
    (de-rinded, chopped)
1 lb turkey or chicken
    livers
4 oz chopped cooked ham
½ teaspoon Tabasco
    sauce
½ level teaspoon mixed
    herbs
1 oz melted butter
2 tablespoons single
    cream
Salt and pepper

Melt butter in a saucepan. Add onion and garlic, and cook until tender, but not browned. Add bacon and livers and simmer gently with lid on pan for about 10 minutes, or until chicken livers are cooked. Allow to cool. Add ham. Put mixture through mincer, and then into a basin. Add Tabasco sauce, mixed herbs, melted butter, cream, and seasoning. Mix well together. Put into a straight-sided dish or small individual dishes, and freeze.

To serve
Thaw at room temperature for 1 hour.
High Quality Storage Life   1 month

Potted Seafood

12 oz cooked lobster,
    crab, scampi or
    prawns (peeled
    weight)
2 oz melted butter
½ teaspoon pepper
Pinch of Cayenne
    pepper
¼ teaspoon ground mace
¼ teaspoon salt

Pound large pieces of seafood, but leave small prawns whole. Put the fish into a saucepan with half the butter and the seasonings, and toss lightly until heated through but not fried. Put into four small pots and leave to cool slightly. Cover with the remaining butter which has been melted but not browned. Cover and freeze.

To serve
Thaw at room temperature for 3 hours and serve with hot toast or brown bread and butter. Potted shellfish can be used as a sandwich filling, or heated as a sauce with plainly cooked white fish.
High Quality Storage Life   3 months

154

Potted Shrimps

Shrimps
Butter
Salt and pepper
Ground mace and cloves
   to taste

Cook freshly caught shrimps, cool in cooking liquid and shell. Pack tightly into waxed cartons. Melt butter, season with salt, pepper and a little mace and cloves. Cool butter and pour over shrimps. Chill until cold. Pack by covering with lids and sealing with freezer tape.

To serve
Thaw in containers at room temperature for 2 hours, or heat in double boiler until butter has melted and shrimps are warm to serve on toast.
High Quality Storage Life 3 months

Prawn Pizza

8 oz self-raising flour
2 oz margarine
6 tablespoons milk
4 oz grated cheese
Salt and pepper
Pinch of Cayenne pepper

Topping
8 oz frozen prawns
2 oz black olives, halved
   and stoned
4 oz sliced tomatoes
1 oz grated cheese
3 tablespoons olive oil
Paprika

Sift flour and scone seasoning into a basin. Add margarine, and rub in until mixture resembles fine breadcrumbs. Add the grated cheese and mix well. Bind with the milk to a firm dough. Roll out to a circle 9 inches in diameter. Decorate the top with 6 oz prawns, and the olives and tomatoes. Sprinkle with grated cheese and oil, and finish with a pinch of paprika. Bake at 400°F, 200°C, Gas Mark 6 for 30 minutes. Cool, then chill and freeze.

To serve
Reheat for 30–40 minutes at 300°F, 150°C, Gas Mark 1–2. Decorate with remaining prawns before serving.
High Quality Storage Life 1 month

Scallops with Dutch Sauce

4 medium-sized scallops
⅛th pint milk
1 oz butter
1 oz cornflour
Mashed potato for piped
   borders
4 oz grated Gouda
   cheese
Salt and pepper to taste

Prepare the scallops, keeping only the white and orange parts, and the deep shells (and liquor if you get it). Rinse if fresh. Poach in a little milk or milk and scallop liquor until tender, between 7 and 10 minutes. Brush the shells with melted butter. Pipe a border of mashed potato round the edge of each shell, and place the scallops in the shells.

Use a frozen basic sauce or make a cheese sauce with the butter, cornflour and almost all the grated cheese. Pour the sauce over the scallops. Sprinkle with the remaining cheese and a few breadcrumbs. Place under a hot grill for 5 minutes.

To serve
Thaw 2 hours at room temperature. Reheat 7–10 minutes in a low oven.
High Quality Storage Life 1 month

Savoury Salmon Plait

1 oz plain flour
1 oz butter
¼ pint milk
2 oz cheese, grated
Salt and pepper
2 oz sweet corn
2 oz button mushrooms,
*   sliced*
8 oz frozen salmon or
*   prawns*
1 × 10-oz pkt frozen
*   puff pastry*
Beaten egg

Melt the butter, add the flour and cook for 2 minutes. Gradually add the milk, return to the heat and stir until the sauce thickens. Add cheese and seasoning to taste. Stir in the sweet corn, mushrooms and defrosted fish. Roll out the pastry to a rectangle 12 inches × 10 inches, trim edges and cut in half lengthways. Spread the filling over 1 half, leaving about 1 inch border. Brush border with beaten egg. Fold the second oblong in half and make diagonal cuts along the fold. Unfold and place over the filling. Seal edges firmly, then flake by cutting with the back of a knife. Brush top with beaten egg. Bake at 425°F, 220°C, Gas Mark 7, for 40 minutes, until golden-brown. Chill and freeze.

To serve
Can be served hot or cold. Thaw for 3 hours at room temperature. Then, if desired, reheat at 350°F, 180°C, Gas Mark 4, for 40 minutes.
High Quality Storage Life   1 month

Yarmouth Straws

6 oz shortcrust pastry
1 beaten egg
1 tablespoon grated
*   Parmesan*
1 large cooked kipper

Roll out pastry into two 3 in. strips. Brush one strip with beaten egg, and sprinkle half the cheese on the other piece. Remove bones from kipper and pound the flesh. Put kipper on one piece of pastry, cover with the other piece and sprinkle on remaining cheese. Cut into ¾ in. fingers. Bake at 350°F, 180°C, Gas Mark 4, for 10 minutes. Cool. Pack in foil trays inside polythene bags.

To serve
Reheat at 325°F, 170°C, Gas Mark 3, for 20 minutes.
High Quality Storage Life   1 month

Quiche Lorraine

4 oz shortcrust pastry
½ oz butter
1 small onion
1 oz streaky bacon
1 egg and 1 egg yolk
2 oz grated cheese
1 gill creamy milk
Pepper

Line a flan ring with pastry, or line a foil dish which can be put into the freezer. Gently soften chopped onion and bacon in butter until golden, and put into pastry case. Lightly beat together egg, egg yolk, cheese, milk and pepper. Add a little salt if the bacon is not very salty. Pour into flan case. Bake at 375°F, 190°C, Gas Mark 5, for 30 minutes. Cool. Pack in foil in rigid container to avoid breakage, and seal with freezer tape.

To serve
Thaw in refrigerator for 6 hours to serve cold. If preferred hot, heat at 350°F, 180°C, Gas Mark 4, for 20 minutes.
High Quality Storage Life   2 months

Salmon Rolls

8 oz shortcrust pastry
2 tablespoons white sauce
1 teaspoon lemon juice
8 oz can pink salmon
Salt and pepper

Roll pastry into a long narrow strip about 3 in. wide. Mix white sauce, lemon juice and drained salmon and season well. Place the mixture along one side of the pastry and roll up to enclose the filling. Cut across in 3-in. lengths. Brush with a little beaten egg and bake at 350°F, 180°C, Gas Mark 4, for 10 minutes. Cool. Pack in foil trays inside polythene bags.

To serve
Thaw at room temperature for 1 hour to serve cold, or heat in a low oven, at 325°F, 170°C, Gas Mark 3, for 20 minutes.
High Quality Storage Life   1 month

Spicy Seafood Quiche

8 oz shortcrust pastry
6 spring onions, in $\frac{3}{4}$-in. lengths
1 oz butter
6 oz peeled prawns
3 eggs
$\frac{1}{4}$ pint single cream
6 tablespoons milk
$1\frac{1}{2}$ oz grated Gruyère
8 oz cooked, flaked fish
Salt
Pinch of dried dill (optional)
$\frac{1}{4}$ teaspoon Tabasco sauce

Roll out pastry and line a 9 in. fluted flan ring. Bake 'blind' for 15 minutes at 425°F, 220°C, Gas Mark 7. Fry the spring onions in the heated butter and add the prawns (reserving a few for decoration). Spread over the base of the pastry case. Beat together the eggs, cream, milk and cheese and add the flaked fish. Add the salt, herbs and Tabasco sauce and pour over the prawn and onion mix. Bake in oven at 350°F, 180°C, Gas Mark 4, for 45–50 minutes. Garnish with prawns. Cool, pack and freeze.

To serve
Thaw at room temperature for 3 hours, or reheat.
High Quality Storage Life   1 month

Meat Loaf

2 lb beef mince
1 lb minced pie veal
1 lb pork mince
3 finely chopped onions
2 carrots
2 crushed garlic cloves
$\frac{1}{4}$ pint milk
4 oz breadcrumbs
1 teaspoon salt
2 crushed bayleaves
2 teaspoons Tabasco sauce
$\frac{1}{2}$ teaspoon thyme
$\frac{1}{2}$ teaspoon allspice
2 eggs

Combine all the ingredients for the loaf together in a large bowl and mix well. Press firmly into a greased baking tin approx. $12 \times 8 \times 1\frac{1}{4}$ in. or into 2 tins. Bake at 350°F, 180°C, Gas Mark 4, for $1\frac{1}{4}$ hours. Cool and pack in foil or polythene for freezing.

To serve
Reheat or serve cold with a spicy tomato sauce.
High Quality Storage Life   2 months

MAIN COURSES

Winter Casserole

4 tablespoons Worcester
    sauce
4 tablespoons water
Salt
1½ lb skirt or stewing
    beef, cut into 2-in.
    pieces
1 oz dripping
4 large carrots
2 leeks
½ lb swede
2 oz flour
½ pint water
½ pint brown ale
Pepper

Mix together Worcester sauce, water and salt. Place beef in marinade for 4 hours or overnight in refrigerator, turning occasionally. Drain meat and reserve marinade. Heat dripping in a pan and brown meat well. Remove to a 4 pint casserole. Add sliced carrot, leeks, swedes to pan and cook in remaining dripping for 3–4 minutes. Blend in flour. Remove from heat, add water, ale, marinade, salt and pepper. Bring to the boil, stirring. Pour over meat in casserole, cover and cook at 325°F, 170°C, Gas Mark 3, for 2½ hours. Pack and freeze.

To serve
Reheat at 325°F, 170°C, Gas Mark 3, for 1¼ hours.
High Quality Storage Life   2 months

Pot Roast Beef with Vegetables

2 lb flank beef (chined
    and tied into round
    shape)
2 carrots
1 turnip
1 onion
Good ⅛th pint stock
Salt and pepper
Thyme, parsley and
    bayleaf
Dripping

Heat dripping in pan until smoking hot and brown meat on all sides. Place chopped vegetables round the meat and add the seasoning and herbs. Pour over the stock. Cover pan with a tight-fitting lid. Simmer gently until meat is tender, about 2 hours. Pack and freeze.

To serve
Reheat in a covered dish at 325°F, 170°C, Gas Mark 3, for 1¼ hours.
High Quality Storage Life   2 months

Spicy Topside

2 lb beef topside
8 oz bacon rashers
½ chopped onion
1 pint brown ale
1 pint water
2 teaspoons salt
2 tablespoons vinegar

Arrange bacon and onion in bottom of deep pan. Add meat, ale, water and salt. Cover pan and simmer till tender, either on top of stove, or at 325°F, 170°C, Gas Mark 3, for 2½ hours. Cool and pack in foil or polythene or rigid container.

To serve
Reheat in covered dish at 325°F, 170°C, Gas Mark 3, for 1¼ hours.
High Quality Storage Life   2 months

Stuffed Steak Casserole

*3 × 8-oz slices chuck
   steak, 1 in. thick
1 oz butter
1 onion
2 oz mushrooms
2 rashers bacon
1 tablespoon chopped
   parsley
1 oz soft white
   breadcrumbs
Salt, pepper and nutmeg
1 beef stock cube
   dissolved in ¼ pint hot
   water
¼ pint red wine
1 pig's trotter (split)*

To make the stuffing, soften the finely chopped onion, mushrooms and bacon in the butter. Add the parsley, crumbs, seasoning and nutmeg. Put a thick layer on two slices of meat. Place one on top of the other and top with the third piece. Tie neatly with tape and place in an oblong casserole. Make up the stock. Add the wine to this and pour into the casserole. Put the trotter on top of the meat. Cover and cook for 4 hours at 275°F, 140°C, Gas Mark 1. Discard the trotter, skim any fat from the sauce and pack for freezing.

To serve
Reheat and slice meat vertically to give stripes of meat and stuffing. The meat may be sliced and served cold with the chopped jellied sauce.
High Quality Storage Life 2 months

Beef in Beer

*1 lb skirt or chuck steak
1 oz flour
1 teaspoon brown sugar
Grated nutmeg
¼ pint hot water
½ pint stout
1 beef stock cube
2 large onions
1 clove garlic
1 bayleaf
1 oz butter*

Cut the meat into 2-in. pieces and toss in flour. Melt the butter in a saucepan or casserole and add the sliced onions to soften without browning. Add the meat and brown on all sides. Season the meat and onions and then add the nutmeg, sugar, garlic and bayleaf. Dissolve the beef cube in the hot water and add to the meat with the stout. Simmer the meat in a casserole with a well fitting lid, for 2½ hours at 275°F, 140°C, Gas Mark 1. Pack and freeze.

To serve
Reheat in a double saucepan or in a covered dish in the oven set at 325°F, 170°C, Gas Mark 3, for 1¼ hours.
High Quality Storage Life 2 months

Braised Beef

*1 lb mixed vegetables
   (carrots, onions,
   celery, leeks, turnips)
3 lb rolled rib beef
2 oz lard or dripping
Salt and pepper
Parsley, thyme and bay
   leaf
Water or stock*

Peel vegetables and cut into neat cubes to make a layer 2 in. thick in a pan which will just fit the beef. Fry the meat in the fat until browned on all sides, and put on top of the vegetables. Add seasoning and herbs, and pour in hot water or stock to a depth of about 1 in. Cover and cook at 325°F, 170°C, Gas Mark 3, for 1½ hours. Cool. Pack in foil or rigid plastic container.

To serve
Return to casserole and heat at 325°F, 170°C, Gas Mark 3, for 1 hour.
High Quality Storage Life 2 months

Braised Brisket with Onions

3 lb brisket
1 oz dripping
4 large onions, skinned
   and cored

Stuffing
3 rashers streaky bacon,
   chopped
4 onion cores, chopped
1 tablespoon soft white
   breadcrumbs
Salt and pepper
1 oz melted butter

Mix the stuffing and fill the onions with it. Make holes in the brisket at intervals with a knife, to insert any remaining stuffing. Tie the joint up tightly, and brown on all sides in the dripping, in a really hot pan. Remove, cool slightly, and wrap in two layers of foil. Seal the edges firmly. Place in a dry meat tin, in a hot oven at 450°F, 230°C, Gas Mark 8–9. Place on a lower shelf, and bake for 2 hours. Add the onions for the last 40 minutes.
Cool, chill and freeze.

To serve
Reheat for 1¼ hours at 350°F, 180°C, Gas Mark 4.
Serve the meat with the onions and with any juices in the foil packet.
High Quality Storage Life   1 month

Meat Balls

¾ lb minced fresh beef
¼ lb minced fresh pork
2 oz dry white
   breadcrumbs
½ pint creamy milk
1 small chopped onion
1½ teaspoons salt
¼ teaspoon pepper
Butter

Mix together beef and pork and soak breadcrumbs in milk. Cook onion in a little butter until golden, and mix together with meat, breadcrumbs and seasoning until well blended. Shape into 1 in. balls, using 2 table-spoons dipped in cold water. Fry balls in butter until evenly browned, shaking pan to keep balls round. Cook a few at a time, draining each batch, and cool. Pack in bags, or in boxes with greaseproof paper between layers, or in foil containers.

To serve
Thaw in wrappings in refrigerator for 3 hours and eat cold. To serve hot, fry quickly in hot fat, or heat in tomato sauce or gravy.
High Quality Storage Life   2 months

Danish Meat Cakes

8 oz chuck steak
8 oz pork fillet
1 large onion
4 oz fresh white
   breadcrumbs
⅜th pint (8 fl. oz)
   bottled soda water, or
   milk
1 beaten egg
Salt and pepper
2 oz butter
2 tablespoons oil

Pass steak, pork and onion twice through fine blade of mincer. Add breadcrunbs and beat in soda water or milk and beaten egg. Add season-ing, cover and chill for 1 hour. The soda water makes them very light. Shape mixture into 8 oblongs, 4 × 2 × ¾ in. thick. Heat butter and oil together in large frying pan and fry meat cakes for 6 minutes on each side. Drain. Pack and freeze.

To serve
Fry in hot fat until golden. Serve with boiled potatoes, red cabbage and beetroot.
High Quality Storage Life   2 months

A reheated freezer casserole of minced meat garnished with mashed potato when thawed.

Pot-roasted stuffed shoulder of lamb (p. 162).

Curried Meat Balls in Vegetable Sauce

1 lb minced fresh beef
1½ oz breadcrumbs
1 tablespoon finely-
  chopped onion
1 teaspoon salt
Pinch of black pepper
2 tablespoons curry
  powder
1 small egg
2 oz butter
2 tablespoons cooking oil
2 tablespoons water

Sauce
4 oz cabbage (finely
  shredded)
2 finely chopped onions
2 de-seeded and chopped
  peppers
1 large peeled and diced
  potato
½ pint boiling water
⅛th teaspoon black
  pepper
½ teaspoon salt
2 tablespoons natural
  yogurt

Mix beef, breadcrumbs, onion, salt, curry powder, pepper and egg very thoroughly. Shape into small balls (1 in. diameter). Heat butter and cooking oil, and fry meat balls until brown. Add water, cover closely and simmer gently for 30 minutes. Shred the cabbage, chop the peppers and onions, and dice the potatoes. Put cabbage, onion, peppers and potato in the boiling water. Add seasoning, cover and simmer for 20 minutes, or until vegetables form a thick sauce. Stir occasionally. Cool, pack and freeze.

To serve
Reheat in double boiler, and stir in yogurt.
High Quality Storage Life   2 months

Jellied Beef

4 lb beef brisket
8 oz lean bacon
Salt and pepper
1 pint red wine
2 oz butter
2 oz oil
½ pint stock
Pinch of nutmeg
Parsley, thyme and
  bayleaf
4 onions
4 carrots
1 calf's foot

Use beef which has not too much fat and see that it is firmly tied. Soak in wine for 2 hours after rubbing all over with salt and pepper. Drain meat and then brown all over in a mixture of butter and oil, together with the chopped bacon. Put in casserole with the wine, stock, nutmeg, herbs, onions, carrots and split calf's foot. Cover and cook at 325°F, 170°C, Gas Mark 3, for 3 hours. Cool slightly and slice beef and put into containers with sliced vegetables. Strain liquid and cool, pour over, cover and freeze.

To serve
Thaw in refrigerator to eat cold, or heat in covered dish at 350°F, 180°C, Gas Mark 4, for 45 minutes.
High Quality Storage Life   2 months

Lamb in Orange Sauce

2 tablespoons oil
2 lb leg or shoulder of
 lamb
1 teaspoon paprika
1 large onion
4 oz mushrooms
⅜th pint (8 fl. oz)
 water
1 teaspoon horseradish
 sauce
Pinch each of rosemary,
 mint leaves, sage
Grated rind of 1 orange
1 teaspoon salt
⅜th pint (8 fl. oz)
 soured cream

Heat the oil and add the lamb. Sprinkle with paprika and add the sliced onions and mushrooms. Cook until the lamb is slightly brown on all sides. Add the water, horseradish, herbs, salt and pepper. Cover and cook over a low heat for 1 hour. Cool, pack and freeze.

To serve
Reheat in double saucepan, or in a covered dish at 325°F, 170°C, Gas Mark 3, for 1¼ hours, and stir in soured cream before serving.
High Quality Storage Life   2 months

Lamb Breast with Kidney Stuffing

1 large breast lamb

Stuffing
1 lamb kidney
4 oz sausagemeat
1 egg
1 level teaspoon salt
½ teaspoon Tabasco
 sauce
Pinch pepper

Have the lamb boned. Put lamb breast on board, boned side up. Chop the kidney. Mix stuffing and spread on lamb. Roll and tie in four places. Weigh the meat, then place in roasting tin and cook in oven for 25 minutes for each pound at 325°F, 170°C, Gas Mark 3. Pack and freeze.

To serve
Reheat in covered dish at 325°F, 170°C, Gas Mark 3, for 1¼ hours. The meat can be thawed in the refrigerator and then sliced and served cold.
High Quality Storage Life   2 months

Pot-Roasted Stuffed Shoulder of Lamb

2 lb shoulder lamb
2 onions
½ parsnip
2 sticks celery
2 carrots
Salt and pepper
Thyme, parsley and
 bayleaf
Dripping

Stuffing
6 oz pork sausagemeat
8-oz can apricots
2 oz breadcrumbs
Salt and pepper

Have the lamb boned. Chop all the vegetables. Mix all stuffing ingredients together in a bowl. Put stuffing into lamb, and tie into a round shape. Heat dripping in frying pan and brown meat on all sides. Place in a saucepan and surround meat with vegetables. Add seasoning and herbs and cover with tight-fitting lid. Cook slowly on top of the stove until meat is tender. The meat may also be cooked in a casserole at 325°F, 170°C, Gas Mark 3, for 2½ hours. Pack and freeze.

To serve
Reheat in a covered dish at 325°F, 170°C, Gas Mark 3, for 1¼ hours.
High Quality Storage Life   2 months

West Country Lamb Casserole

1 oz butter
1 onion
8 oz carrots
1 medium-sized turnip
4 oz button mushrooms
1 lb boned leg or
  shoulder of lamb cut
  into 1-in. cubes
1 oz plain flour
Light stock and ¾ pint
  cider
¼ teaspoon marjoram
Salt and pepper
2 tablespoons single
  cream
Chopped parsley

Melt butter in a pan. Add sliced onion, carrots and turnips and cook 2–3 minutes. Add mushrooms and lamb, and cook for a minute. Add flour and cook for a further minute. Stir in ¾ pint liquid (half stock, half dry cider). Bring to the boil, stirring. Add marjoram and seasoning. Simmer for 45 minutes, cool and freeze.

To serve
Reheat in double saucepan, or in oven set at 350°F, 180°C, Gas Mark 4, for 45 minutes. Stir in cream and garnish with chopped parsley.
High Quality Storage Life   2 months

Lamb and Aubergine Bake

¾ lb cooked minced lamb
2 medium aubergines
1 oz butter
2 tablespoons olive oil
1 large onion
4 oz mushrooms
1 tablespoon breadcrumbs
¼ pint stock
1 level tablespoon
  tomato purée
1 large egg
Salt and pepper

Cut aubergines in slices and sprinkle with salt. Leave to stand for 30 minutes. Drain thoroughly and fry in butter and oil until lightly browned on both sides. Remove from the pan and keep warm. Chop onions and mushrooms. Fry onion in same pan until soft then add mushrooms and fry for a further 2–3 minutes. Mix together the lamb, onion, mushrooms, breadcrumbs, stock, tomato purée, beaten egg and seasoning. Cover the bottom of a casserole or foil container with half the aubergine slices. Put the meat mixture on top and cover with the remaining aubergine slices. Bake uncovered at 350°F, 180°C, Gas Mark 4, for 1 hour. Cool, cover and freeze.

To serve
Reheat without a lid at 350°F, 180°C, Gas Mark 4, for 45 minutes.
High Quality Storage Life   2 months

Pork Steaks in Oatmeal

1 lb thin pork steaks
1 beaten egg
Salt and pepper
4 oz medium oatmeal
Lard

Flatten the steaks with a rolling pin, and cut into small serving portions. Season the egg with the salt and pepper. Dip each piece of meat into the seasoned egg, then into the oatmeal. Press covering on firmly. Fry in hot lard on both sides. After 5 minutes, lower the heat, and continue cooking until brown and tender. Cool, pack and freeze.

To serve
Reheat at 325°F, 170°C, Gas Mark 3, for 30 minutes.
High Quality Storage Life   1 month

Pork Pulao

1 lb lean cooked pork
4 tablespoons vegetable oil
1 onion
2 tablespoons curry powder
¼ teaspoon ground ginger
¾ pint stock
1 cooking apple
1 tablespoon sultanas
¼ teaspoon salt
8 oz long-grain rice

Heat oil and fry finely chopped onion till brown. Remove onion from pan. Fry curry powder and ginger until dark brown. Return onion to pan and add stock, diced meat and apple, sultanas and salt. Heat through quickly, reduce heat, cover and simmer for 15 minutes. Add the long grain rice and simmer very gently until all liquid is absorbed. The rice should be dry and fluffy. Cool and pack in polythene bag or rigid container to freeze.

To serve
Reheat at 300°F, 150°C, Gas Mark 2, for 45 minutes in uncovered dish, occasionally stirring with a fork.
High Quality Storage Life   2 months

Pork Carbonnade

1¼ lb shoulder pork cut into 1-in. squares
1 oz lard
2 leeks
1 crushed garlic clove
2 oz flour
Seasoning
½ pint brown ale
Thyme, parsley and bayleaf
Dash Tabasco sauce
Piece lemon peel
3 oz small mushrooms

Melt lard in flame-proof casserole, and fry chopped leeks and garlic for a minute. Toss pork in seasoned flour, add to leeks and fry for 5 minutes. Add ale, herbs, Tabasco sauce, lemon peel and mushrooms. Bring to the boil, cover and simmer for 1¼ hours. Cool, pack and freeze.

To serve
Reheat at 325°F, 170°C, Gas Mark 3, for 1¼ hours.
High Quality Storage Life   2 months

Pork Fricassée

1¼ lb shoulder pork
¼ pint white wine or cider
1 oz butter
1 oz flour
2 onions
⅛th pint milk
4 oz mushrooms
1 bayleaf
1 sprig thyme
2 parsley stalks
Salt and pepper

Place the pork in a casserole, and add chopped onions, wine, bayleaf, thyme, parsley and seasoning. Cover and cook at 325°F, 170°C, Gas Mark 3, for 1½ hours. Remove herbs, and strain off the liquid. Melt butter in pan, stir in flour and cook for two minutes. Make up milk to ½ pint with meat juices, and add slowly to the roux mixture. Season to taste. Pour over the meat, add mushrooms and return to oven for a further 20 minutes. Pack and freeze.

To serve
Reheat in double boiler and serve with boiled rice.
High Quality Storage Life   2 months

Baked Stuffed Liver

1½ lb liver
1 oz flour
6 oz bacon
2 tablespoons
  breadcrumbs
1 teaspoon chopped
  parsley
½ teaspoon salt
¼ teaspoon pepper
1 small onion
¼ teaspoon grated lemon
  rind
½ pint stock

Toss liver in flour and put into a shallow tin or oven dish. Mix together breadcrumbs, parsley, salt and pepper, finely chopped onion and lemon rind, and moisten with a little stock. Spread over liver and top each slice with a rasher of bacon. Pour on stock and bake at 375°F, 190°C, Gas Mark 5, for 35 minutes. Cool completely. Pack in container, or cover cooking dish with heavy-duty foil lid.

To serve
Reheat at 350°F, 180°C, Gas Mark 4, for 30 minutes.
High Quality Storage Life   1 month

Liver Bake

8 oz pig's liver
8 oz skinless sausages
1 oz butter
2 onions
8 oz tomatoes
Salt and pepper
Pinch sage
¼ pint stock

Cut liver into thin slices. Slice sausages and onions, and peel and slice tomatoes. Melt butter in an oven-proof dish or casserole, and fry onion until soft but not brown. Remove onion and drain off excess fat. Place alternate layers of onion, liver, sausage and tomato in the dish. Season layers. Pour over stock, cover with lid and bake for 30 minutes at 350°F, 180°C, Gas Mark 4. Pack and freeze.

To serve
Reheat in covered dish at 325°F, 170°C, Gas Mark 3, for 1 hour.
High Quality Storage Life   2 months

Oxtail Stew

1 oxtail
1 oz dripping
1 oz plain flour
1 medium onion
4 medium carrots
2 cloves
Salt and pepper

Wipe oxtail and cut into joints. Dust lightly with flour, and fry the joints in dripping until light brown. Work in any remaining flour and add 1½ pints water. Bring to the boil, then add sliced onion and cloves, and season to taste. Simmer for 2 hours. Add sliced carrots and continue cooking for 10 minutes. Cool completely and take off fat, and remove cloves. Pack into containers, leaving headspace.

To serve
Reheat gently, adjusting seasoning to taste, and add 2 tablespoons sherry.
High Quality Storage Life   2 months

Kidney Beef Mince

4 oz bacon rashers
12 oz minced steak
4 tomatoes
2 pig's kidneys
1½ oz butter
1 tablespoon flour
½ pint stock
1 teaspoon
   Worcester sauce
Salt and pepper

Chop and fry bacon in butter until fat runs. Add skinned and chopped tomato, chopped kidney, beef, flour and seasoning. Stir in stock and Worcester sauce. Bring to the boil and pour into a casserole. Cover and bake at 350°F, 180°C, Gas Mark 4, for 45 minutes. Alternatively, the mixture can be simmered in a pan on top of the stove until tender. Pack and freeze.

To serve
Reheat in double boiler or in covered dish at 325°F, 170°C, Gas Mark 3, for 1 hour.
High Quality Storage Life   2 months

Savoury Pie

12 oz minced belly pork
1 large onion
2 tomatoes
1 dessertspoon curry
   powder
Salt and pepper
1 lb mashed potatoes
1 oz lard
Little melted butter

Melt lard and fry curry powder for 2 minutes. Add finely chopped onion and meat, and fry for 5 minutes. Add peeled and chopped tomatoes and seasoning. Turn into a pie dish and cover with mashed potatoes. Brush over with melted butter. Bake in oven for 20 minutes at 400°F, 200°C, Gas Mark 6. Cover and freeze.

To serve
Reheat at 325°F, 170°C, Gas Mark 3, for 1 hour.
High Quality Storage Life   2 months

Stuffed Onions

4 large onions
8 oz cooked minced beef
   or lamb
2 oz fresh breadcrumbs
¼ pint brown gravy
1 teaspoon tomato purée

Peel the onions and boil until just tender. Remove centres and chop finely. Mix with meat, breadcrumbs and gravy, tomato purée, salt and pepper. Fill onions with this mixture and put into a baking tin with a little dripping. Sprinkle with a few breadcrumbs and bake at 400°F, 200°C, Gas Mark 6, for 45 minutes, basting well. Cool. Pack in foil tray, covering with lid of heavy-duty foil.

To serve
Heat at 350°F, 180°C, Gas Mark 4, for 45 minutes and serve with gravy.
High Quality Storage Life   1 month

Beef-Stuffed Green Peppers

4 large green peppers
8 oz Patna rice

Cut peppers in half lengthways, remove seeds and membrane, and rinse 'shells' thoroughly. Cook rice in boiling water until just tender, drain

166

2 tablespoons chopped
parsley
1 teaspoon marjoram or
thyme
1 tablespoon lemon juice
2 tablespoons olive oil
Salt and pepper

and rinse well. Mix with parsley, marjoram or thyme, lemon juice, half the oil, salt and pepper. Fill peppers with this mixture. Pour remaining oil into a shallow baking dish, put in peppers and cover with foil. Bake at 325°F, 170°C, Gas Mark 3, for 1 hour, adding a little more oil if necessary. Cool completely. A little cooked minced meat may be added to the filling. Pack in foil containers.

To serve
Put peppers in an oiled dish, cover with foil, and heat at 350°F, 180°C, Gas Mark 4, for 30 minutes. Home-made tomato sauce is good if poured over the peppers and heated through.
High Quality Storage Life   2 months

Spring Lamb Pie

2½ lb half shoulder or
1½ lb neck fillet of
lamb
1 oz seasoned flour
1 tablespoon oil
1 small onion
½ lb new potatoes cut
into 1-in. cubes
½ pint beef stock
2 level tablespoons
chopped mint
6 oz new carrots,
scraped and sliced
4 oz fresh or frozen peas
Salt and pepper
8 oz puff pastry
Beaten egg for glazing

Remove meat from shoulder if used. Cut lamb into 1 in. cubes and toss in seasoned flour. Heat oil in pan and fry onion gently for 3 minutes. Add lamb and fry for 5 minutes, turning occasionally to brown meat. Add potatoes, stock and mint, and bring to boil, stirring. Cover and simmer for 35 minutes. Add carrots and fresh peas and simmer for a further 10 minutes. If frozen peas are used stir in before covering pastry. Season and spoon into 2 pint pie dish. Cool. Roll out pastry and use to cover pie. Knock up and flute edges. Roll out trimmings and cut leaves to decorate centre of pie. Brush top with beaten egg. Bake at 400°F, 200°C, Gas Mark 6, for 25–30 minutes until pastry is well risen and browned. Cool and pack for freezing.

To serve
Reheat at 350°F, 180°C, Gas Mark 4, for 1 hour.
High Quality Storage Life   2 months

Bacon Pasties

12 oz shortcrust pastry
8 oz minced raw steak
6 oz streaky bacon
4 oz lamb's kidney
1 large onion
Salt and pepper
½ teaspoon
Worcester sauce

Roll out six 7-in. pastry rounds. Chop all ingredients finely and mix well together. Put a spoonful of mixture on each pastry round and form into pasty shapes, sealing edges well. Place on wetted baking sheet and bake at 425°F, 220°C, Gas Mark 7, for 45 minutes. Cool. Pack in foil tray in polythene bag, or in individual polythene bags.

To serve
Thaw 2 hours at room temperature.
High Quality Storage Life   1 month

167

Corned Beef Pie

8 oz shortcrust pastry
2 × 12-oz cans corned beef
6 oz onion
1 tablespoon oil
½ teaspoon salt
Black pepper
1 teaspoon Tabasco sauce
1 egg
4 oz diced cooked carrots
4 oz peas

Divide the pastry in half, roll out and line 8-in. pie dish (use a foil dish in which the pie can be frozen). Mash the corned beef into a basin. Chop onion and fry in oil until soft and transparent. Mix into corned beef with salt, pepper, Tabasco sauce, egg, and vegetables. Put into pastry case and top with remaining pastry. Flute the pie edge and decorate with pastry leaves. Brush with a little egg beten with a pinch of salt. Bake at 400°F, 200°C, Gas Mark 6, for 30 minutes. Cool completely. Wrap in foil, or put into a polythene bag, and freeze.

To serve
Remove from wrappings and leave at room temperature for 3 hours. Pie may be reheated to serve hot.
High Quality Storage Life   1 month

Blackdown Pie

1½ lb potatoes
3 tablespoons milk
1 oz butter
4 oz Cheddar cheese
1 oz butter
1 oz flour
1 medium-sized onion
½ pint dry cider
12 oz minced cooked lamb
4 oz cooked vegetables
2 teaspoons Worcester sauce
Salt and pepper

Boil potatoes, drain well and mash with milk and butter. Add grated cheese, and beat well until melted. To prepare meat mixture, melt butter in a large saucepan, add chopped onion, and cook gently until tender but not brown. Add flour, and cook for a minute, stirring. Remove from heat and gradually add cider. Return to heat, bring to the boil, stirring, and cook for a minute. Remove from heat, stir in lamb, vegetables, sauce and seasoning. Turn meat mixture into a 2 pint ovenproof dish, and spread level. Cover with the mashed potato and mark with a fork, or pipe potato on to meat using a large 'star' nozzle. Bake in a fairly hot oven, 400°F, 200°C, Gas Mark 6, for 20 minutes. Put meat mixture into foil container. Cool and freeze.

To serve
Put into oven set at 350°F, 180°C, Gas Mark 4, for 45 minutes.
High Quality Storage Life   2 months

Summer Chicken Pie

8 oz plain flour
1 teaspoon salt
2 oz lard
2 oz margarine
6–7 tablespoons cold water
2 eggs

Sift together flour and salt. Rub in fat until mixture resembles fine breadcrumbs. Add water and bind together to form a stiff dough; leave to rest in a cool place for 10 minutes. Blend eggs and milk in a large bowl; add tarragon, lemon rind, salt and pepper. Stir in chicken cut into ½-in. strips. Cut off one-third of pastry and keep on one side. Roll out remaining pastry to a circle about 9 in. in diameter, and use to line a 7-in. flan ring, leaving ¼ in. overlapping. Fill with chicken and egg mixture. Cover

¼ pint milk
1 teaspoon dried
    tarragon
Grated rind ½ lemon
Salt and pepper
1 lb cold cooked chicken

pie. Bake at 425°F, 220°C, Gas Mark 7, for 20 minutes. Remove flan ring carefully and reduce oven temperature to 350°F, 180°C, Gas Mark 4. Continue baking for 40 minutes. Cool and wrap in heavy duty foil or polythene.

To serve
Thaw and eat with salad.
High Quality Storage Life   2 months

Deep Chicken Pie

1 boiling chicken
3 rashers bacon
1 tablespoon chopped
    parsley
Pinch of mixed herbs
Salt and pepper
12 oz shortcrust pastry

Boil the chicken for about 3 hours until tender. Take flesh from the bones and put in layers in a foil pie-dish, alternating with finely chopped bacon and parsley and a sprinkling of mixed herbs. Season lightly and cover with a gravy made from the chicken stock thickened with a little cornflour. Cool and cover with pastry. Bake at 450°F, 230°C, Gas Mark 8, for 45 minutes. Cool completely. Pack by putting foil dish into polythene bag.

To serve
Reheat at 350°F, 180°C, Gas Mark 4, for 45 minutes. Pie may be frozen with uncooked pastry, and should then be baked straight from freezer at 450°F, 230°C, Gas Mark 8, for 1 hour.
High Quality Storage Life   2 months

Pigeon Pie

6 pigeons
8 oz chuck steak
Salt, pepper and mace
8 oz shortcrust pastry

Small mushrooms and/or hard-cooked egg yolks make pleasant additions to the pie. Remove the breasts from the pigeons with a sharp knife and put into a saucepan with the steak cut into small pieces. Season with salt, pepper and mace and just cover with water. Simmer with lid on for 1 hour. Cool completely. Put into foil baking dish and cover with pastry, sealing well. Either wrap, seal, label and freeze at once or bake at 425°F, 220°C, Gas Mark 7, for 30 minutes, cool completely, wrap, seal, label and freeze.

To serve
If pastry is uncooked, bake unthawed pie at 400°F, 200°C, Gas Mark 6, for 1 hour. If pastry is cooked, bake unthawed pie at 350°F, 180°C, Gas Mark 4, for 30 minutes.
High Quality Storage Life   2 months

Pork and Apple Pie

1 oz lard
2 large onions
3 sticks celery
1½ lb pork sparerib or
*   shoulder chops cut*
*   into 1-in. cubes*
2 tablespoons
*   Worcester sauce*
½ pint chicken stock
1 level tablespoon
*   cornflour*
2 tablespoons water
Salt and pepper
1 large cooking apple

Pastry:
6 oz flour
¼ level teaspoon salt
1½ oz lard
1½ oz butter
2 tablespoons water
Beaten egg for glazing

Heat lard in a pan and fry chopped onion and celery gently for 5 minutes. Add pork and fry, turning occasionally, for a further 10 minutes. Add Worcester sauce and stock, cover and simmer for 30 minutes. Blend cornflour with water and stir into saucepan. Bring back to the boil, season, add apple and leave to cool. Place in a 1½-pint pie dish or foil container. For the pastry, sift together flour and salt. Rub in fats until the mixture resembles fine breadcrumbs. Add water and mix to a firm dough. Knead lightly until smooth. Roll out and use to cover the pie dish. Decorate top with leaves made from pastry trimmings. Brush with beaten egg. Bake at 400°F, 200°C, Gas Mark 6, for 30–35 minutes until pastry is golden. Cover and freeze.

To serve
The pie may be eaten hot or cold. It may be frozen with a cooked filling and uncooked pastry if this is preferred.
High Quality Storage Life 2 months

Steak and Kidney Pudding

12 oz self-raising flour
¼ teaspoon salt
4½ oz suet
1½ gills cold water
1½ lb chuck steak
½ lb ox kidney
Salt and pepper

Mix flour and salt, stir in suet and mix to a soft but not sticky dough with water. Cut steak and kidney into pieces and toss in a little flour lightly seasoned with salt and pepper. Use two-thirds of the suet pastry to line a large foil basin (about 2½ pint size). Put in meat and half fill with cold water. Cover with a lid of pastry and seal edges. Cover with greased greaseproof paper and steam for 3 hours. Cool and pack by covering basin with lid of heavy-duty foil.

To serve
Steam for 1½ hours.
High Quality Storage Life 2 months

Pork and Sausage Plait

4 oz belly pork
8 oz pork sausagemeat
1 teaspoon basil
8 oz puff pastry
Salt and pepper

Chop the pork very finely or put it through a mincer. Mix thoroughly with sausagemeat, seasoning and half the beaten egg. Form into a long roll, 4-in. thick. Roll out pastry to oblong 10-in. long. Place meat roll down the centre leaving equal borders cut obliquely in ½-in. wide strips, and brush with beaten egg. Fold alternate strips across the filling

1 beaten egg

to form a plait. Glaze with beaten egg and bake at 400°F, 200°C, Gas Mark 6, for 30 minutes. Cover and freeze.

To serve
Reheat in low oven, or thaw and serve cold.
High Quality Storage Life   2 months

Galantine of Beef

1 lb minced stewing
    steak
8 oz sausagemeat
6 oz white breadcrumbs
Salt and pepper
½ teaspoon allspice
1 egg
1 teaspoon Tabasco
    sauce
½ pint beef stock

Glaze
½ pint water
¼ oz gelatine
½ teaspoon gravy
    browning
1 teaspoon meat extract

Grease 2-lb. loaf tin. Mix all the ingredients together until smooth, adding enough stock to give a soft dropping consistency. Press the mixture firmly into the tin, leaving no air spaces and cover with foil or greased, greaseproof paper. Stand tin in a baking tin of water and bake at 375°F, 190°C, Gas Mark 5, for 2 hours. Leave to get quite cold.
To make the glaze, put the water in a small basin with the gelatine, over a saucepan of boiling water. When the gelatine is dissolved, add the browning and extract. Stand the cold galantine on a cake rack and paint it thickly with hot glaze. Wrap and freeze.

To serve
Thaw in the refrigerator and garnish with hard-boiled egg and parsley.
High Quality Storage Life   2 months

Potted Beef

1 lb shin beef
2 bay leaves
2 cloves
Pinch of mace
2 tablespoons water
Salt and pepper
2 oz butter

Cut meat into small pieces, removing fat and gristle. Place in a fireproof dish with the seasonings and water. Cover closely with buttered paper and kitchen foil, all tucked well round the sides. Bake in a low oven, 300°F, 150°C, Gas Mark 2, for 3 hours until the meat is very tender. Lift out bay leaves and cloves. Put meat twice through the mincer, beat well with the juices and the butter. Add salt and pepper if required. Press meat into a foil container and freeze.

To serve
Thaw in refrigerator. Serve in slices with salad or with hot toast.
High Quality Storage Life   2 months

Spiced Pressed Pork

3 lb belly pork (boned)
4 tablespoons vinegar
2 tablespoons oil
½ teaspoon salt
½ teaspoon ground
* nutmeg*
½ teaspoon cinnamon
½ teaspoon ground
* ginger*
¼ teaspoon black pepper

Score the pork rind in diamond shapes. Mix the other ingredients together. Put the pork into a shallow dish, pour over the marinade and allow to stand for at least 3 hours, turning frequently. Wrap the joint in a loose parcel of aluminium foil and place in a roasting tin. Cook for 2 hours at 350°F, 180°C, Gas Mark 4. Remove foil and place the meat between two plates. Put a heavy weight on top and leave until cold.

To serve
Thaw in refrigerator. Cut in slices to serve with salad.
High Quality Storage Life   1 month

Ham and Turkey Loaf

4 oz corn flakes
½ lb cooked ham
½ lb cooked turkey or
* chicken*
1 medium onion
5 level tablespoons
* tomato ketchup*
4 eggs
1 level teaspoon mustard
¼ level teaspoon cloves
Salt and pepper
1½ oz soft brown sugar
1 tablespoon water

Put crushed corn flakes and minced ham, chicken and onion into a large basin. Add tomato ketchup, eggs, mustard, cloves, salt and pepper. Mix all well together. Put into a greased and base-lined 2-lb. loaf tin. Mix together brown sugar and water and spread over the top of the loaf. Bake in a moderately hot oven, 375°F, 190°C, Gas Mark 5, for about 45 minutes. Cool, wrap and freeze.

To serve
Reheat at 325°F, 170°C, Gas Mark 3, for 1 hour and serve with tomato or barbecue sauce. The loaf may be thawed in the refrigerator and served cold with salad.
High Quality Storage Life   1 month

Pork and Bacon Loaf

¾ lb unsmoked back
* bacon*
¾ lb fat pork (belly of
* pork)*
½ lb soft white
* breadcrumbs*
1 onion, finely chopped
1 teaspoon dry mustard
½ teaspoon mixed herbs
1 egg, beaten
6 tablespoons cider
Salt and pepper

Mince the bacon and pork. Mix with all the other dry ingredients in a bowl. Mix the egg into the cider in a jug, and use the mixture to bind the rest. Turn the mixture into a greased 1-lb. loaf tin, cover with greased paper, and bake at 350°F, 180°C, Gas Mark 4, for 1½ hours. Turn out while warm. Cool, pack and freeze.

To serve
Thaw in refrigerator and serve cold.
High Quality Storage Life   1 month

Cold Pork Roll

3 lb belly pork (skinned
    and boned)
6 oz pork sausagemeat
1 onion
Pinch of mixed herbs
Salt and pepper

Place the pork on a board, fat side down. Mix the sausagemeat with grated onion, herbs and seasoning. Spread over the pork. Roll the joint up tightly and tie well with string. Wrap in a pudding cloth of foil, and simmer in a pan of water for 2 hours. Lift out, allow to cool. When cold, remove cloth or foil and string, and wrap for freezing.

To serve
Thaw in refrigerator, slice and serve with salad.
High Quality Storage Life　1 month

Turkey Roll

12 oz cold turkey
8 oz cooked ham
1 small onion
Pinch of mace
Salt and pepper
½ teaspoon mixed fresh
    herbs
1 large egg
Breadcrumbs to cover

Mince turkey, ham and onion finely and mix with mace, salt and pepper and herbs. Bind with beaten egg. Put into greased dish or tin, cover and steam for 1 hour. This may be cooked in a loaf tin, a large cocoa tin lined with paper, or a stone marmalade jar. While warm, roll in breadcrumbs, then cool completely. Pack in heavy-duty foil or in polythene bag.

To serve
Thaw at room temperature for 1 hour, and slice to serve with salads or sandwiches.
High Quality Storage Life　1 month

Taunton Chicken Casserole

1 level tablespoon clear
    honey
1 tablespoon cider
    vinegar
1 tablespoon soy sauce
4 tablespoons dry cider
1½ oz butter
2 onions
4 chicken joints
1 large green pepper
2 level tablespoons plain
    flour
Just under ½ pint dry
    cider
Salt and pepper
15½-oz can peach halves
    (drained)

Put honey, vinegar, soy sauce and dry cider into a small basin and mix well together. Put chicken into a large dish. Pour marinade over chicken and leave for 12 hours, turning once or twice if possible. Remove chicken from marinade. Melt 1-oz butter in a frying pan. Quickly brown chicken joints on both sides. Remove and drain. Fry onion and pepper for 12 minutes. Remove and drain. Melt remaining ½-oz butter in frying pan. Stir in flour and cook for a minute. Remove from heat. Put marinade into a measuring jug and make up to ½ pint with dry cider. Add cider mixture to roux in pan, stirring in gradually. Return to heat and bring to boil stirring. Season. Put chicken, onion and pepper into a deep casserole. Pour cider sauce over chicken. Cover and cook at 375°F, 190°C, Gas Mark 5, for 1 hour. Cool and freeze.

To serve
Put casserole in oven set at 350°F, 180°C, Gas Mark 4, for 45 minutes. Add peach halves and continue heating for 20 minutes. Sprinkle with chopped parsley.
High Quality Storage Life　2 months

Royal Chicken

8 chicken pieces
4 oz bacon
2 oz butter
4 small onions
4 oz mushrooms
½ pint red wine
1 gill stock
Bay leaf, thyme and
    parsley
Salt and pepper
1 tablespoon flour

Wipe the chicken joints. Cut bacon into dice. Melt half the butter and fry the onions until golden, then the bacon and chicken. Add sliced mushrooms, stock, herbs, salt and pepper, cover and cook slowly until the chicken is tender. Take out chicken and mushrooms and keep hot. Skim fat from gravy, and stir in wine. Melt remaining butter, add flour and stir. Add the chicken gravy and simmer until creamy and smooth. Pour over chicken and cool completely. Pack in foil or rigid plastic container, making sure chicken pieces are covered in sauce.

To serve
Put into casserole and heat at 325°F, 170°C, Gas Mark 3, for 1 hour.
High Quality Storage Life   2 months

Pot-Roasted Chicken

3 lb chicken
1½ oz butter
2 sticks celery
6 small onions
2 medium carrots
1 small turnip
½ pint stock
Salt and pepper

Wipe chicken inside and out. Melt butter and brown chicken lightly on all sides. Add sliced vegetables, stock, and salt and pepper. Cover and simmer for 1½ hours, basting sometimes with stock. This dish may be cooked on top of the stove, or in an oven set at 375°F, 190°C, Gas Mark 5. Cool completely and take off fat. Pack in container, leaving headspace.

To serve
Return to casserole and heat at 350°F, 180°C, Gas Mark 4, for 45 minutes. Garnish with chopped parsley before serving.
High Quality Storage Life   2 months

Farmhouse Chicken

4 chicken portions
2 onions
Pinch of tarragon
¾ pint chicken stock
2–3 carrots
1 green pepper

Coat the chicken with flour and fry quickly to seal the meat. Transfer to a casserole. Fry the chopped onions, sliced carrots and green pepper in the fat and add these to the chicken. Pour the stock over the vegetables and chicken, season and cook in the oven, with the lid on the casserole, for 1¼ hours at 350°F, 180°C, Gas Mark 4. Pack and freeze.

To serve
Reheat at 325°F, 170°C, Gas Mark 3, for 1 hour, stirring in 5 fl. oz. single cream just before serving.
High Quality Storage Life   1 month

Creamed Chicken

4 chicken pieces
1 pint chicken stock
1 small onion
2 oz button mushrooms
1 tablespoon chopped
    parsley
1 tablespoon cornflour
Salt and pepper

Brown chicken lightly on all sides in a little butter. Add chopped onion and sliced mushrooms and cook until just soft. Pour on chicken stock (this can be made with a cube if liked) and simmer for 45 minutes. Blend cornflour with a little cold water, and stir into chicken liquid. Add parsley and season lightly. Cool completely. Put chicken pieces into container, pour over sauce, seal and freeze.

To serve
Put into covered oven dish and heat at 350°F, 180°C, Gas Mark 4, for 45 minutes. Serve with rice and peas.
High Quality Storage Life   2 months

Casseroled Turkey

4 turkey joints
1 oz cornflour
Salt and pepper
3 tablespoons oil
8 oz baby carrots
1 onion, finely chopped
¾ pint turkey or chicken
    stock
1 tablespoon tomato
    purée
3 tablespoons cranberry
    sauce
4–6 oz green peas

Skin the turkey and toss in cornflour to which salt and pepper have been added. Heat the oil in a large frying pan and sauté the turkey until it begins to brown. Remove to a casserole dish. Prepare the carrots and add to the casserole. Add the onion to the pan and fry lightly, add the remaining cornflour, mix well and stir in the stock. Bring to the boil, stirring all the time. Stir in the tomato purée and cranberry sauce. Pour over the turkey and carrots. Cook at 350°F, 180°C, Gas Mark 4, for 30 minutes. Stir in the peas and cook for a further 5 minutes. Pour into a freezer tray and allow to cool. Seal, label and freeze.

To serve
Heat at 350°F, 180°C, Gas Mark 4, for 1½ hours.
High Quality Storage Life   2 months

Chicken Pilaff

1 lb chopped cold
    chicken
2 onions
6 rashers streaky bacon
8 oz mushrooms
12 oz Patna rice
2 green peppers
2 pints chicken stock
Salt and pepper
4 oz butter

Melt butter and fry onions, bacon and peppers. Add rice and chicken stock and cook until all the liquid has been absorbed. Then add the chicken and seasoning. Cook until chicken is thoroughly reheated. Cool and freeze.

To serve
Reheat in double boiler or in the oven in an oven dish at 325°F, 170°C, Gas Mark 3, for 45 minutes.
High Quality Storage Life   2 months

Chicken and Turnip Casserole

4 chicken legs
4 young turnips
8 oz baby carrots
8 oz green peas
½ pint stock or water
Salt and pepper
1 bay leaf
2 oz butter
Seasoned flour

Toss the chicken legs in seasoned flour. Melt butter in a pan, lightly fry the chicken legs for 2–3 minutes. Add stock or water to the pan, stir in salt and pepper. Transfer to a casserole. Dice the turnips and add the vegetables and bay leaf. Bake at 375°F, 190°C, Gas Mark 5, for approximately 30 minutes. Pack and freeze.

To serve
Reheat in covered dish at 325°F, 170°C, Gas Mark 3, for 1 hour.
High Quality Storage Life 2 months

Turkey Shepherd's Pie

12 oz cooked turkey
1 onion
1 oz butter
Salt and pepper
½ pint milk
8 oz cranberry sauce
2 lb mashed potato
2 oz Cheddar cheese

Mince together the cooked turkey and onion. Melt the butter in a saucepan. Stir in the flour and cook over a low heat for 1 minute. Remove from the heat and gradually stir in the milk. Bring to the boil, stirring all the time to form a smooth sauce. Season to taste. Stir the turkey and onion mixture into the sauce and pour into a 1½-pint freezer tray. Spread the cranberry sauce over the mixture. Pipe or spread the potato over the cranberry sauce and sprinkle with the grated cheese. Cool, cover and freeze.

To serve
Remove the covering and cook at 350°F, 180°C, Gas Mark 4, for 1–1½ hours.
High Quality Storage Life 2 months

Turkey Cakes

1 lb cold turkey
Salt and pepper
8 oz cold potatoes
½ gill gravy
1 teaspoon tomato
 purée

Mince turkey, season and mix with mashed potato, gravy and tomato purée. Form into small flat cakes. Roll in crumbs or seasoned flour and fry on both sides until golden. Cool. Pack in foil or polythene bag.

To serve
Reheat in oven or frying pan.
High Quality Storage Life 1 month

TOP Creamed chicken (p. 175) with rice and a white sauce (p. 218).
ABOVE Fruit fritters, here made with apple rings (p. 186).

Coley jalousie (p. 180).

Pheasant in Wine

2 young pheasants
12 small onions
2 tablespoons oil
2 tablespoons butter
4 oz small mushrooms
1 pint Burgundy
1 oz plain flour
Salt and pepper

Clean the pheasants. Chop two of the onions with the birds' livers and put half the mixture in each bird. Heat oil and butter together and brown birds all over. Put into a casserole. Remove mushroom stalks and cook in the remaining fat with the wine, until liquid is reduced by half. Mix flour with a little butter and use this to thicken the gravy and pour over the pheasants. Cook onions in boiling salted water until tender, drain and add to casserole. Toss mushrooms in butter and add to other ingredients. Cover and cook at 325°F, 170°C, Gas Mark 3, for 1 hour. Cool. Pack in rigid plastic container or in foil tray.

To serve
Return to casserole and reheat at 325°F, 170°C, Gas Mark 3, for 1 hour. Serve with triangles of fried bread, and garnish with watercress.
High Quality Storage Life   2 months

Pheasant Bayeux

1 pheasant
2 shallots
⅜th pint (8 fl. oz) Calvados
2 oz butter
2 tablespoons water
Thyme, parsley and bayleaf
Salt and pepper
2 sweet eating apples

The pheasant can be cut up either before or after cooking but it is easier to have it done before. The bird should be well hung. Brown the pheasant and chopped shallots in the butter. Flame half the Calvados over it. Add water, herbs, salt and pepper and cook slowly, 325°F, 170°C, Gas Mark 3, for 45 minutes. Add peeled and cored apple rings and Calvados and finish cooking a further 30 minutes or until the bird is tender. Freeze in plastic container.

To serve
Reheat, adding a little thick cream.
High Quality Storage Life   2 months

Normandy Rabbit

1 young rabbit
3 oz butter
4 cloves garlic
1 tablespoon tomato purée
½ pint cider
Salt and pepper

Clean and joint the rabbit and simmer for 30 minutes, with a little salt and pepper. Remove meat from bones in large neat pieces, and fry the rabbit with the garlic cloves until golden. Stir in tomato purée, and season with salt and pepper. Simmer for 2 minutes, then pour on cider. Simmer for 5 minutes and cool. Pack in container, covering rabbit pieces with sauce.

To serve
Reheat gently in double boiler and serve garnished with chopped parsley.
High Quality Storage Life   1 month

Hare in Cider

1½ pints cider
2 oz bacon
1 oz butter
1 tablespoon olive oil
1 large jointed hare
2 oz well-seasoned flour
4 small onions
2 carrots
2 sticks celery
4 long strips orange rind
Good pinch thyme or
   marjoram

Garnish:
Small crescents fried
   bread or puff pastry
Glacé cherries heated in
   a little cider
Tiny onions cooked in
   cider or fried button
   mushrooms

Fry the diced bacon in the melted butter and oil. Have the back of the hare cut into 4–6 pieces and each leg into two. Coat with seasoned flour and fry until richly-browned. Coat and fry rib cage, head and liver. Remove hare, stir in remaining flour and brown. Add cider to make a smooth sauce. Return hare, except liver, to pan with the onions, left whole, sliced carrots and celery, orange rind and herbs. Cover and cook at 325°F, 170°C, Gas Mark 3, for 2–2½ hours. Pack into containers and freeze.

To serve
Reheat in a covered casserole at 325°F, 170°C, Gas Mark 3, for 1 hour, and garnish to taste.
High Quality Storage Life   2 months

Fish Pie (Pastry)

½ lb cooked haddock or
   cod (fresh or smoked)
3 tomatoes
4 oz button mushrooms
Juice of ½ lemon
1 tablespoon chopped
   parsley
1 oz butter
1 oz flour
½ pint milk
Salt and pepper
Pinch of ground mace
½ lb flaky or puff pastry
Beaten egg to glaze

Cut the cooked fish into even-sized pieces, and arrange in layers with the tomatoes and mushrooms in the bottom of a pie dish. Sprinkle with parsley and lemon juice. Melt the butter in a saucepan and stir in the flour. Gradually blend in the milk, and stir over a gentle heat until the sauce thickens. Season with salt and pepper and a pinch of mace. Pour over the fish. Cool and freeze.

To serve
Roll out the pastry to a little larger than the pie dish. Cut off a thin strip of pastry and press round the rim of the dish using a little water to seal. Brush with water. Lift the remaining pastry and cover pie dish. Press edges together to seal, cut away surplus with a knife and decorate as required. Brush with beaten egg and place in oven at 400°F, 200°C, Gas Mark 6, and cook for 45 minutes or until the pastry is cooked and the filling thawed.
High Quality Storage Life   1 month

Fish Pie (Potato)

1 lb cooked white fish
1 lb cooked potato
⅛th pint milk
2 oz butter
2 tablespoons chopped parsley
Salt and pepper
½ pint white sauce

Flake the fish. Mash the potato with warmed milk, butter, parsley and seasoning. Mix the fish with the sauce, and put in base of greased pie dish or foil container. Spread potato mixture on top. Pack by putting container into polythene bag, or covering with a lid of heavy duty foil. Freeze until firm.

To serve
Reheat at 400°F, 200°C, Gas Mark 6, for 1 hour.
High Quality Storage Life　1 month

Sea Pie

4 oz shortcrust pastry
8 oz cooked cod or haddock
4 oz prawns or shrimps
½ pint milk
1 oz plain flour
1 oz butter
3 oz grated cheese
Salt and pepper

Line 9-in. pie plate or foil dish with pastry and bake blind for 15 minutes. Flake fish and prepare prawns or shrimps if fresh. Melt butter, add flour and cook gently for 1 minute. Stir in milk, and bring to the boil, stirring all the time. Add fish, prawns or shrimps, cheese and seasonings. Cool slightly and pour into pastry case. Bake at 400°F, 200°C, Gas Mark 6, for 20 minutes. Cool completely. Pack in polythene bag, heavy-duty foil or carton to avoid crushing.

To serve
Thaw at room temperature for 2 hours to eat cold, or reheat at 325°F, 170°C, Gas Mark 3, for 30 minutes to eat hot.
High Quality Storage Life　1 month

Salmon Kedgeree

1 lb cooked salmon
8 oz Patna rice
3 oz butter
Salt and pepper
1 tablespoon chopped parsley
2 hard-boiled egg yolks

Flake the fish. Cook rice in fast-boiling salted water for about 20 minutes until tender, and drain well. Mix with flaked fish, melted butter, seasonings, parsley and chopped egg yolks. For a supper dish, 4 oz chopped button mushrooms cooked in a little butter may be added. Pack in foil container covered with lid of heavy-duty foil, or in polythene bag.

To serve
Thaw in refrigerator for 3 hours, then reheat in double saucepan over boiling water. The dish may be put into a cold oven straight from the freezer and heated at 400°F, 200°C, Gas Mark 6, for 45 minutes. Heating will be speeded if the dish is stirred occasionally.
High Quality Storage Life　1 month

Coley Jalousie

*1 small pkt frozen
    puff pastry*
½ oz margarine or butter
⅜ oz flour
¼ pint milk
½ oz tomato purée
½ teaspoon salt
1 small onion
*½ lb coley (cooked and
    flaked)*
Egg to glaze
*Garnish with quartered
    tomatoes and prawns*

Melt butter or margarine and stir in flour, cook the roux for a few moments. Remove the saucepan from heat and stir in milk, return to heat and bring back to the boil, stirring continuously. Season the sauce, and add the cooked flaked fish, very finely chopped onion and tomato puree. Cover this mixture and put aside to cool.

Divide the pastry in half, roll out the first half to form a rectangle. Place on a baking sheet and spread with cool fish mixture, leaving a ½-in. border around the edge of the pastry. Roll out the second half of the pastry the same size as the first. Fold this piece of pastry in half lengthways, and make a series of diagonal cuts down the folded edge to within about a ½ in. of the cut edge, to form a herringbone pattern when unfolded.

Brush lightly with water around the edge, and fit over the fish mixture, seal the edges to the bottom layer of the pastry. Knock up the edges with a knife, and glaze with beaten egg. Cook at 425°F, 220°C, Gas Mark 6, for about 30 minutes, until golden brown. Cool, wrap and freeze.

To serve
Reheat at 350°F, 180°C, Gas Mark 4, for 45 minutes and serve hot with peas or a salad.
High Quality Storage Life   1 month

Fish Cakes

1 lb cooked white fish
1 lb mashed potato
*4 teaspoons chopped
    parsley*
2 oz butter
Salt and pepper
2 small eggs

Mix flaked fish, potato, parsley, melted butter and seasonings together and bind with egg. Divide the mixture into sixteen pieces and form into flat rounds. Coat with egg and breadcrumbs and fry until golden. Cool quickly. Pack in polythene bags or foil containers, separating fish cakes with waxed paper or Cellophane. Fish cakes may also be frozen uncovered on baking sheets and packed when solid.

To serve
Reheat in oven or frying-pan with a little fat, allowing 5 minutes' cooking on each side.
High Quality Storage Life   1 month

Macaroni Cheese

8 oz macaroni
4 oz butter
4 tablespoons flour
1½ pints milk

Optional – chopped ham, chopped cooked onions or mushrooms. Cook macaroni as directed and drain well. Melt butter, blend in flour and work in milk, cooking to a smooth sauce. Over low heat, stir in cheese and seasoning. Mix macaroni and cheese and cool. Pack into foil container.

10 oz cheese
1 teaspoon salt
Pepper

To serve
Cover with foil and heat at 400°F, 200°C, Gas Mark 6, for 1 hour, removing foil for the last 15 minutes to brown top.
High Quality Storage Life   2 months

Simple Risotto

1 onion
2½ oz butter
12 oz rice
2 pints chicken stock
1 oz cheese
Salt and pepper

Chop onion finely and cook in half the butter until soft and transparent. Add the rice and cook, stirring well, until it is buttered but not brown. Add stock which has been heated very gradually, adding more until it has been absorbed. Cook over a low heat for about 30 minutes until the liquid has been taken up and the rice is soft but firm. Stir in cheese, remaining butter, salt and pepper, and cool. This mixture may be frozen on its own, or with the addition of cooked peas, mushrooms, flaked fish or shellfish, chopped ham or chicken, or chicken livers, which should be added during the last 10 minutes' cooking. Pack in waxed or rigid plastic container, or polythene bags.

To serve
Reheat gently over direct heat, and serve sprinkled with grated cheese. Risotto may be reheated in covered dish in low oven.
High Quality Storage Life   2 months

Spanish Rice

8 oz Patna rice
2 oz oil
4 oz lean bacon
12 oz onions
6 oz mushrooms
8 oz tomatoes
Salt and pepper

Slightly undercook rice in boiling salted water and drain well. Heat oil and cook chopped bacon and onions gently for 10 minutes. Add sliced mushrooms and peeled and sliced tomatoes and continue cooking until tender and well blended. Stir in rice and seasoning and cool. Pack in waxed or rigid plastic containers, or in polythene bags.

To serve
Reheat gently over direct heat, or use to fill green peppers, aubergines or marrow.
High Quality Storage Life   2 months

Gnocchi

1 onion
1 bay leaf
1 pint milk
5 tablespoons polenta or
   semolina
Salt and pepper
1½ oz grated cheese
½ oz butter
1 teaspoon French
   mustard

Topping
2 oz butter
2 oz grated cheese

Put onion and bay leaf in milk and bring slowly to the boil with the lid on the pan. Remove onion and bay leaf, stir in polenta or semolina and mix well. Season with salt and pepper and simmer 15 minutes until creamy. Remove from heat, stir in cheese, butter and mustard, and spread out on a tin about ¾-in thick. When cold and set, cut in squares. Pack in overlapping layers in foil tray, brush with melted butter and grated cheese, and cover with foil, or put in polythene bag.

To serve
Thaw at room temperature for 1 hour, then bake at 350°F, 180°C, Gas Mark 4, for 45 minutes until golden and crisp.
High Quality Storage Life 2 months

SWEET COURSES AND ICES

Fruit Cream

1 lb raspberries,
   currants,
   gooseberries or
   blackberries
¾ pint water
6 oz sugar
2 tablespoons cornflour

Clean fruit. Bring water to boil, add fruit and sugar, and boil until fruit is soft. Mix cornflour with a little cold water, blend into hot liquid, and bring back to boil. Cool. Pack in serving dish covered with foil.

To serve
Thaw in refrigerator for 1 hour and serve with cream.
High Quality Storage Life 1 month

Fruit Mousse

¼ pint fruit purée
1 oz caster sugar
¼ pint double cream
2 egg whites
Juice of ½ lemon

Mix fruit purée and sugar. Whip cream lightly, and whip egg whites stiffly. Add lemon juice to fruit, then fold in cream and egg white. A little colouring may be added if the fruit is pale. Pack in serving dish covered with foil.

To serve
Thaw in refrigerator without lid for 2 hours.
High Quality Storage Life 1 month

Fruit Whip

1 lb rhubarb or
gooseberries or
blackcurrants
Sugar
½ pint evaporated milk

Prepare fruit and stew in very little water with sugar to taste until tender. Put through a sieve and fold into whipped evaporated milk. This may be made with whipped cream, but the tinned milk is less rich for small children or old people. Pack in individual dishes and cover with foil.

To serve
Thaw at room temperature for 2 hours.
High Quality Storage Life   2 months

Blackberry and Apple Mousse

1 lb cooking apples
8 oz blackberries
¼ pint water
4 oz caster sugar
Juice of 1 lemon
½ oz gelatine
2 egg whites

Peel and slice the apples into a pan with the blackberries, water and 3 oz sugar. Cover and simmer 15 minutes. Sprinkle lemon juice with gelatine and leave to soak. Take cooked fruit from heat, add gelatine and stir until dissolved. Put through a sieve, and leave purée to cool and thicken. Whisk egg whites stiffly, fold in remainder of sugar, and fold into fruit purée. Pour into a serving dish which can be used in the freezer, and leave until cold. Pack by covering with a lid of heavy-duty foil.

To serve
Thaw in refrigerator for 3 hours, and decorate with cream.
High Quality Storage Life   2 months

Brown Bread Mousse

½ pint milk
2 egg yolks
2 oz caster sugar
Vanilla essence to taste
4 oz brown breadcrumbs
2 level teaspoons
gelatine
2 tablespoons water
2 egg whites

Heat milk and whisk into yolks and sugar. Return to pan and cook gently until custard thickens, stirring continuously, or cook in a double boiler. Add vanilla essence and cool. Stir in breadcrumbs. Dissolve gelatine in water over a pan of hot water and stir into mixture. Whisk egg whites until stiff and fold in. Pour into wetted 1 pint mould and leave to set. Wrap and freeze.

To serve
Thaw in refrigerator and unmould. This is good with fresh fruit and whipped cream.
High Quality Storage Life   2 months

Lemon Puddings

2 oz cornflakes
3 eggs
4 oz caster sugar
1 tablespoon grated
  lemon peel
3 tablespoons lemon
  juice
½ pint double cream

Crush cornflakes and sprinkle a little in each of six paper or foil jelly cases. Beat egg whites to soft peaks and gradually beat in sugar until stiff peaks form. In another bowl, beat yolks until thick and beat in lemon peel and juice until well mixed. Whip cream lightly, then fold egg yolk mixture and cream into egg whites until just mixed. Put mixture into cases and sprinkle with more cornflake crumbs. Pack by putting foil lid on each dish.

To serve
Thaw in refrigerator for 30 minutes.
High Quality Storage Life 1 month

Coffee Pudding

3 oz caster sugar
4 oz butter
4 oz fresh white fine
  breadcrumbs
5 tablespoons strong
  black coffee

Cream butter and sugar until light and fluffy. Work in breadcrumbs and coffee until completely mixed. Press into dish. Pack by covering serving dish with foil lid.

To serve
Thaw uncovered in refrigerator for 45 minutes, cover with whipped cream and decorate with nuts.
High Quality Storage Life 1 month

Raisin Shortcake

4 tablespoons orange
  juice
4 oz seedless raisins
6 oz plain flour
2 oz caster sugar
4 oz butter

Put orange juice and raisins into a pan and bring slowly to the boil; leave until cold. Sieve flour into a basin and work in the sugar and butter until the mixture looks like fine breadcrumbs. Knead well and divide dough into two pieces. Form into equal-sized rounds. Put one on a greased baking sheet, spread on raisin mixture and top with second round of dough, pressing together firmly and pinching edges together. Prick well. Bake at 350°F, 180°C, Gas Mark 4, for 45 minutes, mark into sections, and remove from tin when cold. Pack in foil.

To serve
Thaw in wrappings for 3 hours.
High Quality Storage Life 4 months

Baking-Day Cheescake

2 oz digestive biscuit
    crumbs
1 lb cottage cheese
1 teaspoon lemon juice
1 teaspoon grated
    orange rind
1 tablespoon cornflour
2 tablespoons double
    cream
2 eggs
4 oz caster sugar

Use an 8-in. cake tin with removable base to bake this cheesecake. Butter sides and line base with buttered paper. Sprinkle with crumbs. Sieve cottage cheese and mix with lemon juice, orange rind and cornflour. Whip cream and stir in. Separate eggs, and beat egg yolks until thick, then stir into cheese mixture. Beat egg whites until stiff and beat in half the sugar, then stir in remaining sugar. Fold into cheese mixture and put into baking tin. Bake at 350°F, 180°C, Gas Mark 4, for 1 hour, and leave to cool in the oven. Remove from tin. Pack in foil after freezing, and then in box to avoid crushing.

To serve
Thaw in refrigerator for 8 hours.
High Quality Storage Life   1 month

Cumberland Tart

8 oz shortcrust pastry
½ pint thick sweet
    applesauce
2 oz butter
1 oz sugar
1 egg
4 oz plain flour

Icing:
2 oz butter
2 oz icing sugar

Line baking tin with pastry and cover with applesauce. Cream butter and sugar, beat in egg, and add flour. Put on top of applesauce and bake at 400°F, 200°C, Gas Mark 6, for 30 minutes. Leave until cold. Cream butter and icing sugar until light and fluffy and spread on top of tart. Freeze before wrapping. Pack in foil or polythene bag.

To serve
Remove wrappings and thaw at room temperature for 3 hours.
High Quality Storage Life   2 months

Blackcurrant Saucer Pies

10 oz plain flour
½ teaspoon salt
5 oz mixed margarine
    and lard
1 oz caster sugar
3 tablespoons water
12 oz blackcurrants
2 oz caster sugar

Sieve together flour and salt. Rub in fat until mixture resembles fine breadcrumbs. Add 1 oz sugar and bind together with water to form a firm dough. Roll out pastry and cut into 8 circles big enough to line old saucers. Put a circle on 4 saucers. Mix blackcurrants with sugar and divide fruit between saucers. Moisten edges of pastry and put second circle on top. Gently press edges of pastry together to seal, then trim edges. Decorate with a fork or pointed knife. Bake at 375°F, 190°C, Gas Mark 5, for 30 minutes. Cool and wrap individual pies in heavy duty foil or polythene.

To serve
Thaw, sprinkle with sugar, and serve with cream or ice cream.
High Quality Storage Life   3 months

Danish Cherry Tart

8 oz shortcrust pastry
8 oz stoned cooking
  cherries
4 oz ground almonds
6 oz icing sugar
2 eggs

Line a pie plate or foil dish with pastry and prick the pastry well. Fill with cherries. Mix ground almonds, sugar and eggs one at a time to a soft paste. Pour over cherries and bake at 400°F, 200°C, Gas Mark 6, for 25 minutes. Cool. Pack in foil or polythene bags.

To serve
Thaw in wrappings at room temperature for 3 hours.
High Quality Storage Life   2 months

Basic Pancakes

4 oz plain flour
¼ teaspoon salt
1 egg and 1 egg yolk
½ pint milk
1 tablespoon oil or
  melted butter

Sift flour and salt and mix in egg and egg yolk and a little milk. Work together and gradually add remaining milk, beating to a smooth batter. Fold in oil or melted butter. Fry large or small thin pancakes. Pack in layers separated by Cellophane and put in foil or polythene bag.

To serve
Separate the pancakes, put on a baking sheet and cover with foil, and heat at 400°F, 200°C, Gas Mark 6, for 10 minutes, or thaw and use cold with ice cream filling.
High Quality Storage Life   2 months

Fruit Fritters

4 oz plain flour
Pinch of salt
1 egg and 1 egg yolk
½ pint milk
6 eating apples or 6
  bananas or 1 large
  can pineapple rings
1 tablespoon melted
  butter
1 tablespoon fresh white
  breadcrumbs

Prepare batter by mixing together flour, salt, egg and egg yolk and milk, and folding in melted butter and breadcrumbs. Peel, core and slice apples into ¼-in. rings, or cut bananas in half lengthways. Dip fruit into batter and fry until golden in deep fat. Drain on absorbent paper and cool. Pack in polythene bags, foil or waxed containers, separating fritters with Cellophane or waxed paper.

To serve
Put in a single layer on baking tray, thaw and heat at 375°F, 190°C, Gas Mark 5, for 10 minutes. Toss in sugar before serving.
High Quality Storage Life   1 month

Sugar and Spice Fritters

¼ pint cider
4 oz plain flour
Pinch of salt
1 egg

Sift flour and salt into a basin, make hollow in centre and drop in egg yolk and olive oil. Make to a smooth batter about the consistency of single cream with the cider. Fold in the stiffly whisked egg white just before using. Mix the sugar and spice, peel and core the apples and cut

1 tablespoon olive oil

4 tablespoons soft brown sugar

Good pinch ground cloves or cinnamon

Small cooking apples

into slices ⅓ in. thick. Dip first into the sugar, coating evenly and then into the batter. Fry until crisp and brown on first side, turn. Drain on kitchen paper. Cool, pack and freeze. Mixing the batter with cider instead of milk gives a very crisp, slightly sweet batter.

To serve
Put in a single layer on baking tray, thaw and heat at 375°F, 190°C, Gas Mark 5, for 10 minutes. Toss in sugar before serving.
High Quality Storage Life 1 month

Loukomades with Chocolate Sauce

Dough

7 oz plain flour

½ oz fresh yeast

1 level teaspoon thin honey

¼ pint milk

1 oz melted margarine

2 oz caster sugar

1 level teaspoon ground cinnamon

Chocolate sauce

4 oz plain chocolate

2 tablespoons honey

2 tablespoons lemon juice

1 level tablespoon cornflour

¼ pint water

2 oz unsalted butter

For the dough, sieve flour with ½ teaspoon of salt into a large mixing bowl. Cream together yeast and honey, add milk and margarine and pour into the flour, beating to form a smooth dough. Knead well on a floured board. Divide into 20 pieces and shape each into a ball. Place on a greased baking tray and leave in a warm place until double in size. Fry in hot deep fat until golden brown; drain well. Cool, pack in polythene bags, label, seal, freeze. Place all the ingredients for the chocolate sauce in a pan and dissolve over a gentle heat, stirring continuously, then boil for a few seconds until it thickens; allow to cool. Place in a rigid container, seal, label and freeze until required.

To serve
Allow loukomades to thaw, toss in sugar and cinnamon, place in serving dish.
Allow the sauce to thaw, reheat in a saucepan and use to pour over loukomades before serving.
High Quality Storage Life 1 month

Apple Strudel

8 oz puff pastry

1 oz melted butter

2 large cooking apples

1 oz currants

1 oz sultanas

2 oz sugar

1 level teaspoon mixed spice

3 sweet biscuits

Roll out the pastry as thinly as possible – approximately 14 in. × 15 in. Brush with melted butter. Slice apples thinly, and crush biscuits. Mix the other ingredients and sprinkle over the pastry. Roll up the pastry and filling and seal the edges. Wrap in polythene and freeze.

To serve
Place on a baking sheet and bake at 425°F, 220°C, Gas Mark 7, for 45 minutes. Dust lightly with icing sugar, and return to the oven for 2–3 minutes to glaze. Serve warm or cold with cream.
High Quality Storage Life 3 months

Baked Apple Dumplings

8 apples
Sugar
8 oz shortcrust pastry
Butter

Core apples, leaving ¼-in. core at bottom of each to hold filling. Fill with sugar and put a knob of butter in each. Put each apple on a square of pastry and seal joins. Bake at 425°F, 220°C, Gas Mark 7, for 25 minutes. Cool. Pack in containers or foil dishes and cover with foil lids.

To serve
Put in oven while still frozen and heat at 375°F, 190°C, Gas Mark 5, for 20 minutes, serving with cream, custard or hot apricot jam.
High Quality Storage Life 1 month

Fruit Crumble

1 lb apples, plums or
   rhubarb
6 oz plain flour
3 oz brown sugar
4 oz butter or margarine

Clean and prepare fruit by peeling and/or slicing and arrange in greased pie dish or foil container, sweetening to taste (about 3 oz sugar to 1 lb. fruit). Prepare topping by rubbing fat into flour and sugar until mixture is like breadcrumbs. Sprinkle topping on fruit and press down. Pack the fruit crumble uncooked by covering with heavy duty foil, or by putting container into polythene bag.

To serve
Put container into cold oven and cook at 400°F, 200°C, Gas Mark 6, for 30 minutes, then at 375°F, 190°C, Gas Mark 5, for 45 minutes.
High Quality Storage Life 6 months (apples may discolour; a little lemon juice will help to prevent this).

Swedish Applecake

3 oz fresh brown
   breadcrumbs
1 oz butter
2 tablespoons brown
   sugar
1 lb apples

Gently fry breadcrumbs in butter until golden brown. Cook apples in very little water until soft, and sweeten to taste. Stir brown sugar into buttered crumbs and arrange alternate layers of buttered crumbs and apples in buttered dish, beginning and ending with a layer of crumbs. Press firmly into dish and cool. Pack by covering with foil lid.

To serve
Thaw without lid in refrigerator for 1 hour, turn out and serve with cream.
High Quality Storage Life 1 month

Apple Lucerne

½ pint cider
2 lb cooking apples
2 oz sultanas
2 oz soft brown sugar
1 level teaspoonful
  ground cinnamon
1 Swiss roll
1 oz butter
1 dessertspoon olive oil

Heat the cider in a pan, adding the apples as they are peeled and cored. Add the sultanas and cook until the apples are soft. Beat in the sugar and spice. Transfer to a foil container. Cut the Swiss roll into 12 slices and arrange over the apple. Melt butter and oil together and brush over Swiss roll. Bake for 15 minutes at 400°F, 200°C, Gas Mark 6, until the roll is crisp and lightly browned. Cool, cover and freeze.

To serve
Heat at 325°F, 170°C, Gas Mark 3, for 45 minutes and serve with jam sauce.
High Quality Storage Life   2 months

Orange Castles

4 oz butter
4 oz sugar
2 eggs
4 oz self-raising flour
Grated rind of 1 orange

Cream butter and sugar until light and fluffy. Beat in eggs one at a time with a little flour. Stir in orange rind and a little milk to moisten together with rest of flour. Put into 8 individual buttered castle pudding moulds, cover tops with foil and steam for 45 minutes. Cool, and remove from moulds. Pack in foil, or leave in moulds and cover with foil.

To serve
Reheat in foil in oven or steamer for 20 minutes and serve with custard or a little jam.
High Quality Storage Life   2 months

Belgian Cheese Tart

8 oz puff pastry
8 oz full fat soft or curd
  cheese
2 eggs
¼ pint double cream
Grated rind and juice of
  ½ lemon
1½ oz caster sugar

Roll out pastry thinly on a floured surface and line an 8-in. flan ring, taking care not to stretch pastry. Prick base well. Chill for 30 minutes. Line with foil and baking beans and bake 'blind' at 425°F, 220°C, Gas Mark 7, for 15 minutes. Remove foil and beans and bake for further 5 minutes. Mix eggs into cheese gradually, beating until smooth. Stir in cream, lemon rind and juice and sugar. Do not beat. Turn into flan case and return to oven at 350°F, 180°C, Gas Mark 4, for 25 minutes, until filling is set. Cover and freeze.

To serve
Thaw in refrigerator.
High Quality Storage Life   2 months

189

Marmalade Pudding

2 oz soft white
    breadcrumbs
8 oz marmalade
2 oz butter
$\frac{1}{4}$ pint milk
1 egg

Put breadcrumbs and marmalade in a basin and pour over butter heated with milk. Mix well and add beaten egg. Turn into a greased foil pudding basin and steam for $2\frac{1}{2}$ hours. Cool completely. Pack by covering basin with heavy-duty foil lid, or by putting basin in a polythene bag.

To serve
Steam for 1 hour and serve with cream or custard.
High Quality Storage Life   2 months

Picnic Cheesecakes

8 oz plain flour
1 teaspoon salt
2 oz lard
2 oz margarine
3 tablespoons cold water
15-oz can drained
    apricot halves
1 egg
$1\frac{1}{2}$ oz caster sugar
8 oz full fat soft or curd
    cheese
2 tablespoons soured
    cream
1 tablespoon plain flour
Rind and juice of 1
    lemon

Sift together flour and salt. Rub in fat until mixture resembles fine breadcrumbs. Add water and mix to a stiff dough. Knead lightly and rest pastry in a cool place for 10 minutes. Roll out and line six $4\frac{1}{2}$-in. foil baking cases. Line with foil and beans and bake 'blind' at 375°F, 190°C, Gas Mark 5, for 10 minutes. Remove beans and foil, and leave cases to cool. Keep 6 apricot halves for decoration. Chop remaining apricots and divide between cases. Whisk egg yolk and sugar until light and fluffy, and add cheese and soured cream. Blend flour with lemon rind and juice and add to cheese mixture. Mix well together until smooth. Whisk egg white until just stiff, fold into mixture and spoon into pastry cases. Bake at 375°F, 190°C, Gas Mark 5, for 35 minutes. Wrap cooled cheesecakes in foil and freeze. Do not decorate unless for immediate use.

To serve
Thaw and decorate if liked.
High Quality Storage Life   2 months

Pear and Chocolate Ice-Box Flan Cake

2 × 7-in. sponge flan
    cases
1 tablespoon white rum
1 × 8-oz carton bought
    chocolate spread
$\frac{1}{8}$th pint double cream
    ($\frac{1}{2}$ 6-oz carton)
4 oz softened unsalted
    butter
1 × 15-oz can pear
    halves in syrup,
    drained
1 oz chopped mixed nuts

Place one of the flan cases on a foil plate. Sprinkle the centre (not the rim) with the rum. Turn $\frac{1}{2}$ the chocolate spread into a basin. Whip the cream stiffly, and add it with $\frac{1}{2}$ the butter to the chocolate. Mix all three together until smooth and well blended. Fill it into the centre of the flan case. Sprinkle with nuts. Cut the drained pear halves in half horizontally, and place them in a flat layer on the chocolate mixture.
Mix the remaining 4 oz chocolate spread and 2 oz butter until blended, and mix in the remaining nuts. Fill the second flan case with this mixture, using some in a thin layer on the rim. Invert the case on to the first case, enclosing the pears. Wrap the cake in foil and freeze.

To serve
Thaw the cake for 3 hours in the refrigerator. Sprinkle with icing sugar

just before serving.
High Quality Storage Life 2 months

Coffee Ice-Box Torte

4 oz butter
4 oz caster sugar
2 large eggs
1 tablespoon coffee
essence
3 tablespoons brandy
2 × 7-in. Victoria
sandwich cakes,
home-made or bought

Cream the butter until soft, and whisk in the sugar gradually. Whisk until well-blended, light and fluffy. Add the eggs, one at a time whisking well after each addition. Stir in lightly the coffee essence and brandy. Slice each cake into 3 horizontal layers, making 6 in all. Place the bottom layer of 1 cake in a 7-in. cake tin with a fixed bottom, lined with foil. Smooth over it one-fifth of the coffee mixture. Continue building up the layers in the same way, ending with a top cake layer. Put the base of a loose-bottomed cake or sandwich tin on top, and weight it lightly so that cake and coffee cream layers are pressed together. Freeze.

3 oz butter
6 oz sifted icing sugar
1 level dessertspoon
instant coffee powder
Finely-chopped walnut
pieces
6-oz carton double
cream

To serve
Thaw for 3 hours in the refrigerator. Turn the cake out on to a serving plate, and decorate with the following mixture:
Beat the butter until creamy, and add the icing sugar gradually. Beat until smooth, trickling in the coffee powder as you beat. Spread this mixture round the sides of the cake, and press the chopped walnuts into it. Whip the cream until stiff, and use it to decorate the top of the cake.
High Quality Storage Life 2 months

Choco-Cherry Ice-Box Layer Cake

2 tablespoons
finely-grated plain or
bitter chocolate
Glacé cherries
4 oz margarine
6 oz icing sugar
2 medium eggs
2 tablespoons cocoa
1 teaspoon coffee
essence
Fingers of dry or stale
plain cake (chocolate,
spice, Madeira,
sponge, etc. not fruit
cake)

Line an oblong foil freezer pan with a second layer of foil. Scatter the grated chocolate over the bottom of the pan. Cut the cherries in half, and press them, cut side up, into the chocolate in a regular pattern. Make sure they touch the bottom of the pan, so that their tops will show when you unmould the cake.
Cream the margarine until very soft, then sift the icing sugar gradually and cream them together. Sift and mix in the cocoa, then stir in the coffee essence. Blend them thoroughly.
Cover the grated chocolate with dots of the creamed mixture, and, with the back of a spoon, spread them carefully over the chocolate to make a smooth cream layer. On this, place a layer of cake fingers, closely packed, side by side. Repeat these layers (now, or later when you have other cake to spare) until the pan is full; the top layer should be a cake layer. Cover the cake tightly with foil, and freeze.

To serve
Invert the cake on to a plate, and peel off the foil. Let the cake thaw for 2–3 hours in the refrigerator.
High Quality Storage Life 2 months

Orange Ice-Box Layer Cake

Make this like the Choco-Cherry Ice-Box Cake above, with these substitutes: use 2 tablespoons finely-chopped hazelnuts and 1 teaspoon grated orange peel for the grated chocolate and nuts; use 1–2 tablespoons concentrated frozen orange juice (to suit your taste) instead of the cocoa and coffee essence; add 1 teaspoon orange-flavoured liqueur if you wish.

Ice Cream Making

Home-made ice cream for the freezer is best made with pure cream and gelatine or egg yolk. For immediate use, evaporated milk may be used, but the flavour is not so good (before using, the unopened tin of milk should be boiled for 10 minutes, cooled and left in a refrigerator overnight).

Ice cream should be frozen quickly, or it will be 'grainy' and will keep this rough texture during long storage. The correct emulsifying agent will help to give smoothness. Egg, gelatine, cream or sugar syrup will stop large ice crystals forming; gelatine gives a particularly smooth ice. Whipped egg whites give lightness.

Freezing diminishes sweetness, but too much sugar will prevent freezing. The correct proportion is one part sugar to four parts liquid. Whatever emulsifying agent is used, preparation is similar. The mixture should be packed into trays and frozen until just solid about $\frac{1}{2}$ in. from the edge. The mixture should be beaten quickly in a chilled bowl, then frozen for a further hour. This 'freezing and beating' technique should be repeated for up to three hours. Some freezer owners save time by packing the ice cream into storage containers and freezing after the first beating, but results are not so smooth, and it is preferable to complete the ice cream before packing for storage.

Custard Ice

$\frac{3}{4}$ *pint creamy milk*
1 vanilla pod
2 large egg yolks
2 oz sugar
Small pinch of salt
$\frac{1}{3}$ *pint thick cream*

Scald milk with vanilla pod. Remove pod and pour milk on to egg yolks lightly beaten with sugar and salt. Cook mixture in a double boiler until it coats the back of a spoon. Cool and strain and stir in the cream. Pour into freezing trays and beat twice during a total freezing time of about 3 hours. Pack into containers, cover and seal, and store in freezer.

Gelatine Ice

$\frac{3}{4}$ *pint creamy milk*
1 vanilla pod
1 dessertspoon gelatine

Heat $\frac{1}{4}$-pint milk with vanilla pod to boiling point. Soak gelatine in 2 tablespoons cold water, then put into a bowl standing in hot water until the gelatine is syrupy. Pour warm milk on to the gelatine, stir in sugar,

Loukomades with chocolate sauce (back left) with pancakes, a Swedish applecake in a foil dish, a sweet pie (filled with mince-meat), an unmoulded steam pudding with peach sauce and a useful loaf cake.

Animal fun biscuits (p. 244).

3 oz sugar
Pinch of salt

salt and remaining milk. Remove vanilla pod and freeze mixture, beating twice during 3 hours total freezing time. Pack into containers, cover and seal, and store in freezer. This mixture is particularly good for using with such flavourings such as chocolate or caramel.

Cream Ice

1 pint single cream
1 vanilla pod
3 oz sugar
Pinch of salt

Scald cream with vanilla pod, stir in sugar and salt, and cool. Remove vanilla pod and freeze mixture to a mush. Beat well in a chilled bowl and continue freezing (about 2 hours total freezing time). Pack into containers, cover, seal and label, and store in freezer.

Flavouring for Ice Creams, Basic

Flavourings should be strong and pure (e.g. vanilla pod or sugar instead of essence; liqueurs rather than flavoured essences), as they are affected by low temperature storage. Flavourings may be varied by using one of the basic recipes and adjusting to the required flavour.

Butterscotch   Cook the sugar in the recipe with 2 tablespoons butter until well browned, then add to hot milk or cream.

Caramel   Melt half the sugar in the recipe with a moderate heat, using a heavy saucepan, and add slowly to the hot milk.

Chocolate   Melt 2 oz unsweetened cooking chocolate in 4 tablespoons hot water, stir until smooth, and add to the hot milk.

Coffee   Scald 2 tablespoons ground coffee with milk or cream and strain before adding to other ingredients.

Peppermint   Use oil of peppermint, and colour lightly green.

Praline   Make as caramel flavouring, adding 4 oz blanched, toasted and finely chopped almonds.

Egg Nog   Stir in several tablespoons rum, brandy or whisky to ice cream made with egg yolks.

Ginger   Add 2 tablespoons chopped preserved ginger and 3 tablespoons ginger syrup to basic mixture.

Maple   Use maple syrup in place of sugar, add 4 oz chopped walnuts.

Pistachio   Add 1 teaspoon almond essence and 2 oz chopped pistachio nuts, and colour lightly green.

Flavourings for Ice Creams, Mixed

Mixed flavour ice creams can be prepared by adding flavoured sauces or crushed fruit to vanilla ice cream, or by making additions to some of the basic flavours. Crushed fruit such as strawberries, raspberries or canned mandarin oranges may be beaten into vanilla ice cream before packing.

Continued overleaf

Chocolate or butterscotch sauce can be swirled through vanilla ice. Chopped toasted nuts or crushed nut toffee pair with vanilla, coffee or chocolate flavours. A pinch of coffee powder may be used in chocolate ice cream, or a little melted chocolate in coffee ice; one of the chocolate- or coffee-flavoured liqueurs may also be used.

Brown Bread Ice Cream

½ pint double cream
¼ pint single cream
3 oz sieved icing sugar
4 oz brown breadcrumbs
    from a day-old loaf
1 tablespoon rum
2 eggs, separated

Whisk double cream until just stiff and gradually whisk in single cream. Fold in icing sugar and breadcrumbs. Mix together rum and egg yolks and fold in. Whisk egg whites until almost stiff and fold into mixture. Pour into freezing trays or 2 pint polythene container and freeze until firm. This ice cream does not need beating during freezing.

To serve
Scoop into small glasses and serve with sweet biscuits and fresh fruit.

Coffee Ice

4 heaped tablespoons
    freshly-ground coffee
1 pint water
3 oz caster sugar
½ pint single cream

Put coffee into a hot dry coffee pot, pour on boiling water, and leave to stand for 10 minutes. Strain and mix with sugar. Cool and mix with cream. Freeze for 45 minutes, stir and continue freezing for 1½ hours. Pack in waxed or rigid plastic containers.

To serve
Pile into small cups and serve with sweet biscuits.
High Quality Storage Life   2 months

Gooseberry Sorbet

2 lb green gooseberries
6 oz caster sugar
1½ pints water
Juice of 1 lemon
Green vegetable
    colouring
2 tablespoons
    Maraschino
2 tablespoons white rum

Cook gooseberries with sugar and water, add lemon juice and a little green colouring and put through a sieve. Cool and freeze to a thick batter. Add Maraschino and rum, and continue freezing. This ice will not become solid. Pack in waxed or rigid plastic containers.

To serve
Scoop into glasses.
High Quality Storage Life   2 months

Lemon Cream Ice

2 lemons
3 oz granulated sugar

Thinly peel the lemons and add to the water and sugar. Simmer together gently for 5 minutes. Leave to cool. Remove the peel, and add the juice

¼ pint water
¼ pint double cream

from the lemons. When cold, add slowly to the whipped cream. Pour into the ice tray, cover with foil and freeze for 2–3 hours. Take it out and stir after half an hour and one hour. Pack to store.

To serve
Scoop into glasses.
High Quality Storage Life   1 month

Lemon Water Ice

8 oz caster sugar
1 pint water
Rind and juice of 3
   lemons
1 egg white

Dissolve the sugar in the water over a low heat, add thinly peeled lemon rind and boil gently for 10 minutes. Leave to cool. Add the lemon juice, strain into the ice cube tray. Place in the ice-making compartment of the refrigerator, set at coldest. Leave to half freeze. Turn the half frozen mixture into a bowl. Fold in the stiffly whisked egg white. Replace in the tray and refreeze. Pack in rigid container for storage.

To serve
Scoop into glasses.
High Quality Storage Life   1 month

Orange Cream Ice

½ pint double cream
½ pint orange juice
Caster sugar

Whip cream to hold its shape. Stir in ¼ pint orange juice and add the rest a little at a time. Sugar to taste. Freeze for 1 hour and stir well. Pack for storage.

To serve
Scoop into glasses.
High Quality Storage Life   1 month

Tea Ice

2 oz tea
1 pint water
3 eggs
½ teaspoon vanilla
   essence
3 oz caster sugar
½ pint double cream

Warm a teapot, put in the tea and pour on boiling water. Leave to infuse for 5 minutes, strain and leave until completely cold. Beat the whole eggs with the sugar and vanilla essence for about 5 minutes, until white and thick. Add the cold tea by degrees, whipping all the time. Fold in thickly whipped cream and freeze for 2 hours, stirring once during freezing. Pack in waxed or rigid plastic container.

To serve
Scoop out and serve with small sweet biscuits.
High Quality Storage Life   2 months

Orange Sorbet

2 teaspoons gelatine
½ pint water
6 oz sugar
1 teaspoon grated lemon
    rind
1 teaspoon grated
    orange rind
½ pint orange juice
4 tablespoons lemon
    juice
2 egg whites

Soak gelatine in a little of the water and boil the rest of the water and sugar for 10 minutes to a syrup. Stir gelatine into syrup and cool. Add rinds and juices. Beat egg whites stiff but not dry, and fold into mixture. Freeze to a mush, beat once, then continue freezing allowing 3 hours total freezing time. This ice will not go completely hard. Pack into containers, cover, seal, label and store in freezer. For party occasions, this ice may be packed into fresh fruit containers. Scoop out oranges or lemons, wash them and fill with sorbet. Pack into containers, seal, label and store in freezer. If the ice has not been prepacked into fruit cases, the containers may be prepared before serving. To do this, scoop out oranges and lemons, wash and put into freezer wet so that they get a frosted surface. Thirty minutes before serving, scoop out the ice from its large container into the cases and leave in the freezer until serving time. The same recipe may be used for a lemon sorbet, using only lemon juice and rind instead of a mixture of orange and lemon.

Viennese Red Currant Ice

1 lb redcurrants
4 oz redcurrant jelly
1 pint water
1 large ripe tomato
4 oz raspberries
Juice and rind of
    ½ lemon
3 oz caster sugar
Red vegetable colouring
4 egg yolks
2 tablespoons white rum
    or brandy
½ pint double cream

Remove currants from stalks and simmer with redcurrant jelly, hot water, tomato, raspberries, juice and rind of lemon, sugar and colouring until the fruit is a pulp. Cool and add well-beaten egg yolks and rum or brandy. Rub through a sieve, and freeze to a batter. Add whipped cream and continue freezing for 2 hours. Pick into waxed or rigid plastic containers.

To serve
Scoop into glasses.
High Quality Storage Life   2 months

Rum Raisin Ice Cream

4 oz raisins
4 tablespoons rum
4 eggs
4 oz icing sugar
½ pint double cream

Soak raisins in rum for 30 minutes. Whisk yolks and sugar until fluffy. Whip cream until thick and fold into egg mixture. Add the raisins. Whisk egg whites until stiff and fold into mixture. Freeze for 1 hour, then stir mixture. Pack in container for freezing and label.

To serve
Scoop into glasses.
High Quality Storage Life   1 month

196

Coupe Rouge

*1 family sweet vanilla
  ice cream
4 oz small strawberries
4 oz raspberries
4 oz redcurrants
4 maraschino cherries
4 teaspoons maraschino
  juice*

Place a scoop of ice cream in each of four glasses. Sprinkle with a few strawberries, top with another layer of ice cream and then divide the raspberries between the glasses. Finish with a further scoop of ice cream and decorate with strings of redcurrants. Top each with a maraschino cherry and a little of the juice. Serve with wafer biscuits.

Chocolate Cream Lolly

*3 heaped teaspoons
  drinking chocolate
1 teaspoon boiling water
3 tablespoons single
  cream
Approx. ¼ pint milk*

Put the chocolate into a measure, add the boiling water and mix well. Stir in a little milk, then the cream and add the rest of the milk to make ⅓ pint. Pour into the moulds. Place in freezing compartment to set. Unmould and wrap in foil for storage.

High Quality Storage Life   1 month

Chocolate Nut Lolly

*3 heaped teaspoons
  drinking chocolate
1 tablespoon boiling
  water
1 tablespoon black
  treacle
Approx. ⅓ pint milk
Chopped almonds or
  walnuts*

Put the chocolate into a measure, add the boiling water and mix well. Pour in a little of the milk, stir, then add the treacle. Stir again and continue stirring as the rest of the milk is added to make up to ⅓ pint. Sprinkle some chopped nuts into each mould, pour in the mixture, sprinkle more nuts on the top. Place in freezing compartment to set. Unmould and wrap in foil for storage.

High Quality Storage Life   1 month

Chocolate Raspberry Lolly

*3 heaped teaspoons
  drinking chocolate
1 teaspoon boiling water
1 teaspoon raspberry
  milk shake syrup
Approx. ⅓ pint milk*

Put the drinking chocolate into a measure, add the boiling water and mix well. Add a little milk, mix further, then stir in the raspberry syrup. Top up to ⅓ pint with the milk. Pour into the moulds. Place in freezing compartment to set. Unmould and wrap in foil for storage.

High Quality Storage Life   1 month

Blackcurrant Yogurt Sorbet

8 oz blackcurrant purée
2 oz icing sugar
10 oz natural yogurt
Juice of ½ lemon
½ oz gelatine
4 tablespoons water
2 egg whites

Combine blackcurrant purée, sugar, yogurt and lemon juice in a bowl. Dissolve gelatine in water over a pan of hot water. Stir this into purée mixture. When mixture begins to set, fold in egg whites, whisked until just stiff. Pour into ice tray and freeze. Pack for storage.

To serve
Scoop into glasses.
High Quality Storage Life   1 month

Ice Cream Bombes

Ice cream bombes or moulds are both decorative and delicious and are a good way of using small quantities of rather special flavours. They may be made with either bought or home-made ice cream, or with a combination of both. Any metal mould or bowl can be used; metal jelly moulds are excellent for the purpose. Special double-sided moulds can also be bought, can be covered with foil for storage.

The ice cream should be slightly softened before using in a mould, and pressed firmly into the container with a metal spoon; each layer should be pressed down and frozen before a second layer is added or the flavours and colours may run into each other. Moulds may also be lined with one flavour ice cream, and the centre filled with another flavour, or with mixtures of fruit, liqueurs and ice cream.

Bombes are unmoulded by turning on to a chilled place and covering the mould with a cloth wrung out in hot water, shaking slightly to release the ice cream. It is a good idea to unmould the bombe about an hour before serving, then wrap the ice cream in foil and return to the freezer to keep firm.

Flavourings for Bombes

Melon Bombe   Line mould with pistachio ice cream and freeze 30 minutes. Fill with raspberry ice cream mixed with chocolate chips and wrap for storage. This looks like a watermelon when cut in slices.

Raspberry Bombe   Line mould with raspberry ice cream, freeze for 30 minutes and fill with vanilla ice cream.

Coffee Bombe   Line mould with coffee ice cream, freeze 30 minutes. Fill with vanilla or chocolate ice cream flavoured with chopped maraschino cherries and syrup. Decorate with coffee bean sweets.

Three-Flavour Bombe   Line mould with vanilla ice cream, freeze 30 minutes. Put in thin lining of praline ice cream and freeze 30 minutes. Fill centre with chocolate ice cream.

Tutti Frutti Bombe   Line mould with strawberry ice cream, freeze 30 minutes. Fill with lemon sorbet mixed with drained canned fruit cocktail.

Raspberry-Filled Bombe   Line mould with vanilla or praline ice cream and freeze 30 minutes. Fill with crushed fresh raspberries beaten into whipped cream and lightly sweetened.

Peach-Filled Bombe   Line mould with vanilla ice cream and freeze 30 minutes. Fill with whipped cream mixed with chopped drained canned peaches, lightly sweetened and flavoured with light rum.

Recipes using frozen cream and ice cream

Chocolate Cream Truffles

4 oz plain chocolate
6 dessertspoons commercial frozen dairy cream
2 teaspoons pure vanilla essence
1 lb sifted icing sugar
Cocoa

Melt the chocolate in a basin over hot water. Stir in the cream and essence, and gradually add the icing sugar. Leave in a cool place until firm. Roll into 24 equal-sized balls. Toss in cocoa. Freeze.

To serve
Thaw for 2–3 hours at room temperature.
High Quality Storage Life   1 month

Iced New-style Mince Pies

1 × ½-lb packet frozen vol-au-vent cases
1 dessertspoon mincemeat per case
1 large spoonful family sweet vanilla ice cream for each case
1 beaten egg (optional)

Cook the vol-au-vent cases as instructed on the packet. Brush with beaten egg to glaze if desired. Let the cases become quite cold. Then fill each with mincemeat, top with ice cream and place a pastry lid on top.

Collettes

4 oz cooking chocolate
1 oz butter
¼ pint commercial frozen dairy cream
2 tablespoons rum or brandy
Flaked almonds
5 oz plain chocolate

Melt the cooking chocolate in a basin over hot water. Using a pastry brush, coat the insides of paper cases with 3 layers, letting each set before adding the next. Remove paper cases, when fully set.
Prepare the filling: melt the butter and plain chocolate in basin over hot water. Stir in the defrosted cream and flavouring. Leave in a cool place until thick. Using a forcing bag and rose tube pipe the filling into the cases. Decorate each with a flaked almond. Chill and freeze.

To serve
Thaw at room temperature for 2–3 hours.
High Quality Storage Life   1 month

Full Cream Fudge

1 lb granulated sugar
½ pint commercial frozen dairy cream
2 oz butter
3 tablespoons water
¼ pint milk
1–2 teaspoons pure vanilla essence

Place all the ingredients in a thick-based saucepan. Stir over gentle heat until all are dissolved and blended. Boil steadily until mixture reaches 238°F, 114°C (soft ball). Remove from heat and beat until thick and cloudy. Pour into a well-greased tin and allow to set. Cool and cut into squares. Chill, pack and freeze.

To serve
Thaw at room temperature for 2–3 hours.
High Quality Storage Life 1 month

TEATIME FOOD

FREEZER
FILLINGS FOR
SANDWICHES

Creamed fillings are delicious for frozen sandwiches. You can cream meat, cheese and fish with butter, margarine or cream cheese, or try one of these more exciting recipes. Go easy on seasonings such as pepper and curry powder which become stronger during storage. Slices of cucumber, watercress or lettuce can be slipped into the sandwiches when thawed.

Kipper Cream Paste

7½-oz packet frozen kipper fillets
2 tablespoons lemon juice
2 oz soft margarine
Salt
Freshly-ground black pepper
3 tablespoons single cream or top milk

Poach kipper fillets in a little water until cooked (about 6–8 minutes). Drain and cool. Skin and flake fish and pound together with lemon juice and margarine. Season and stir in cream or milk. Spreads 8 large slices of bread (especially nice with brown bread).

Devilled Ham Spread

4 oz ham, minced or finely chopped
2 oz soft margarine
1 teaspoon Worcester sauce
¼ level teaspoon made mustard
Salt and pepper

Cream ham with margarine and stir in all other ingredients. Spreads 8 large slices of bread.

Liptauer Cheese Spread

4 oz cream cheese
2 oz soft margarine
¼ level teaspoon made
 mustard
3 chopped anchovy
 fillets
3 chopped gherkins
Salt and pepper
¼ level teaspoon paprika

Beat together cream cheese and margarine until smooth and add mustard, anchovies and gherkins. Season well and stir in paprika. Spreads 8 large slices of bread.

Rosy Cheese Spread

6 oz cream cheese
1½ tablespoons tomato
 chutney or ketchup

Blend cream cheese with chutney or ketchup, using more or less according to taste. If necessary, thin with a little sweet or soured cream.

Kipper Pâté

1 lb frozen boned
 kippers
4 oz butter
1 onion, finely chopped
Freshly-ground black
 pepper
Juice of 1 lemon
3 tablespoons double
 cream
Chopped parsley
1 hard-boiled egg

Poach kippers until tender. Allow to cool, then remove skin and tail. Melt 1 oz of the butter in a pan, and sauté the onion until translucent. Pound together or process in a blender the kippers, onion and cooking butter, remaining butter, lemon juice, cream and parsley. Pour into individual ramekins. Set in refrigerator or freeze when chilled.

To serve
Thaw at room temperature for 1 hour. Decorate with parsley and chopped hard-boiled egg.

White Bread

2½ lb white bread flour
1 oz fresh yeast
2 oz fat (butter, lard or
 margarine)
½ oz salt
1½ pints warm water

Warm a large bowl and put in flour. Make a well in centre and sprinkle salt round edge. Cream yeast with a little warm water and pour into the well. Add remaining water and warmed fat and mix well to a consistency like putty. Leave to prove until double its size. Divide into loaf tins and leave to prove again until bread reaches top of tins. Bake at 450°F, 230°C, Gas Mark 8, for 45 minutes, turning bread once in the oven. Cool on a rack and leave overnight. Pack in polythene bags or in heavy duty foil.

To serve
Thaw in wrappings at room temperature for 3 hours.
High Quality Storage Life   8–12 months

Currant Bread

1½ lb white bread flour
4 oz sugar
Pinch of salt
1 oz fresh yeast
4 oz warm butter
½ pint warm milk
8 oz mixed dried fruit
2 oz chopped mixed peel

Using a large warm bowl, mix flour, sugar and salt, and add yeast creamed with a little sugar. Work in butter and milk, knead well and leave to prove for 1½ hours. Work in fruit and peel, and put into loaf tins or shape into buns. Prove for 45 minutes. Bake at 375°F, 190°C, Gas Mark 5, for 45 minutes, turning loaves after 20 minutes; small buns should be baked for 20 minutes. Cool on a wire tray, brushing with a mixture of milk and sugar to give a sticky finish. Store overnight in a tin. Pack in polythene bags or in heavy duty foil.

To serve
Thaw in wrappings at room temperature for 3 hours (loaves), 1½ hours (buns).
High Quality Storage Life   2 months

Bridge Rolls

2½ lb white bread flour
1 oz fresh yeast
4 oz butter or
    margarine
½ oz salt
2 eggs
1 pint warm milk

Make the bread dough as for White Bread, whisking the eggs into the milk before adding to the flour. Shape rolls into small sausage shapes and prove for 30 minutes. Paint with milk, and bake at 450°F, 230°C, Gas Mark 8, for 15 minutes. Cool on rack. Pack in polythene bags.

To serve
Thaw in wrappings at room temperature for 45 minutes.
High Quality Storage Life   10–12 months

Croissants

1 oz butter
¼ pint warm milk
1 heaped teaspoon salt
1½ tablespoons sugar
1 oz fresh yeast
    dissolved in a little
    warm water
12 oz white bread flour
4 oz butter
1 egg yolk beaten with a
    little milk

Put butter in bowl, pour on warm milk and add salt and sugar. Cool to lukewarm, then add yeast and gradually add flour to give a soft dough. Cover dough with damp cloth and leave for 2 hours. Knead dough, chill thoroughly, and roll into a rectangle. Spread butter lightly and evenly over dough. Fold over dough to a rectangle and roll again. Chill, roll and fold twice more at intervals of 30 minutes. Roll dough out to ¼ in. thickness and cut into 4 in. squares. Divide each square into 2 triangles, and roll each triangle up, starting at longest edge and rolling towards the point. Bend into crescent shapes, put on floured baking sheet, brush with beaten egg and milk, and bake at 425°F, 220°C, Gas Mark 7, for 15 minutes. Cool. Pack into polythene bags. Store carefully.

To serve
Thaw in wrappings at room temperature for 30 minutes, then lightly heat in the oven or under the grill.
High Quality Storage Life   2 months

Baps

1 lb white bread flour
2 oz lard
1 level teaspoon sugar
2 level teaspoons salt
1 oz yeast
*½ pint lukewarm milk
and water*

Sieve the flour and rub in the lard and sugar. Dissolve the salt in half the liquid, and cream the yeast into the rest of the liquid. Mix into the flour, knead and prove until double in size. Divide into pieces and make into small flat rounds about 4 ins. across. Brush with milk, put on a greased baking sheet, prove again, and bake at 450°F, 230°C, Gas Mark 8, for 20 minutes. Cool on a rack. Pack in polythene bags. Baps may be split, buttered and filled before freezing.

To serve
Thaw in wrappings at room temperature for 1 hour.
High Quality Storage Life   Unfilled: 10–12 months. Filled: 1 month.

Brioche

8 oz white bread flour
1 oz yeast
*2 tablespoons warm
water*
3 eggs
6 oz melted butter
1 teaspoon salt
1 tablespoon sugar

Put 2 oz flour in a warm bowl and mix with yeast creamed with a little warm water. Put the little ball of dough into a bowl of warm water and it will expand and form a sponge. Put remaining flour into a bowl and beat in eggs thoroughly. Add butter, salt and sugar and continue beating. Add yeast sponge removed from water, and mix well. Cover with damp cloth and prove for 2 hours, then knead dough and leave in cool place over-night. Half-fill castle pudding tins with dough and prove 30 minutes. Bake at 450°F, 230°C, Gas Mark 8, for 15 minutes. Cool. Pack in polythene bags.

To serve
Thaw in wrappings at room temperature for 45 minutes. Brioche may also be heated with the tops cut off and the centres filled with sweet or savoury mixtures (e.g. creamed mushrooms, chicken or shrimps).
High Quality Storage Life   2 months

Tea Cakes

8 oz white bread flour
Pinch of salt
½ oz butter
½ oz fresh yeast
1 teaspoon sugar
1 egg
¼ pint milk
2 oz sultanas

Warm flour and salt and rub in butter. Cream yeast and sugar and mix into the flour together with the egg, milk and sultanas. Knead well and leave in a warm place until double in size. Knead again and divide into three, shaping into round flat cakes. Put on greased tins and prove for 10 minutes. Bake at 450°F, 230°C, Gas Mark 8, for 12 minutes. Brush over with milk and sugar immediately after removing from the oven. Cool. Pack in polythene bags.

To serve
Thaw in wrappings at room temperature for 45 minutes.
High Quality Storage Life   2 months

Doughnuts

8 oz white bread flour
1 teaspoon salt
2 teaspoons sugar
½ oz yeast
¼ pint lukewarm milk
½ oz margarine
Raspberry jam

Sieve flour and salt, and mix in sugar. Whisk yeast in half the milk; add melted margarine to remaining milk and cool to lukewarm. Mix both liquids into flour and knead well, then leave to prove for 1 hour. Knead lightly, divide into 16 pieces and form into balls. Flatten balls, put jam in centre, and fold edges to enclose jam, pressing together firmly. Prove for 20 minutes. Fry until golden in hot fat and drain very thoroughly on kitchen paper. Pack in polythene bags.

To serve
Heat straight from freezer at 400°F, 200°C, Gas Mark 6, for 8 minutes, then roll in caster sugar and serve at once.
High Quality Storage Life   1 month

Danish Pastries

8 oz white bread flour
½ level teaspoon salt
2½ oz sugar
½ oz yeast
¼ pint warm water
3 oz butter

Put flour and salt in a warm basin. Cream yeast with a little of the sugar and put into the flour together with the remaining sugar and water. Mix to a soft, slightly sticky dough, and leave to rise in a warm place until increased by one-third in volume. Form butter into a rectangle and dust with flour. Flatten dough with hands and fold with the fat in the centre like a parcel. Roll and fold twice like puff pastry. Leave in a cold place for 20 minutes, then roll and fold twice more and leave for 20 minutes. Roll out to ¼ in. thick. Fold squares of pastry over fillings of dried fruit, jam, marzipan or chopped nuts, to make envelope shapes. Brush pastries with a mixture of melted butter, milk and egg, and bake without proving at 375°F, 190°C, Gas Mark 5, for 30 minutes. Cool. The pastries may be frozen un-iced or with a light water icing. Pack in foil trays with foil lid, or put trays into polythene bags.

To serve
Thaw at room temperature, removing wrappings if iced, for 1 hour.
High Quality Storage Life   2 months

Basic Scones

1 lb plain white flour
1 teaspoon bicarbonate
of soda
2 teaspoons cream of
tartar
3 oz butter
¼ pint milk

Sift together flour, soda and cream of tartar and rub in butter until mixture is like breadcrumbs. Mix with milk to soft dough. Roll out, cut in rounds, and place close together on greased baking sheet. Bake at 450°F, 230°C, Gas Mark 8, for 12 minutes. Cool.
Fruit Scones   Add 1½ oz sugar and 2 oz dried fruit.
Cheese Scones   Add pinch each of salt and pepper and 3 oz grated cheese. Pack in sixes or dozens in polythene bags.

Thaw in wrappings at room temperature for 1 hour, or heat at 350°F, 180°C, Gas Mark 4, for 10 minutes with a covering of foil.
High Quality Storage Life　2 months

Drop Scones

8 oz plain white flour
¼ level teaspoon salt
½ level teaspoon
　bicarbonate of soda
1 level teaspoon cream
　of tartar
1 level tablespoon sugar
1 egg
¼ pint milk

Sieve together flour, salt, soda and cream of tartar. Stir in sugar and mix to a batter with egg and milk. Cook in spoonfuls on lightly greased griddle or frying pan. When bubbles appear on the surface, turn quickly and cook other side. Cool in a cloth to keep soft. Pack in foil, with a sheet of Cellophane or greaseproof paper between layers.

To serve
Thaw at room temperature for 1 hour, and butter.
High Quality Storage Life　2 months

Celery and Herb Yogurt Scones

8 oz wholemeal flour
1 teaspoon baking
　powder
½ teaspoon bicarbonate
　of soda
½ teaspoon salt
2 oz butter
1 level teaspoon basil
3 sticks celery
5 oz carton natural
　yogurt

Sift together flour, baking powder, bicarbonate of soda and salt. Rub in butter until mixture is like fine breadcrumbs. Add basil and finely chopped celery and mix well. Using a knife, bind mixture with yogurt to form a soft dough. Pat out to a rectangle about ¾ in. thick on a floured board. Cut out into 1½-in. diameter scones. Place on greased and floured baking tray and bake at 400°F, 200°C, Gas Mark 6, for 12–15 minutes. Cool. Pack in polythene bag.

To serve
Heat at 325°F, 170°C, Gas Mark 3, for 20 minutes and serve hot with butter.
High Quality Storage Life　2 months

Wholemeal Fruit Scones

4 oz wholemeal flour
2 teaspoons baking
　powder
4 oz plain white flour
½ teaspoon salt
1½ oz butter or
　margarine
½ oz sugar
1 oz dried fruit
¼ pint milk

Sieve flours, baking powder and salt, and rub in fat. Mix with sugar and fruit and mix to a soft dough with milk. Roll out ½ in. thick and cut out with 2-in. cutter. Brush over with egg or milk and bake at 450°F, 230°C, Gas Mark 8, for 10 minutes. Cool on a rack. Pack in a polythene bag.

To serve
Thaw at room temperature for 30 minutes, or reheat in a moderate oven for 15 minutes, then split and butter.
High Quality Storage Life　2 months

Cottage Cheese and Walnut Teabread

*8 oz sieved cottage
    cheese
6 oz soft brown sugar
3 eggs
2 oz chopped walnuts
Grated zest of 2 oranges
8 oz self-raising flour
1 level teaspoon baking
    powder*

Cream cottage cheese and sugar together and beat in eggs, one by one. Stir in walnuts and orange zest. Sift together flour and baking powder and fold into mixture. Line a 2-lb. loaf tin with greaseproof paper and brush with oil. Spoon in mixture and bake at 350°F, 180°C, Gas Mark 4, for 45–50 minutes until risen and browned. Leave 5 minutes in the tin, then remove, peel off greaseproof and cool. Wrap in polythene or foil and freeze.

To serve
Thaw at room temperature for 3 hours, slice and butter.
High Quality Storage Life   2 months

Choux Pastry

*¼ pint water
2 oz lard
2¼ oz plain flour
Pinch of salt
2 small eggs*

Bring water and lard to boil in pan and immediately put in flour and salt. Draw pan from heat and beat until smooth with wooden spoon. Cook for 3 minutes, beating very thoroughly, cool slightly and beat in whisked eggs until the mixture is soft and firm but holds its shape. Pipe in finger lengths on baking sheets and bake at 425°F, 220°C, Gas Mark 7, for ½ hour. Cool. Pack in polythene bags.

To serve
Thaw in wrappings at room temperature for 2 hours, fill with whipped cream, and top with chocolate or coffee icing.
High Quality Storage Life   1 month

Rich Fruit Loaf

*3 oz butter
3 oz soft brown sugar
3 oz currants
1 oz chopped mixed peel
8 oz plain wholemeal
    flour
1 egg
¼ pint ale
½ teaspoon bicarbonate
    of soda*

Cream the butter and sugar, and gradually work in fruit, peel and flour. Beat the egg with the ale, and stir in the bicarbonate of soda. Add to the butter and flour mixture, mix thoroughly and pour into 1-lb. loaf tin which has been well greased. Bake at 350°F, 180°C, Gas Mark 4, for 1 hour. Cool. Pack in heavy-duty foil or polythene.

To serve
Thaw without wrappings at room temperature for 3 hours, and cut in slices to serve spread with butter.
High Quality Storage Life   4 months

Honey Loaf

4 oz butter

Cream butter and sugar until light and fluffy, and mix in honey

4 oz caster sugar
6 tablespoons honey
1 egg
10½ oz plain flour
3 teaspoons baking
   powder
1 teaspoon salt
¼ pint milk

thoroughly. Beat in egg. Sieve flour, baking powder and salt, and stir into creamed mixture alternately with milk. Put into greased 2-lb. loaf tin and bake at 350°F, 180°C, Gas Mark 4, for 1¼ hours. Cool, then pack in polythene bag or foil.

To serve
Thaw in wrappings for 3 hours, slice and spread with butter.
High Quality Storage Life　4 months

Tea Loaf

1 lb mixed dried fruit
8 oz sugar
½ pint warm tea
1 egg
2 tablespoons
   marmalade
1 lb self-raising flour

Soak fruit with sugar and tea overnight. Stir egg and marmalade into fruit and mix well with flour. Pour into two 1-lb. loaf tins and bake at 325°F, 170°C, Gas Mark 3, for 1¾ hours. Cool in tins for 15 minutes before turning out. Cool and pack in polythene bags or foil.

To serve
Thaw in wrappings for 3 hours, slice and butter.
High Quality Storage Life　4 months

Yogurt Cake

4 oz butter
Rind of 1 lemon
6 oz caster sugar
Chopped peel
6 oz self-raising flour
3 eggs
6 oz natural yogurt

Cream butter and sugar, add lemon rind and beat well. Add egg yolks one at a time and beat in. Add sifted flour alternately with the yogurt and stir in the peel. Whisk egg whites until stiff and fold into the batter. Spoon into a greased loaf tin and bake at 350°F, 180°C, Gas Mark 4, for 1 hour. Turn out onto a wire tray and cool. Wrap and freeze.

To serve
Thaw at room temperature for 3 hours, and top with thin lemon icing.
High Quality Storage Life　2 months

Very Light Spongecake

3 eggs
5 oz caster sugar
3 oz plain flour

Separate yolks and whites of eggs and whisk whites until very stiff. Put the mixing bowl over a saucepan of hot, but not boiling, water and gradually beat in yolks and sugar. Beat for 5 minutes, then fold in sifted flour very carefully. Bake in an 8-in. greased tin with greaseproof paper on the bottom at 400°F, 200°C, Gas Mark 6, for 45 minutes. Cool thoroughly. Pack in polythene bag or heavy duty foil.

To serve
Thaw in wrappings at room temperature for 3 hours.
High Quality Storage Life　10 months

Simple Honey Cake

4 oz butter
2 oz Barbados sugar
3 tablespoons honey
2 lightly-beaten eggs
8 oz wholemeal flour
3 teaspoons baking
  powder
1 teaspoon ground
  cinnamon
Milk
1 oz halved blanched
  almonds

Cream butter and sugar and work in honey. Add eggs, flour sifted with baking powder and cinnamon, and a little milk to make a smooth dropping consistency. Grease 7-in. square tin, and scatter almonds in the bottom. Pour in cake mixture and bake at 350°F, 180°C, Gas Mark 4, for 1 hour. Cool. Pack in heavy-duty foil or polythene.

To serve
Thaw without wrappings at room temperature for 3 hours.
High Quality Storage Life   4 months

Victoria Sandwich

4 oz margarine
4 oz caster sugar
2 eggs
4 oz self-raising flour

Cream margarine and sugar until light and fluffy and almost white. Break in eggs one at a time and beat well. Fold in sifted flour. Bake in two 7-in. greased tins at 325°F, 170°C, Gas Mark 3, for 30 minutes. Leave in tins for 2 minutes, then cool on wire rack. Pack in polythene bag or heavy duty foil with a piece of Cellophane or greaseproof paper between the two layers.

To serve
Thaw in wrappings at room temperature for 3 hours, fill and ice as required.
High Quality Storage Life   4 months

Sponge Drops

2 eggs
3 oz caster sugar
3 oz plain flour
¼ teaspoon baking
  powder
Pinch of salt

Separate yolks and whites. Add salt to whites and whisk until very stiff. Gradually whisk in sugar and yolks alternately until the mixture is thick and creamy. Fold in flour sifted with baking powder. Put in spoonfuls on greased and floured baking sheets. Dust with sugar and bake at 450°F, 230°C, Gas Mark 8, for 5 minutes. Cool thoroughly. Pack in polythene bags.

To serve
Thaw in wrappings at room temperature for 1 hour, then sandwich together with jam, or with jam and whipped cream, and dust with icing sugar.
High Quality Storage Life   10 months

Scones (p. 204) with desserts and pastries finished with commercially-frozen cream.

Walnut brownies (p. 213), chocolate fudge cake (p. 214), and feather squares (p. 214).

Dundee Cake

8 oz butter
8 oz caster sugar
5 eggs
8 oz self-raising flour
½ teaspoon grated
  nutmeg
12 oz mixed currants
  and sultanas
3 oz ground almonds
3 oz chopped glacé
  cherries
2 oz chopped candied
  peel
2 oz split blanched
  almonds

Cream butter and sugar until fluffy and add eggs one at a time with a sprinkling of flour to stop curdling. Beat well after adding each egg. Stir in flour, ground almonds and the fruit lightly coated with a little of the flour. Put into greased and lined 10-in. tin, smooth top and arrange almonds on top. Bake at 325°F, 170°C, Gas Mark 3, for 2½ hours. Cool thoroughly. Pack in polythene bag or heavy duty foil.

To serve
Thaw in wrapping at room temperature for 3 hours.
High Quality Storage Life 4 months

Luncheon Cake

4 oz butter
8 oz caster sugar
3 eggs
6 oz plain flour
½ teaspoon baking
  powder
¼ teaspoon salt
½ teaspoon grated
  nutmeg
2 tablespoons milk
2 tablespoons honey
¼ teaspoon bicarbonate
  of soda
8 oz walnuts
1 lb seedless raisins

Cream butter and sugar until light and fluffy. Beat eggs together and add to creamed mixture with sifted flour, baking powder, salt and nutmeg. Stir in milk. Mix honey and bicarbonate of soda together and add to mixture, and stir in walnuts and raisins. Put mixture into greased and floured 2-lb. loaf tin. Bake at 325°F, 170°C, Gas Mark 3, for 2¼ hours. Cool in tin before turning out. Pack in polythene bag or foil.

To serve
Thaw in wrappings at room temperature for 3 hours.
High Quality Storage Life 4 months

Apple Cake

4 oz self-raising
  wholemeal flour
Pinch of salt
3 oz Barbados sugar
2 oz butter
1 egg
1 lb crisp eating apples

Sieve flour and salt. Cream sugar and butter together until light and fluffy and beat in egg. Peel and core apples and cut in fine slices. Add flour and apples to butter mixture and put into greased 7-in. cake tin. Bake at 375°F, 190°C, Gas Mark 5, for 45 minutes until golden brown. Cool on rack. Pack in heavy-duty foil or polythene.

To serve
Thaw at room temperature for 3 hours and sprinkle with brown sugar.
High Quality Storage Life 2 months

Light Christmas Cake

8 oz butter
8 oz caster sugar
4 large eggs
10 oz plain flour
1 teaspoon baking
  powder
2 oz chopped orange
  peel
3 oz sultanas
3 oz currants
2 oz glacé cherries
3 oz glacé pineapple
Grated rind of ½ lemon
Milk

Cream butter and sugar until light and fluffy. Beat in eggs one at a time, adding a little flour each time. Gradually work in flour sifted with baking powder, and fruit (chop the cherries and pineapple), and grated lemon rind. Add a little milk if necessary to make a soft consistency. Grease and line 10-in. round tin and put in mixture. Bake at 350°F, 180°C, Gas Mark 4, for 1½ hours. Cool. Pack in heavy-duty foil or polythene.

To serve
Thaw at room temperature for 3 hours.
High Quality Storage Life   4 months

Blackberry Cake

4 oz butter
4 oz sugar
1 egg
8 oz plain flour
2 teaspoons baking
  powder
¼ teaspoon salt
¼ pint milk

Topping
8 oz ripe blackberries
2 oz butter
4 oz sugar
2 oz flour
½ teaspoon cinnamon

Cream butter and sugar and beat in the egg. Gradually add flour sifted with baking powder and salt, and beat to a smooth batter with the milk. Pour into buttered rectangular tin (about 7 × 11 in.). Sprinkle thickly with well-washed and drained blackberries. Make a topping by creaming the butter and sugar and working in the flour and cinnamon to a crumbled consistency. Sprinkle on blackberries and bake at 350°F, 180°C, Gas Mark 4, for 1 hour. Cool in tin. Pack tin in polythene bag. A baking tin may be made from heavy-duty foil if it is not possible to spare one for the freezer.

To serve
Remove wrappings and thaw at room temperature for 2 hours. Cut in squares.
High Quality Storage Life   4 months

Orange Juice Cake

5 eggs
7 oz caster sugar
8 oz plain flour
Pinch of salt
2 teaspoons baking
  powder
1 teaspoon lemon juice
Scant ¼ pint orange
  juice

Separate eggs, and beat the yolks until foamy. Add half the sugar and continue to beat until the sugar has dissolved. Sift flour, salt and baking powder and add alternately with the fruit juices. Whip egg whites until stiff, fold in remaining sugar, and fold into cake mixture. Put into 8-in. cake tin, and bake at 350°F, 180°C, Gas Mark 4, for 1 hour. Cool completely. Pack in polythene bag or in heavy-duty foil.

To serve
Thaw at room temperature for 3 hours, and dust with icing sugar.
High Quality Storage Life   2 months

Almond Pull-apart Cake

Pastry dough
10 tablespoons
 lukewarm water
2 level teaspoons caster
 sugar
1 oz fresh yeast
1 lb plain flour
Pinch salt
8 oz butter (unsalted)
2 oz caster sugar
2 eggs, beaten
¼ teaspoon vanilla
 essence

Filling
6 oz ground almonds
3 oz caster sugar
3 oz sieved icing sugar
1 large beaten egg

Icing
4 oz sieved icing sugar
Water to mix

Put lukewarm water into a small basin. Add 2 teaspoons sugar. Sprinkle yeast over the liquid. Leave to stand for 10 minutes. Sieve flour and salt into a large basin. Rub in 2 oz butter. Stir in the sugar. Make a well in the centre and add yeast mixture, eggs and vanilla essence. With the hand, mix ingredients together until a soft dough is formed. Knead dough on a lightly floured board for about 10 minutes, or until smooth and elastic. Wrap loosely in foil. Refrigerate for ½ hour. Beat butter until soft enough to spread. Roll out chilled dough to a rectangle approximately 14 × 10 in. Mark lightly into three. Spread half the softened butter over centre third of dough. Fold left-hand third of pastry over butter. Seal edges with a rolling pin. Spread remaining butter on top, and fold right-hand third of pastry over that. Seal the edges. Wrap loosely in foil and chill for ½ hour. Roll out to a rectangle 16 × 8 in. Fold both narrow ends in to meet at the centre, then fold in half, making 4 layers. Wrap in foil and chill for 20 minutes. Repeat the procedure twice more, the second time folding the dough in half only.

To make the filling
Put the ground almonds, caster sugar and icing sugar into a basin. Add the beaten egg and mix to a paste. Roll out pastry dough to a rectangle 16 × 12 in. Cut in half, making two rectangles 16 × 6 in. Spread almond filling over the rectangles. Cut each rectangle into 8 strips. Roll up each strip. Stand rolls in rows of four in a freezer tray. Bake in a moderate oven at 350°F, 180°C, Gas Mark 4, for about 1 hour. When cooked, cool quickly, place lid on tray, label and freeze.

To serve
Allow to thaw for 5–6 hours and ice. Put icing sugar into a basin and add enough water to mix to a thick consistency. Trickle icing over the cake.
High Quality Storage Life   2 months

Cherry Almond Cake

7 oz self-raising flour
Pinch of salt
4 oz butter or margarine
4 oz caster sugar
3 eggs
1 oz ground almonds
6 oz glacé cherries

Wash and dry cherries. Mix flour and salt. Cut up cherries in 4 pieces, and toss in a little of the flour. Cream butter or margarine until soft, and add sugar, beating until light and fluffy. Beat in eggs one at a time, with a little of the flour. Stir in almonds, cherries and remaining flour. Put into greased and lined 6-in. tin. Bake at 350°F, 180°C, Gas Mark 4, for 1 hour 20 minutes. Cool completely. Pack in polythene bag or in heavy-duty foil.

To serve
Thaw at room temperature for 3 hours.
High Quality Storage Life   2 months

Gingerbread

8 oz golden syrup
2 oz butter
2 oz sugar
1 egg
8 oz plain flour
1 teaspoon ginger
1 oz candied peel
1 teaspoon bicarbonate
  of soda
Milk

Melt syrup over low heat with butter and sugar, and gradually add to sifted flour and ginger together with beaten egg. Mix bicarbonate of soda with a little milk and beat into the mixture, and add chopped peel. Pour into rectangular tin and bake at 325°F, 170°C, Gas Mark 3, for 1 hour. Cool in tin. Pack baking tin into polythene bag or heavy-duty foil, or cut gingerbread in squares and pack in polythene bags or boxes.

To serve
Thaw in wrappings at room temperature for 2 hours.
High Quality Storage Life   2 months

Coffee Kisses

6 oz self-raising flour
Pinch of salt
3 oz butter or margarine
2 oz caster sugar
1 egg yolk
1 teaspoon liquid coffee
  essence

Icing
2 oz butter
3 oz icing sugar
1 teaspoon liquid coffee
  essence

Sift flour and salt, rub in butter or margarine, and stir in sugar. Mix to a stiff paste with the egg yolk and coffee essence. Shape into 24 small balls and put on a greased baking tray. Bake at 375°F, 190°C, Gas Mark 5, for 15 minutes. Cool on a rack. Mix icing by gradually beating together butter, icing sugar and coffee essence until soft and fluffy. Sandwich 'kisses' together in pairs. Pack in box or polythene bag.

To serve
Thaw at room temperature for 1 hour, and dust with icing sugar.
High Quality Storage Life   2 months

Filled Chocolate Cookies

8 oz butter
4 oz caster sugar
8 oz self-raising flour
2 oz cocoa
1 teaspoon vanilla
  essence

Filling
2 oz cocoa
Strong coffee
2 oz butter
Sugar and vanilla to
  taste

Cream butter, sugar and essence, and work in cocoa and flour gradually. Divide into walnut-sized pieces, roll into balls, and put out at regular intervals on a buttered tin. Flatten with a fork dipped in water, and bake at 350°F, 180°C, Gas Mark 4, for 12 minutes. Lift carefully off tin and cool. Cook the cocoa in a little strong coffee to make a thick cream, remove from the heat and beat in the butter. Add sugar and vanilla to taste and leave until cold. Sandwich together pairs of cookies with this filling. Pack in boxes to avoid crushing.

To serve
Thaw in wrappings at room temperature for 1 hour.
High Quality Storage Life   3 months

Lemon Crispies

6 oz caster sugar
6 oz butter
2 eggs
6 oz self-raising flour
½ teaspoon vanilla
  essence

Icing
4 oz caster sugar
2 tablespoons lemon
  juice

Soften the butter but do not let it melt. Add the sugar, eggs and vanilla essence and beat together lightly. Stir in the flour until well mixed and drop in teaspoonfuls, spaced well apart, on a lightly greased baking sheet. Bake at 375°F, 190°C, Gas Mark 5, for 25 minutes. Just before the biscuits come out of the oven, mix the sugar and lemon juice to a thin paste. Spread this over the biscuits while they are still warm. Cool and pack carefully in a single layer in a box for freezing.

To serve
Thaw at room temperature for 3 hours.
High Quality Storage Life   2 months

Fig Squares

4½ oz rolled oats
5 oz plain flour
1 level teaspoon
  bicarbonate of soda
8 oz soft brown sugar
6 oz melted butter
¼ teaspoon almond
  essence

Filling
8 oz dried figs
3 oz caster sugar
½ gill boiling water
2 teaspoons lemon juice
½ oz butter

Make the filling first so that it can cool. Cut up the figs, removing any hard stems. Cook them slowly with the other ingredients until soft and thick. Cool.
Make the biscuits by mixing together the rolled oats, flour, bicarbonate of soda and sugar. Add the butter and the almond essence and mix very thoroughly together. Divide into two portions. Press half firmly into a lightly greased shallow tin about 13 × 9 in. Spread the fig filling carefully over this layer. Press on the remaining oat mixture, patting down lightly with a fork. Bake at 375°F, 190°C, Gas Mark 5, for 45 minutes, and mark into squares while still warm. Pack into bags and freeze.

To serve
Thaw at room temperature for 3 hours.
High Quality Storage Life   2 months

Walnut Brownies

6 oz margarine
2 level tablespoons
  cocoa
6 oz caster sugar
2 eggs
2 oz plain flour
2 oz chopped walnuts

Melt 2 oz margarine, stir in the cocoa and set aside. Cream the remaining butter with the sugar until lighter in colour and texture, and gradually beat in the eggs. Fold in the sieved flour; add the walnuts and cocoa mixture. Turn into a greased and base-lined 7-in. tin and bake in a moderate oven, 350°F, 180°C, Gas Mark 4, for approximately 45 minutes. Leave to cool in the tin. Turn out and wrap in foil or polythene to freeze.

To serve
Thaw at room temperature and sprinkle with caster sugar, or cover with melted plain chocolate. Cut in squares.
High Quality Storage Life   2 months

Chocolate Fudge Cake

4 oz butter

2 tablespoons golden syrup

8 oz crushed sweet biscuits

1 oz stoned raisins

2 oz quartered glacé cherries

5 oz plain chocolate

Chocolate peppermint creams and ice cream or fudge icing

Fudge Icing

2 oz chocolate

1 oz butter

6 oz icing sugar

Grease and base-line a 1-lb. loaf or round tin. Melt butter and syrup in a saucepan. Stir in biscuits, fruit and melted or chopped plain chocolate. Press firmly into prepared tin and leave in a cool place to set. Later turn out on to a board. Either top with chocolate peppermint creams, grill for 1 minute, then top with ice cream, or ice. For the fudge icing, melt chocolate and butter with 3 dessertspoonfuls of water, over a gentle heat. Remove from heat. Stir in sifted icing sugar and beat until cool and thick. Spread icing over cake. Freeze on an open tray, and wrap in foil or polythene for storage.

To serve

Thaw at room temperature for 2 hours. If preferred, the cake can be frozen without icing, which can be added after thawing.

High Quality Storage Life   2 months

Feather Squares

3 large eggs

3 oz caster sugar

3 oz plain flour

1 level tablespoon cocoa

Filling

4 oz plain chocolate

½ pint double cream

½ teaspoon vanilla essence

Icing

2 oz plain chocolate

A knob of butter

1 heaped tablespoon sifted icing sugar

1 oz plain chocolate, melted

Whisk eggs and sugar, in a bowl placed over a pan of hot water, until thick and creamy. Fold in sifted flour and cocoa and pour mixture into a greased and base-lined 12 × 8 in. tin. Bake in a hot oven, 400°F, 200°C, Gas Mark 6, for 15 minutes, or until cooked. Cool on a wire rack. Slice in half for the filling. Place the 4 oz chocolate in a pan with the cream and heat gently until melted, stirring continuously. Pour into a bowl and refrigerate for at least an hour. Add vanilla essence and beat to a mousse-like texture. Spread thickly over one piece of cake and lift the other on top. Freeze on an open tray, and wrap in foil or polythene for storage.

To serve

Thaw at room temperature for 2 hours, and ice. For the icing, melt chocolate and butter together in a basin over hot water and leave until melted. Beat in the icing sugar and 1 tablespoonful warm water, until smooth. Spread over the top of the cake. Cut into squares or slices. Place the chocolate in a greaseproof paper piping bag, cut off the tip and pipe zig-zag lines over the top of each slice.

High Quality Storage Life   2 months

SAUCES AND STUFFINGS

Chicken Stock

1 chicken carcass
1 quart water
1 carrot
1 onion
1 stick celery
Sprig parsley
Pinch of salt

Break up carcass and put in pan with sliced vegetables, water and salt. Simmer for 2 hours, strain and cool. Remove fat from surface. Put into cartons, seal, label and freeze.

To serve
Thaw in saucepan over low heat.
High Quality Storage Life 2 months

Meat Stock

*1 lb shin beef (including
  bone)*
1 quart water
1 carrot
1 small onion
Parsley and bayleaf
6 peppercorns
½ teaspoon salt

Put meat and bones into water, cover and simmer for 2 hours. Cut vegetables in small pieces, fry lightly and add to liquid together with seasoning. Simmer for 2 hours, strain and cool. Remove fat and put into cartons, seal, label and freeze.

To serve
Thaw in saucepan over low heat.
High Quality Storage Life 2 months

Apple Sauce

Apples
Sugar
Lemon juice

Slice the apples but do not peel them. Put them into a casserole with water barely to cover. Put on a lid and cook at 325°F, 170°C, Gas Mark 3, for 45 minutes until the apples are soft. Sieve the apples and sweeten to taste, adding a good squeeze of lemon juice. Cool and pack into small containers.

To serve
Thaw for 3 hours at room temperature.
High Quality Storage Life 1 year

Bread Sauce

1 small onion
4 cloves
½ pint milk
*2 oz fresh white
  breadcrumbs*
½ oz butter
Salt and pepper

Peel onion and stick with cloves. Put all ingredients into saucepan and simmer for 1 hour. Remove onion, beat sauce well, and season further to taste. Cool. Pack in small waxed containers.

To serve
Thaw in top of double boiler, adding a little cream.
High Quality Storage Life 1 month

Brown Sauce

1 oz bacon
1 oz butter
½ small onion
1 small carrot
2 mushrooms
½ pint meat stock
Parsley, thyme and
*   bayleaf*
2 tablespoons tomato
*   purée*
Salt and pepper
1½ tablespoons
*   cornflour*

Chop the bacon and fry it in the butter for 2 minutes. Chop the onion and slice the carrot and mushrooms. Add to the butter and fry until lightly brown. Take off the heat, and gradually add the stock, herbs, tomato purée, salt and pepper. Simmer very gently for 1 hour, stirring occasionally. Strain, and reheat, adding the cornflour which has been mixed to a paste with a little water. Cook for 2 minutes to thicken. Cool and pack into a rigid container.

To serve
Reheat in a double saucepan, or in a bowl over hot water. Serve as it is, or with the addition of wine, sherry or onions to taste.
High Quality Storage Life   2 months

Cranberry Sauce

1 lb cranberries
12 oz sugar
¾ pint water

Rinse the cranberries. Dissolve the sugar in water over a gentle heat. Add the cranberries and cook gently for 15 minutes until the cranberries burst. Cool and pack into small containers.

To serve
Thaw at room temperature for 3 hours.
High Quality Storage Life   1 year

Curry Sauce

2 medium onions
1 tablespoon curry
*   powder*
1 tablespoon cornflour
1 pint stock
1 tablespoon vinegar
1 tablespoon chutney
1 tablespoon sultanas

Slice onions and fry in a little butter until soft. Add curry powder and cook for 1 minute. Gradually add stock and cornflour blended with a little water. Add remaining ingredients and simmer 15 minutes. Cool. This sauce may also be frozen with the addition of some small chicken, lamb or beef pieces, but should then only be stored for 2 months. Pack in containers, or in brick form or ice.cube trays, wrapping frozen bricks or cubes in foil for storage.

To serve
Reheat in a double boiler, stirring gently.
High Quality Storage Life   6 months

Gooseberry Sauce

1 lb gooseberries
1 oz butter

Wash gooseberries, but do not top and tail them. Put in a pan with 2 tablespoons water and the butter. Cover and cook 15 minutes on low

tablespoons caster sugar

heat until soft. Put through a sieve and then reheat purée with sugar until dissolved. Chill and pack in small containers.

To serve
Reheat gently and use with fish, or with steamed puddings.
High Quality Storage Life   3 months

Goulash Sauce

2 oz butter
2 large onions
2 tablespoons paprika
2 tablespoons plain flour
1 tablespoon tomato purée
1 pint meat stock
Parsley, thyme and bayleaf
1 clove garlic
1 green or red pepper
2 large tomatoes

Melt the butter and fry the sliced onions for 2 minutes. Add the paprika and cook slowly for 1 minute. Stir in the flour, tomato purée, stock and herbs. Crush the garlic. Cut the pepper into shreds and peel the tomatoes. Add to the other ingredients and bring to the boil. Simmer for 10 minutes. Cool and pack into a rigid container.

To serve
Reheat in a double saucepan, or in a bowl over hot water. Add 4 tablespoons sour cream just before using.
High Quality Storage Life   2 months

Green Pepper Sauce

2 tablespoons dripping
1 large green pepper
1 large onion
½ teaspoon garlic salt
1 tablespoon cornflour
½ pint meat stock
16-oz can tomatoes

Melt the dripping and add the sliced pepper and onion and the garlic salt. Cook until tender. Blend the cornflour with the stock and add to the sauce. Boil for 1 minute. Stir in the tomatoes with their juice. Simmer for 5 minutes, cool and pack into a rigid container.

To serve
Reheat in a double saucepan, or in a bowl over hot water.
High Quality Storage Life   2 months

Spaghetti Sauce

1 large chopped onion
1 clove garlic
2 tablespoons olive oil
1 lb minced beef
1 lb chopped tomatoes
6 oz tomato purée
½ pint water
1 teaspoon salt
½ teaspoon pepper
1 bay leaf

Fry onion and crushed garlic in oil, add beef and cook until browned. Add all the other ingredients and simmer slowly for 1 hour until thick and well blended. Cool. Pack in containers, in brick form, or in ice cube trays, wrapping frozen bricks or cubes in foil for storage.

To serve
Thaw gently over direct heat.
High Quality Storage Life   2 months

Tomato Sauce

1 lb tomatoes
1 oz butter
1 small onion
1 small carrot
1 oz ham
1 pint stock
Parsley, thyme, bay leaf
1 oz cornflour

Cut tomatoes in slices. Melt butter and fry sliced onion and carrot until golden. Add tomatoes, ham, stock and herbs and simmer for 30 minutes. Put through a sieve, thicken with cornflour, season again to taste, and cook for 5 minutes stirring well. Cool. Pack in containers, in brick form, or in ice cube trays, wrapping bricks or cubes when frozen in foil.

To serve
Thaw in double boiler, stirring gently.
High Quality Storage Life   12 months

White Sauce

1 small onion
1 carrot
1 bayleaf
1 oz butter
1 pint milk
1 oz cornflour
Salt and pepper

Cut onion and carrot into slices and simmer with bayleaf in milk for 15 minutes. Melt butter in pan, work in cornflour and cook for 2 minutes, stirring carefully. Add milk gradually, beating thoroughly, and season to taste. Cool, put into containers, seal, label and freeze.

To serve
Thaw in top of double boiler.
High Quality Storage Life   2 months

Apricot Nectar Sauce

4 heaped tablespoons
  apricot jam
1 tablespoon lemon juice
1 tablespoon water
1 dessertspoon sherry
2 tablespoons shredded
  almonds or desiccated
  coconut

Gently heat the jam, lemon juice and water until melted and well blended together. Cool and stir in sherry and almonds, or coconut. Pack into a rigid container.

To serve
Thaw at room temperature and serve cold.
High Quality Storage Life   2 months

Chocolate Sauce

4 oz plain chocolate
½ oz butter
2 tablespoons water
2 level tablespoons
  golden syrup
2 drops pure vanilla
  essence

Heat the chocolate and butter in a small saucepan over a low heat until melted. Add the water, syrup and vanilla essence. Stir well and heat through. Cool and pack into a rigid container.

To serve
Thaw at room temperature to serve cold, or heat gently.
High Quality Storage Life   2 months

Dundee Apple Sauce

1 lb cooking apples
Sugar
4 tablespoons chunky
 marmalade

Simmer the apples in very little water until they form a thick pulp. Sweeten to taste and stir in the marmalade. Cool and pack into a rigid container.

To serve
Thaw at room temperature to serve cold, or heat gently.
High Quality Storage Life 1 year

Lemon Butterscotch Sauce

4 oz Demerara sugar
½ pint water
Rind and juice of
 ¼ lemon
1 oz butter
1 tablespoon arrowroot

Dissolve the sugar in half the water. Add a strip of lemon rind and the butter. Boil for 5 minutes until reduced by half. Blend the arrowroot with the remaining water. Stir into the syrup and add the lemon juice. Bring to the boil and boil for 1 minute. Cool and pack into a rigid container.

To serve
Reheat gently in a double saucepan, or in a bowl over hot water.
High Quality Storage Life 2 months

Peach Sauce

1 lb ripe peaches
4 oz caster sugar
1 tablespoon lemon juice

Peel and stone the peaches. Crush the fruit with a stainless fork, and put through a sieve. Mix with the sugar and lemon juice. Pack into small containers.

To serve
Thaw in the refrigerator with the lid on until the last possible minute to prevent discolouration.
High Quality Storage Life 6 months

Raspberry Sauce

Raspberries
Sugar

Put raspberries in pan with very little water and heat very slowly until juice runs. Put through a sieve and sweeten to taste. Pack into small waxed or rigid plastic containers.

To serve
Thaw in container in refrigerator for 2 hours. Serve with puddings or ice cream.
High Quality Storage Life 1 year

Strawberry Sauce

1 lb strawberries
6 oz caster sugar
Juice of 2 lemons

Hull and wash fruit, and put through a sieve. Stir in sugar and lemon juice which has been strained, and continue stirring until sugar has dissolved. Pack into waxed or rigid plastic container.

To serve
Thaw in refrigerator and serve cold over ice cream, cakes or puddings.
High Quality Storage Life   1 year

Sweet Cider Sauce

4 oz jam
½ pint cider
2 teaspoons cornflour

Put the jam and the cider into a saucepan and bring slowly to the boil. Simmer for 5 minutes. Strain and return to the pan with the cornflour which has been mixed to a smooth paste with a little extra cider. Bring to the boil and stir until the sauce thickens a little. Cool and pack into a rigid container.

To serve
Reheat gently in a double saucepan, or in a bowl over hot water.
High Quality Storage Life   2 months

Walnut Fudge Sauce

4 tablespoons soft brown
   sugar
4 tablespoons
   evaporated milk
2 tablespoons golden
   syrup
1 oz butter
1 tablespoon chopped
   walnuts

Put the sugar, milk, syrup and butter into a small saucepan, and heat gently until the sugar has dissolved, and the ingredients are well blended. Do not boil. Add the walnuts. Cool and pack into a rigid container.

To serve
Reheat gently and serve hot.
High Quality Storage Life   2 months

Brandy Butter

2 oz butter
2 oz icing sugar
2 tablespoons brandy

Cream butter and sugar and work in brandy. Pack into carton, pressing down well, cover, seal, label and freeze.

To serve
Put into refrigerator 1 hour before serving time.
High Quality Storage Life   2 months

220

Parsley Butter

2 oz butter
2 teaspoons lemon juice
2 teaspoons chopped
 parsley
Salt and pepper

Cream butter and work in other ingredients. Form butter into a roll, wrap in greaseproof paper and polythene and freeze.

To serve
Cut off in slices when required to serve with grilled meat or fish.
High Quality Storage Life   2 months

Apricot Stuffing (for turkey, chicken or pork)

4 oz butter
4 cups breadcrumbs
Salt
½ cup chopped celery
4 oz dried apricots

This recipe will be enough for a chicken or a joint of pork. Quantities should be doubled for a 12-lb. turkey.
Melt butter and stir in breadcrumbs, salt and celery. Cook apricots in a little water, and when cool, cut in strips. Add apricots to stuffing mixture, and moisten with a little of the apricot cooking liquid. Pack in cartons or polythene bags and freeze.
High Quality Storage Life   1 month

Bacon and Green Pepper Stuffing (for chicken)

½ cup chopped onion
½ cup chopped celery
4 oz melted butter
4 cups breadcrumbs
1 finely-chopped green
 pepper
4 crumbled fried bacon
 rashers
Salt and pepper

Soften the onion and celery in butter and stir in breadcrumbs. Add green pepper and bacon, and season with salt and pepper. Moisten with a little stock if necessary. Pack into cartons or polythene bags and freeze.
High Quality Storage Life   2 weeks

Basic Poultry Stuffing

2 oz shredded suet
4 oz soft white
 breadcrumbs
2 teaspoons chopped
 parsley
1 teaspoon chopped
 thyme
Grated rind of ½ lemon
Salt and pepper
1 standard egg

Mix all the ingredients together, binding with egg. Pack into cartons or polythene bags and freeze.
High Quality Storage Life   1 month

Brazil Nut Stuffing (for turkey or capon)

4 oz butter
2 cups chopped Brazil
    nuts
½ cup chopped onion
½ cup diced celery with
    leaves
1 teaspoon salt
¼ teaspoon pepper
½ teaspoon Tabasco
    sauce
¼ teaspoon thyme
8 cups lightly-packed
    breadcrumbs
2 tablespoons parsley
2 tablespoons boiling
    water or stock

The quantities in this recipe are enough for a 12-lb. turkey; the recipe should be halved for a 6-lb. capon.

Melt the butter and add nuts, onion, celery, salt and pepper, Tabasco and thyme. Cook until the nuts are lightly browned. Stir in bread-crumbs and parsley and moisten with boiling water or stock. Pack in cartons or polythene bags.
High Quality Storage Life   1 month

Chestnut Stuffing (for turkey)

1 lb chestnuts
2 oz soft white
    breadcrumbs
1 oz melted butter
2 teaspoons fresh mixed
    herbs
2 standard eggs
Salt, pepper and dry
    mustard

Peel chestnuts, and then simmer in a little milk until tender. Sieve and mix with breadcrumbs, butter, herbs and eggs. Add salt and pepper and a pinch of dry mustard. Pack in cartons or polythene bags.
High Quality Storage Life   1 month

Chestnut and Sausage Stuffing (for turkey)

1 lb cooked and mashed
    chestnuts
1 lb sausagemeat
2–3 minced shallots (or
    1 onion) cooked in
    butter
3 sticks chopped celery
2 eggs
½ glass cream or a little
    milk
Seasoning

Mix all ingredients, and moisten with a little stock if necessary. Pack in cartons or polythene bags.
High Quality Storage Life   1 month

Fruit Stuffing (for duck)

*2 cups small bread
  cubes*
*2 tablespoons melted
  butter*
2 fl oz water
1 large orange
2 oz seedless raisins
1 large eating apple
2 oz walnuts
Salt
Nutmeg
*4 fl oz red wine or
  Madeira*

Toast the bread cubes lightly and toss in melted butter. Mix with water, chopped orange sections, raisins, chopped apple and walnuts, a good pinch of salt and of nutmeg and the red wine or Madeira. Leave to stand for 1 hour. Pack into cartons or polythene bags and freeze.
High Quality Storage Life · 2 weeks

Lemon, Thyme and Mushroom Stuffing (for chicken)

8 oz breadcrumbs
*6 oz cleaned, shredded
  suet*
2 teaspoons thyme
*Grated rind and juice of
  1 lemon*
Salt and pepper
Pinch of nutmeg
4 oz chopped mushrooms
4 oz streaky bacon
2 beaten eggs

Fry the diced bacon and mushrooms in a little butter, mix all the ingredients together and bind with the beaten egg. If necessary, add a little stock to make it more moist. Pack into cartons or polythene bags.
High Quality Storage Life   1 month

Mint or Watercress Stuffing (for chicken)

*1½ tablespoons
  finely-chopped onion*
*3 tablespoons chopped
  celery*
6 tablespoons butter
*½ cup fresh mint or 1½
  cups finely-cut
  watercress*
Salt and pepper
*3 cups fine dry
  breadcrumbs*

Cook onion and celery in half the butter for 2 minutes. Add mint or watercress and season generously with salt and pepper. Cook until liquid evaporates and stir in remaining melted butter and breadcrumbs. Pack in cartons or polythene bags.
High Quality Storage Life   1 month

Raisin and Nut Stuffing (for turkey)

4 oz butter
10 cups breadcrumbs
Salt and pepper
½ teaspoon thyme
1 cup broken walnuts
1 cup chopped seeded
   raisins

Melt butter and stir in all ingredients. Pack in cartons or polythene bags and freeze.
High Quality Storage Life   1 month

Sausage Stuffing (for turkey)

1 lb sausagemeat
2 oz streaky bacon
Liver from turkey
1 onion
1 standard egg
2 oz fresh white
   breadcrumbs
Salt and pepper
2 teaspoons fresh mixed
   herbs
Stock

Put sausagemeat into a bowl. Mince bacon, liver and onion. Mix with sausagemeat, egg, breadcrumbs, seasonings and herbs, and moisten with a little stock if necessary. Pack in cartons or polythene bags and freeze.
High Quality Storage Life   2 weeks

Savoury Sausage Stuffing

1½ lb sausagemeat
1 dessertspoon mixed
   herbs
2 finely-chopped onions
1 beaten egg

Mix together all the ingredients and pack into cartons or polythene bags. Any stuffing left over can be made into sausage meat balls and baked separately.
High Quality Storage Life   2 weeks

Ice cream layer cake with strawberries.

Dishes frozen in foil which are good for entertaining week-end house guests.

Part VII ENTERTAINING FROM THE FREEZER

DINNER PARTIES

The freezer is invaluable for dinner party preparation since a complete meal can be assembled and frozen weeks ahead, at leisure; or one or two courses may be thus organised, leaving the hostess free to concentrate on the tricky preparation of just one course or special seasonal dish. A wise hostess does not attempt to offer three hot courses, and, for ease of serving, many now offer a cold first and third course with a hot main course. In the summer, this pattern is sometimes varied so that a hot soup precedes a cold meal, or a hot pudding finishes one.

It is as well to remember when preparing a special dinner that commercially-frozen foods are recognisable by many people today, and a better illusion is created by serving home-made frozen dishes with fresh vegetables in season, or with fresh herbs as a garnish, or a salad; bulk ice-cream too is better converted into a more elaborate pudding than served 'straight', in the way a home-made ice or sorbet can be offered. The vital point to remember about planning a dinner party around frozen food is that while a great deal of last-minute preparation and strain is avoided, there must be great care in organising thawing and heating preparations so that the meal is served in perfect condition.

Overleaf are menus for dinner-parties which are easy to assemble.

DINNER PARTY MENU 1
Coquilles St. Jacques
Coq au Vin
Fresh Vegetables in Season
Duchesse Potatoes
Stuffed Peaches

Coquilles St. Jacques

8 scallops (fresh or frozen)
½ pint dry white wine
1 small onion
Parsley, thyme and bayleaf
4 oz butter
Juice of 1 lemon
4 oz small mushrooms
1 tablespoon cornflour
Salt and pepper
2 oz grated cheese

Clean scallops and put in a pan with wine, chopped onion and herbs. Simmer 5 minutes, no longer as they become tough, and drain scallops, keeping liquid. Melt half the butter, add lemon juice and cook sliced mushrooms until just soft. Drain mushrooms. Add remaining butter to pan and pour in liquid from scallops. Simmer 2 minutes, then thicken with cornflour mixed with a little water. Stir in salt and pepper and grated cheese. Cut scallops in pieces, mix with mushrooms and a little sauce, and divide between 8 scallop shells or individual dishes. Coat with remaining sauce. If liked, pipe edges with creamed potato. Pack by putting shells on to trays, freezing, then wrapping in foil.

To serve
Heat frozen scallops at 400°F, 200°C, Gas Mark 6, for 20 minutes, after sprinkling surface with a few buttered breadcrumbs (these may also be frozen).
High Quality Storage Life   1 month

Coq au Vin

2 × 3 lb chicken
8 oz bacon
20 small white onions
2 oz butter
2 oz oil
2 tablespoons brandy
Salt and pepper
1 tablespoon tomato purée
1 pint red wine
Parsley, thyme and bayleaf

Chicken joints may be used for this dish; otherwise clean and joint chickens. Cut bacon into small strips, simmer in water for 10 minutes and drain. Peel the onions. Melt the butter and oil and lightly fry bacon until brown. Remove from pan and then brown the onions and remove from pan. Fry chicken joints until golden (about 10 minutes), then add bacon and onions. Cover and cook over low heat for 10 minutes. Add brandy and ignite, rotating the pan until the flame dies out. Add salt and pepper, tomato purée, wine, herbs and nutmeg, and crushed garlic and simmer on stove or in oven for 1 hour. Remove chicken pieces and put into freezer container. Cook mushrooms in a little butter and add to chicken pieces. Thicken gravy with cornflour, cool, and pour over chicken and mushrooms. Pack by covering container with lid or foil.

226

Pinch of nutmeg
12 oz button mushrooms
1 garlic clove
1 tablespoon cornflour

To serve
Put chicken and sauce in covered dish and heat at 400°F, 200°C, Gas Mark 6, for 45 minutes.
High Quality Storage Life   1 month

Duchesse Potatoes

2 lb cooked potatoes
4 oz butter
2 eggs
Salt and pepper
Pinch of nutmeg

Put potatoes through a sieve, and beat well with butter and eggs to give a piping consistency, seasoning well. A little hot milk may be added if mixture is stiff. Pipe in pyramids on to baking sheets lined with oiled paper. Pack frozen shapes into bags of suitable quantities.

To serve
Put on to baking sheets, brush with egg and cook at 400°F, 200°C, Gas Mark 6, for 20 minutes.
High Quality Storage Life   1 month

Stuffed Peaches

8 large ripe peaches
4 oz ground almonds
3 oz icing sugar
1½ oz butter
Grated rind of 1 lemon
1 tablespoon orange juice
4 tablespoons sherry

Peel peaches and cut in halves. Mix ground almonds with icing sugar, soft butter and lemon rind and work in orange juice to give a soft paste. Form paste into eight small balls. Put peaches together round stuffing and put on oven dish. Pour on sherry and sprinkle thickly with icing sugar. Bake at 400°F, 200°C, Gas Mark 6, for 15 minutes and cool quickly. Pack in individual containers, or by covering container in which peaches have been cooked in foil.

To serve
Thaw at room temperature for 2 hours, uncover and heat at 375°F, 190°C, Gas Mark 5, for 10 minutes. Serve with cream.
High Quality Storage Life   1 month

DINNER PARTY SERVING PLAN	2 hours before dinner	Remove Stuffed Peaches from freezer
	1½ hours before dinner	Remove Coq au Vin from freezer and put in oven
	20 minutes before dinner	Remove Coquilles St. Jacques and Duchesse Potatoes from freezer and put in oven
	15 minutes before dinner	Begin cooking fresh vegetables
	After first course	Put Stuffed Peaches in oven

DINNER PARTY MENU 2
Tomato Soup
Beef Olives
Creamed Spinach
Pears in Red Wine

Tomato Soup

2 lb tomatoes
2 oz mushrooms
2 medium onions
1 leek
2 sticks celery
Juice of 1 lemon
Parsley, thyme and bay
    leaf
2 oz butter
3 pints stock
2 oz rice flour
2 egg yolks
$\frac{1}{4}$ pint creamy milk
Pinch of sugar
Salt and pepper
Red colouring

Cut tomatoes in slices. Slice mushrooms, onions, leek and celery and cook lightly in butter. Add the lemon juice, herbs and stock and tomatoes and simmer for 30 minutes. Sieve the mixture. In a bowl, mix egg yolks, rice flour and milk until creamy and add a little of the hot tomato mixture, stirring gently. Add remaining liquid and cook very gently for 10 minutes without boiling. Season to taste with salt and pepper and sugar, and colour if necessary. Pack after cooling into cartons, leaving headspace.

To serve
Reheat in a double boiler, stirring gently.
High Quality Storage Life   2 months

Beef Olives

1 lb chuck steak
1 oz fat
2 onions
2 carrots
$\frac{1}{2}$–$\frac{3}{4}$ pint hot beef stock
Salt and pepper

Forcemeat
3 oz breadcrumbs
2 oz cleaned, shredded
    suet
Juice $\frac{1}{2}$ lemon
1 tablespoon chopped
    parsley
1 tablespoon thyme
1 onion
Egg to bind

Cut the meat into thin pieces about 4×3 in. Spread on a board and flatten each piece. Make the forcemeat and spread some on each piece of meat. Roll up and secure with fine string or cotton. Chop the carrot and onion. Heat the fat and fry the meat and onion in it, add the carrot, bay leaf seasoning and stock. Cover and simmer until tender. Remove the string and thicken the gravy by blender in $\frac{1}{2}$ oz flour and bringing to the boil. Cool and pack, covering beef olives with gravy.

To serve
Reheat in a covered dish in the oven at 375°F, 190°C, Gas Mark 5, for 1 hour.
High Quality Storage Life   2 months

228

Creamed Spinach

Spinach leaves
2 oz butter
1 oz flour
¼ pint milk
Top of milk or cream
Sea-salt

Wash leaves well. Cook gently in a large saucepan with water. Turn from time to time until tender. Drain. In same saucepan melt butter, add flour and milk to make a thick white sauce. Return spinach to saucepan and mix very thoroughly, cutting with a knife against the side of the pan. Finally add top of milk or cream. Freeze in cartons.

To serve
Reheat in a double boiler stirring gently.
High Quality Storage Life   2 months

Pears in Red Wine

8 eating pears
8 oz sugar
¼ pint water
¼ pint Burgundy
2-in. cinnamon stick

Peel pears but leave whole with stalks on. Dissolve sugar in water and add cinnamon stick. Simmer pears in syrup with lid on for 15 minutes, then add burgundy and uncover the pan. Continue simmering for 15 minutes. Drain pears and put into individual leakproof containers. Reduce syrup by boiling until it is thick, then pour over pears, and cool. Pack into leakproof containers since the syrup does not freeze solid; the pears lose moisture on thawing and thin the syrup, but the effect is lessened if they are packed in individual containers.

To serve
Thaw in refrigerator for 8 hours.
High Quality Storage Life   2 months

DINNER PARTY SERVING PLAN	8 hours before dinner	Remove Pears in Wine from freezer and put into refrigerator
	1 hour before dinner	Put Beef Olives into oven
	30 minutes before dinner	Gently reheat Tomato Soup and Spinach in double boilers, or in bowls over hot water

DOUBLE DINNER PARTY MENU 3
Cod's Roe Pâté
Hereford-style Pheasant
Fresh Vegetables in Season
Ice-cream Layer Cake

Note: The quantities suggested will make two pâtés, Hereford Pheasants and Ice-cream Layer Cakes – one of each for your dinner-party, and one to keep for some future unexpected or planned occasion.

Cod's Roe Pâté

24 oz smoked cod's roe
½ pint double cream
2 crushed garlic cloves
Juice of 1 lemon
2 dessertspoons olive oil
Black pepper
Cucumber and mint
  sprigs to garnish

Scrape roe into bowl and mix to a smooth paste with cream, garlic, lemon, oil and pepper. Pack into small containers with lids.

To serve
Thaw in refrigerator for 3 hours, stirring occasionally to blend ingredients. Serve in stemmed glasses or glass bowls, decorated with cucumber and mint springs.
High Quality Storage Life   1 month

Hereford-style Pheasant

1½ pints dry cider
2 large pheasants
Seasoned flour
8 oz butter
2 small chopped onions
2 crushed cloves garlic
Thyme, parsley and
  bayleaf
8 rashers streaky bacon
8 small dessert apples
2 oz flour
1 × 10-oz carton fresh
  soured cream
2–4 teaspoons paprika
Salt and pepper
Watercress sprigs or
  pheasant tail feathers
  to garnish

Measure the cider. Dust the pheasant with seasoned flour and fry in half the melted butter until lightly browned. Transfer to a casserole. Fry the onion and garlic in the butter, pour in the cider, stir and bring to the boil. Pour over the pheasants and add the herbs and the rinds from the bacon. Cover with the lid, and cook at 325°F, 170°C, Gas Mark 3, for about 1¾ hours. Remove herbs and bacon rind.
Wash and core the apples. Make 16 bacon rolls from the rashers; bake-fry in a shallow pan in the remaining butter until the bacon is cooked and the apples golden. Remove and keep warm. Add the flour to the pan, and then the strained liquid from the pheasants. Cook for 3 minutes, remove from heat and stir in soured cream and paprika. Test for seasoning. Put pheasants and sauce in 2 freezer containers, garnish with apples and bacon rolls, and dust with a little paprika. Cover and freeze.

To serve
Reheat one bird at 375°F, 190°C, Gas Mark 5, for 1 hour. Transfer to a serving dish suitable for carving, and garnish bird. If preferred, the bacon rolls and apple may be omitted from the freezer recipe, and added at serving time together with the finishing touches for the sauce.
High Quality Storage Life   2 months

Ice-Cream Layer Cake

½ gallon strawberry ice
cream
½ gallon vanilla ice
cream
16 tablespoons
strawberry jam
1 lb strawberries
2 pints double cream

Slightly soften ice creams and press into sponge cake tins to make 4 strawberry layers and 4 vanilla layers. Cover each tin with foil and freeze until firm. Unmould ice cream and arrange in 2 stacks of alternate layers spread with strawberry jam (this is best done on a foil-covered cake board). Cover with whipped cream and strawberries and freeze uncovered for three hours. Wrap in foil for storage.

Note: This cake may be made without the cream and strawberries, which can be added just before serving. Fresh strawberries may also be chopped and added to the strawberry ice cream before moulding in the tins.

DINNER PARTY
SERVING PLAN

3 hours before dinner — Remove required quantity of Cod's Roe Pâté from the freezer and put into the refrigerator

1 hour before dinner — Put 1 Hereford-style pheasant into oven

30 minutes before dinner — Remove ice-cream layer cake from the freezer and put into the refrigerator. Prepare fresh vegetables

DINNER PARTY MENU 4
Pheasant Pâté
Cod Creole
Frozen Peas or Beans
Mashed Potatoes
Rum Babas

Pheasant Pâté

8 oz calf's liver
4 oz bacon
1 small onion
Salt and pepper
1 large cooked pheasant
Powdered cloves and
allspice

Cook liver and bacon lightly in a little butter and put through a mincer with the onion. Season with salt and pepper. Remove meat from pheasant in meat pieces and season lightly with cloves and allspice. Put a layer of liver mixture into a dish (foil pie dish, loaf tin or terrine), and add a layer of pheasant. Continue in layers finished with liver mixture. Cover and steam for 2 hours. Cool with heavy weights on top. Pack by covering container with foil lid and sealing with freezer tape, or by turning pâté out of cooking utensil and wrapping in heavy-duty foil.

To serve
Thaw in wrappings in refrigerator for 6 hours, or at room temperature for 3 hours.
High Quality Storage Life   1 month

Cod Creole

1 oz butter
1 finely-chopped onion
1 tablespoon flour
¾ lb canned tomatoes
4 tablespoons tomato purée
¼ pint chicken stock
Dash Tabasco sauce
Pinch of sugar
Salt
Thyme, parsley and bay leaf
1 lb cod, cut into wedges

Melt the butter and sauté the onion until soft. Stir in the flour and then add the tomatoes, tomato purée, stock, Tabasco sauce, sugar, salt, thyme, parsley and bay leaf. Add the cod, bring to the boil and simmer for 15 minutes. Adjust for seasoning. Cool and put into freezer container.

To serve
Heat with a lid on at 350°F, 180°C, Gas Mark 4, for 45 minutes. Garnish with grated lemon rind.
High Quality Storage Life 2 months

Rum Babas

6 oz self-raising flour
Pinch of salt
2 oz butter
3 oz caster sugar
2 eggs
2 tablespoons milk

Syrup
4 oz granulated sugar
½ pint water
4 tablespoons rum
1 tablespoon lemon juice

Sift flour and salt. Cream butter and sugar, and beat in eggs one at a time, adding a little flour with each. Beat in milk with a little more flour, then stir in remaining flour. Divide mixture into twelve individual baba rings, or one large ring tin. Bake at 375°F, 190°C, Gas Mark 5, for 15 minutes (25 minutes for large one). Cool on a rack. Make syrup by dissolving sugar in water, boiling without stirring for 10 minutes, then adding rum and lemon juice. Prick warm babas with a skewer and pour over hot syrup, basting well. Cool. Pack in rigid plastic container.

To serve
Remove from container and thaw at room temperature for 3 hours. Sprinkle with a little rum and serve with thick cream.
High Quality Storage Life 3 months

DINNER PARTY SERVING PLAN	6 hours before dinner	Remove Pheasant Pâté from freezer and put into refrigerator
	3 hours before dinner	Remove Rum Babas from freezer and put on to a serving dish, sprinkling with a little rum
	45 minutes before dinner	Put Cod Creole into oven
	15 minutes before dinner	Remove vegetables and potatoes from the freezer and prepare

DINNER PARTY MENU 5
Seafood Mousse
Spicy Lamb Casserole
Mashed or Jacket Potatoes
Nut Ice Cream

Seafood Mousse

½-pint packet aspic
    powder
8 oz cooked lobster, crab
    or scampi
1 tablespoon dry white
    wine
¼ pint double cream
Salt and Cayenne
    pepper

Make up the aspic as directed on the packet, but with only ¼ pint water. Leave until cold. Pound together the shellfish and wine, and put the mixture through a sieve (or whirl it in a blender). Gradually add the aspic, a little at a time. Whip the cream to a soft peak and gradually fold into the crab mixture. It is best if this is done with the crab mixture in a bowl on crushed ice. Add salt and Cayenne pepper to taste. Put into a soufflé dish, cover and freeze.

To serve
Thaw in refrigerator for 3 hours and garnish with chopped parsley.
High Quality Storage Life   2 months

Spicy Lamb Casserole

2 lb middle neck lamb
2 tablespoons cooking oil
1 chopped onion
8 oz button onions
1 oz flour
1 pint stock
Salt
¼ teaspoon Tabasco
    sauce
Thyme, parsley and bay
    leaf
8 oz carrots
2 oz sweetcorn
4 oz peas

Brown the lamb in the oil and remove from the pan. Sauté the chopped and button onions until beginning to turn brown. Add the flour and then replace the meat. Pour in the stock and season with salt, pepper sauce and herbs. Bring to the boil, adding the carrots and sweetcorn, and simmer for 1 hour or until the meat is tender. Ten minutes before cooking finishes adjust for seasoning and add the peas. Cool and pack for freezing.

To serve
Reheat at 375°F, 190°C, Gas Mark 5, for 1 hour. Peas may be added during reheating if preferred.
High Quality Storage Life   2 months

Nut Ice Cream

6 oz mixed nuts
  (walnuts, almonds,
  hazels, brazils)
6 oz caster sugar
Pinch of salt
1 pint cream
2 eggs
1 teaspoon vanilla
  essence

Blanch and chop nuts fairly finely. Mix sugar, salt and nuts and add the cream gradually. Put in a double boiler and cook over hot water for 10 minutes. Remove from stove and stir in the beaten eggs very slowly. Freeze to a mush, beat and return to freezer until firm. This ice is also delicious if coffee essence is used instead of vanilla (use 2 teaspoons). Pack in waxed or rigid plastic container.

To serve
Scoop into small dishes and serve with sweet wafers, or use in tartlets with canned fruit.
High Quality Storage Life   3 months

DINNER PARTY
SERVING PLAN

3 hours before dinner	Remove Seafood Mousse from freezer and put into refrigerator
1 hour before dinner	Remove Nut Ice Cream from freezer and put into ice-making compartment of refrigerator
	Put Spicy Lamb Casserole into oven
	Prepare potatoes, or remove them from freezer to reheat

DINNER PARTY MENU 6
Green Pea Soup
Hawaiian Gammon Pot Roast
Green Salad
Lemon Crumb Pudding

Green Pea Soup

2 lb green peas
1 oz butter
1 small onion
1 small lettuce
Mixed herbs
3 pints stock
Salt and pepper

Put peas, butter, grated onion, shredded lettuce, and a small bunch of herbs in a pan with a tight-fitting lid. Cook slowly for 10 minutes. Add stock, salt and pepper, and simmer for 1½ hours. Put through a sieve and cool. Pack in waxed or rigid plastic containers, leaving headspace.

To serve
Reheat gently, adjusting seasoning to taste, and stir in ½ gill cream just before serving. Fried or toasted croûtons, or small pieces of crisp bacon are good garnishes for this soup.
High Quality Storage Life   2 months

Hawaiian Gammon Pot Roast

2 lb corner of gammon, soaked in cold water
1 pint cider
3 tablespoons white vinegar
Dash of Tabasco sauce
Freshly-ground black pepper
4 tablespoons honey
8-oz tin pineapple cubes and juice
8 oz small peeled potatoes
8 oz button mushrooms
2 teaspoons arrowroot, 2 tablespoons water, mixed together

Place the gammon in a pan with cold water. Bring to the boil and simmer for 20–30 minutes. Drain off the liquid. Replace the gammon into a clean pan and pour over the cider, vinegar, Tabasco sauce, pepper, honey, pineapple cubes and juice. Bring to the boil and simmer for 30 minutes. Add the potatoes and cook for a further 15 minutes or until the gammon is tender. Add mushrooms 10 minutes before the end of cooking.

Place the meat in a serving dish and keep hot. Pour a little of the juice on to the arrowroot and water. Return to the pan and bring to the boil, stirring all the time. Pour the sauce over the gammon. Cool and pack for freezing.

To serve
Reheat at 325°F, 170°C, Gas Mark 3, for 1¼ hours.
High Quality Storage Life   2 months

Lemon Crumb Pudding

8 oz white breadcrumbs
4 oz butter or margarine
4 oz sugar
Grated rind and juice of 1 lemon
Apricot jam or pineapple jam

Mix together crumbs, softened butter, sugar and lemon juice and rind. Spread jam liberally in the bottom of an oven dish which can be used in the freezer, or in a foil pie dish. Put on mixture and bake at 350°F, 180°C, Gas Mark 4, for 30 minutes. Cool completely. Pack by putting basin in polythene bag or by covering dish with heavy-duty foil lid.

To serve
Heat at 325°F, 170°C, Gas Mark 3, for 45 minutes, and serve with cream or custard.
High Quality Storage Life   2 months

1¼ hours before serving   Put Hawaiian Gammon Pot Roast in oven
45 minutes before serving   Put Lemon Crumb Pudding in oven
15 minutes before serving   Reheat Green Pea Soup. Make Salad.

DINNER PARTY MENU 7
Potted Crab
Pork with Orange Sauce
New Potatoes
Green Salad or Peas
Apple Cake

Potted Crab

8 oz fresh crabmeat
4 oz butter
1 teaspoon black pepper
1 teaspoon ground mace
Pinch of Cayenne
    pepper
Juice of ½ lemon

Heat ½ oz butter in a pan, and add pepper, mace and Cayenne pepper. When butter is hot, add crab and lemon juice, and stir well until crab is hot but not brown. Pack into small waxed or plastic cartons. Heat the rest of the butter until it is foamy, skim, and pour over crab, covering it completely. Leave until butter is hard. Pack by covering carton with lids.

To serve
Thaw overnight in refrigerator, turn out, and serve with hot toast and lemon slices.
High Quality Storage Life   2 months

Pork with Orange Sauce

6 large lean pork chops
2 medium onions
2 tablespoons vinegar
½ pint orange juice
    (fresh, tinned or
    frozen)
1 tablespoon brown
    sugar

Toss the meat very lightly in a little seasoned flour and cook in a little oil until browned. Remove from oil and cook sliced onions until just soft. Return chops and onions to pan, pour over orange juice, vinegar and sugar and simmer gently for 30 minutes until chops are cooked through. Cool. Pack in foil trays, covering with sauce, and with foil lid.

To serve
Heat with lid on at 375°F, 190°C, Gas Mark 5, for 45 minutes. Garnish with fresh orange slices or segments.
High Quality Storage Life   1 month

Apple Cake

1 lb cooking apples
    (peeled, cored and
    sliced)
1–2 tablespoons water

Put apples, water and sugar into a saucepan. Cook gently until soft. Mash well with a fork. Stir in the sultanas. Allow to cool. Melt butter and sugar in a frying pan. Add cinnamon, almonds and breadcrumbs and fry gently until golden brown, turning frequently. Arrange apple mixture

1–2 *tablespoons brown*
  sugar
2 *oz sultanas*
2½ *oz butter*
2½ *oz brown sugar*
1 *level teaspoon*
  cinnamon
2 *oz finely-chopped*
  almonds
4 *oz crumbs from a*
  brown or wholemeal
  loaf

and crumbs in layers in a freezer tray, starting and finishing with a layer of crumbs; press down lightly. Cool quickly. Place lid on freezer tray and freeze.

To serve
Remove lid and bake in a fairly hot oven for about 1 hour until crisp and golden brown. Serve hot or cold with whipped cream.
High Quality Storage Life 2 months

DINNER PARTY
SERVING PLAN

8 hours before dinner	Remove Potted Crab from freezer and put into refrigerator
1 hour before dinner	Put Apple Cake into oven
45 minutes before dinner	Put Pork with Orange Sauce into oven
15 minutes before dinner	Prepare Salad or Peas (from freezer) and potatoes (fresh or from freezer)

COCKTAIL AND OTHER PARTIES

Make your selection from the following recipes. They must either be thawed an hour or two ahead of the party, or reheated. It is always a good idea to have one or two hot items for serving with drinks.
The only supplements you will need will be nuts, olives, crisps, and a few raw vegetables for use with the dips.

Cheese Cigarettes

2½ *tablespoons butter*
2 *tablespoons plain flour*
¾ *cup creamy milk*
¼ *teaspoon salt*
½ *lb Parmesan cheese*
2 *egg yolks*
¼ *teaspoon Cayenne*
  pepper
3 *loaves thinly-sliced*
  bread

Melt butter, blend in flour and gradually add milk and salt. Cook on low heat, stirring well, until thick. Remove from heat and stir in cheese, beaten egg yolks and Cayenne pepper. Put in refrigerator in covered bowl, and leave to cool to spreading consistency. Remove crusts from bread slices and flatten each slice with rolling pin. Spread with cheese paste and roll like cigarettes. Enough for 60 to 70 'cigarettes'. Pack after freezing unwrapped on trays, into polythene bags.

To serve
Thaw at room temperature for 1 hour and fry in deep fat heated to 475°F until brown. Drain on absorbent paper and serve hot.
High Quality Storage Life 1 month

Crab and Cheese Rolls

4 oz butter
8 oz full fat soft cheese
1 lb fresh or canned
    crabmeat
2 loaves thinly-sliced
    bread

In a double boiler, melt butter and blend in cheese until just warm. Cool and add crabmeat. Remove crusts from bread slices, roll each slice with a rolling pin, and spread with crab and cheese mixture. Roll up like cigarettes and cut each roll in half. Enough for 70 to 80 rolls. Pack after freezing unwrapped on trays, into polythene bags.

To serve
Put rolls on baking tray, brush with melted butter, thaw for 30 minutes at room temperature and bake at 400°F, 200°C, Gas Mark 6, for 10 minutes.
High Quality Storage Life 2 weeks

Cheese Toasts

8 oz Cheddar cheese
8 rashers grilled lean
    bacon
1 medium onion
1 teaspoon cream
1 teaspoon dry mustard
2 loaves thickly-sliced
    bread

Mince together cheese, bacon and onion and mix with cream and mustard Cut bread into rounds or slices without crusts, and toast on one side only. Spread mixture on other side. Enough for 60 pieces of toast. Pack after freezing unwrapped on trays into foil or polythene.

To serve
Thaw at room temperature for 1 hour, and grill under medium heat for 4 minutes.
High Quality Storage Life 2 weeks

Creamy Cheese Balls

Full fat soft cheese
Walnuts or onions
Salt and pepper
Chopped nuts or crushed
    crisps

Mash cheese with finely chopped walnuts or onions and season well with salt and pepper. Roll balls about $\frac{3}{4}$ in. diameter, and roll in chopped nuts or crushed crisps. Arrange on foil trays or foil-wrapped cardboard. Pack with foil overwrap, or in polythene bag.

To serve
Thaw at room temperature for 1 hour and put on to cocktail sticks.
High Quality Storage Life 1 month

Cocktail Grapes

White grapes
Cream cheese
Roquefort cheese
Grated onion

Split grapes and remove seeds. Blend equal parts cream cheese and Roquefort cheese and season highly with grated onion, salt and Worcester sauce. Stuff grapes with filling and arrange on foil trays or foil-wrapped cardboard. Pack with foil overwrap, or in polythene bag.

Salt
Worcester sauce

To serve
Thaw at room temperature for 1 hour.
High Quality Storage Life   2 weeks

Blue Cheese Spread

8 oz Danish Blue cheese
4 oz soft butter
2 tablespoons port
2 tablespoons chopped
 parsley
1 small onion

Blend together cheese, butter, port and parsley with a fork (put bowl in pan of hot water to make this easier). Add minced or grated onion. Pack in small waxed or rigid plastic containers.

To serve
Thaw in refrigerator for 3 hours and spread on small salted biscuits.
High Quality Storage Life   2 weeks

Creamy Cheese and Liver Spread

1 lb full fat soft cheese
8 oz liver sausage
Worcester sauce
Salt and pepper

Blend together cheese and liver sausage until smooth, and season well with sauce, salt and pepper. Pack into small waxed or rigid plastic containers.

To serve
Thaw in refrigerator for 3 hours, and serve on toast or biscuits, as a canapé spread, or as a sandwich filling.
High Quality Storage Life   2 weeks

Crab and Cheese Dip

2 oz Danish Blue cheese
2 oz cream cheese
½ teaspoon Worcester
 sauce
1 clove garlic
1 teaspoon lemon juice
6 oz fresh or canned
 crabmeat

Blend together cheeses and gradually work in sauce, crushed garlic, lemon juice and crabmeat. Pack in waxed or rigid plastic container.

To serve
Thaw in refrigerator for 3 hours and serve in a bowl surrounded by crisps.
High Quality Storage Life   2 weeks

Ham and Horseradish Dip

8 oz cooked ham
1 tablespoon chopped
 parsley
1 tablespoon grated
 horseradish
4 oz cream cheese

Put ham through mincer and blend in parsley, horseradish and cream cheese. Pack in waxed or rigid plastic container.

To serve
Thaw in refrigerator for 3 hours and serve in a bowl surrounded by crisps or small salted biscuits.
High Quality Storage Life   2 weeks

Orange Cheese Dip

4 oz full fat soft cheese
1 tablespoon grated
   orange rind
¼ teaspoon salt
Pinch of paprika

Blend together cheese, orange rind, salt and paprika. Pack in waxed or rigid plastic container.

To serve
Thaw in refrigerator for 3 hours, and serve in a bowl with crisps.
High Quality Storage Life 2 weeks

Salmon Rolls

8 oz shortcrust pastry
2 tablespoons white
   sauce
1 teaspoon lemon juice
8-oz can pink salmon
Salt and pepper

Roll pastry into a long narrow strip about 3 in. wide. Mix white sauce, lemon juice and drained salmon and season well. Place the mixture along one side of the pastry and roll up to enclose the filling. Cut across in 3-in. lengths. Brush with a little beaten egg and bake at 350°F, 180°C, Gas Mark 4, for 10 minutes. Cool. Pack in foil trays inside polythene bags.

To serve
Thaw at room temperature for 1 hour to serve cold, or heat in a low oven 325°F, 170°C, Gas Mark 3, for 20 minutes.
High Quality Storage Life 1 month

Both cocktail and special dishes can be prepared for a buffet party. Likewise, some or all of the dishes below can be used, depending on the number of people to be catered for; there is a choice of meat or fish. Supplement these party dishes with salads and plenty of crusty bread. A rice salad can be prepared if you have rice in the freezer. The meal can finish with fruit and cheese, or with any cold sweet dish from the freezer.

BUFFET PARTY MENU
Vol au Vents with Creamy Chicken Filling
Iced Prawn Curry
Chicken Puffs with Sour Cream Sauce
Beef Galantine
Summer Ratatouille

Vol au Vents with Creamy Chicken Filling

1 pkt (12) frozen
   vol-au-vent cases
Egg to glaze

Cook the vol-au-vents according to the instructions on the packet. To make the filling, melt the butter in a saucepan and stir in the flour. Gradually add the stock and milk and bring to the boil, add the chopped

Filling

1 oz butter
2 tablespoons flour
¼ pint chicken stock
¼ pint milk
2 cooked chicken joints,
*   meat removed and*
*   chopped*
4 tablespoons chopped,
*   canned pimento*
2 tablespoons single
*   cream*
½ teaspoon Tabasco
*   sauce*
Additional seasoning if
*   desired*

chicken, pimento, cream, Tabasco sauce and any additional seasonings desired. Fill the vol-au-vent cases with the chicken mixture and freeze.

To serve
Reheat or serve cold, sprinkled with parsley.
High Quality Storage Life   1 month

Iced Prawn Curry

1 small onion
1 tablespoon oil
1 tablespoon flour
2 tablespoons curry
*   powder*
8-oz can tomatoes
½ teaspoon salt
1 teaspoon sugar
1 tablespoon chutney
¼ teaspoon Tabasco
*   sauce*
Juice ½ lemon
8 oz peeled prawns
¼ pint mayonnaise
2 tablespoons single
*   cream*
8 oz long grain rice

French Spicy Dressing
¼ teaspoon salt
¼ teaspoon pepper
¼ teaspoon Tabasco
*   sauce*
1 tablespoon vinegar
3 tablespoons salad oil
*   beaten together*

Sauté the onion in the oil until soft. Stir in flour and curry powder. Gradually add the tomatoes, salt, sugar, chutney and sauce. Bring to the boil, cover and cook gently for 30 minutes stirring frequently. Remove from heat and add the lemon juice and peeled prawns. Allow to become quite cold and freeze. Cook the long grain rice, drain the rice with cold water and freeze.

To serve
Mix rice thoroughly with the spicy French dressing. Arrange the rice on a serving dish. Thaw the curry for 2 hours and mix with mayonnaise and cream. Serve garnished with hard-boiled egg, whole prawns and chopped parsley.
High Quality Storage Life   1 month

Chicken Puffs with Sour Cream Sauce

12 chicken drumsticks
Liver pâté
1 lb puff pastry

Wrap the chicken drumsticks in foil and then roast, boil, poach or grill until tender. Remove the skin and allow to cool. Spread pâté on to chicken drumsticks. Cut out strips of puff pastry and wind round drumsticks from top to bottom. Bake in a hot oven at 425°F, 220°C, Gas Mark 7, until the pastry is cooked, about 25 minutes. Cool and freeze.

To serve
Reheat or serve cold with various sauces based on sour cream, such as: (a) chopped cucumber in sour cream; (b) chopped chives in sour cream.
High Quality Storage Life 1 month

Beef Galantine

12 oz minced fresh beef
*2 oz fresh white
    breadcrumbs*
1 medium onion
3 oz shredded suet
Salt and pepper
1 teaspoon mixed herbs
1 egg

Grate the onion, and mix together all ingredients, binding with the egg. Form into a neat roll or oblong. Dip a cloth in boiling water, flour well, and put the galantine in this. Steam for $2\frac{3}{4}$ hours. Unwrap the cloth and cool galantine completely. Pack galantine in freezer paper, heavy-duty foil or polythene.

To serve
Thaw in refrigerator for 6 hours, or at room temperature for 3 hours. Roll galantine in crisp breadcrumbs.
High Quality Storage Life 1 month

Summer Ratatouille

2 medium onions
1 lb tomatoes
3 small aubergines
*2 small green or red
    peppers*
4 small courgettes
*2 cloves garlic, peeled
    and crushed*
3 tablespoons olive oil
Salt
*$\frac{1}{4}$ teaspoon Tabasco
    sauce*
12 coriander seeds

Chop the onions and skin the tomatoes. Cut the aubergines into $\frac{1}{2}$-in. dice, place in a colander and sprinkle with salt. Seed and cut the peppers into dice. Slice the courgettes into $\frac{1}{4}$-in. slices. Gently cook the chopped onion and crushed garlic in the oil. Rinse the aubergines and dry on kitchen paper. Add to the onion with courgettes, tomatoes and peppers. Season with salt and pepper sauce. Add the coriander seeds, cover closely and simmer very slowly for 40 minutes. Cool and freeze.

To serve
Thaw at room temperature for 3 hours. Garnish with chopped parsley.
High Quality Storage Life 2 months

242

CHILDREN'S PARTY MENU
Sandwiches
Hot Sausages on Sticks
Basket Cakes
Name Cakes
Sugar Plum Layer Cake
Animal Fun Biscuits

The sandwiches can be small open sandwiches, or ribbon, pinwheel or rolled sandwiches. Avoid jam, honey, or hard-boiled egg in freezer fillings. The sausages can be stored in the freezer until cooked and served. Prepare the cakes from your favourite chocolate cake recipe, or use bought cakes, and freeze them without icing. Thaw for 2 hours at room temperature before preparing as Basket Cakes and Name Cakes. It is best to freeze the big cake iced, but without decorations; they should be added just before serving.

Basket Cakes

14 chocolate buns
4 oz butter
8 oz sifted icing sugar
2 oz grated plain chocolate
Angelica, cut into thin strips
A piping bag with a small star pipe attached

Cream butter and icing sugar to make a smooth buttercream, adding a little pink food colouring. Spread a little round the side of each bun and pipe stars over the top. Bend angelica to form handles and stick one into each bun. If angelica is hard, soak in hot water to soften. Coat the edges in grated chocolate and place buns on a plate.

Name Cakes

14 chocolate buns in paper cases
4 oz icing sugar, sieved
Knob of softened butter
2 oz melted plain chocolate

Add a little water to the icing sugar, making a spreading consistency. Beat in the butter and a little pink food colouring. Spread icing on top of the buns and leave to set. Later pipe a child's name in chocolate on each bun.

Sugar Plum Layer Cake

8 oz soft margarine
8 oz caster sugar
4 eggs
8 oz self-raising flour
3 level tablespoons
  cocoa
2 oz plain chocolate
1 banana
1 tablespoon redcurrant
  jelly
A little pink food
  colouring

Frosting
2 egg whites
12 oz granulated sugar
$\frac{1}{4}$ level teaspoon cream
  of tartar
1 packet marshmallows
Pink candle holders and
  birthday candles

Use two $8\frac{1}{2}$-in. tins, greased and base-lined. Make up the Victoria Sponge mixture by creaming margarine and sugar well, until lighter in colour and texture. Beat eggs carefully into mixture with a teaspoon of flour; fold in sifted flour and a pinch of salt. Divide mixture in half, adding sifted cocoa and the chocolate chopped into small pieces, to one half, spread in a cake tin. Mash banana, add to remaining mixture with the redcurrant jelly and a little pink colouring, spread in tin. Bake cake in a moderately hot oven, 375°F, 190°C, Gas Mark 5, for 35–40 minutes until springy to the touch and cooked through. Turn out and cool on a wire tray. Cut cakes in half making four layers. Place the egg whites, sugar, cream of tartar and 4 tablespoonfuls of water into a bowl, place over a pan of hot water. Stir until sugar had dissolved; this will take 5–8 minutes. Add a few drops of pink food colouring, whisk mixture until thick and standing in peaks. Adjust colouring if necessary. Spread the frosting quickly on each layer of cake and pile up, alternating the colours. Lift cake on to a board, and freeze. Wrap for storage. A butter icing may be used instead and will have a longer storage life.

To serve
Thaw at room temperature for 3 hours. Snip marshmallows with scissors to resemble waterlilies. Push a candle holder and candle into the centre of each and place the required number on the cake.
High Quality Storage Life   1 month

Animal Fun Biscuits

Plain biscuit mixture
3 oz butter or margarine
2 oz caster sugar
1 egg yolk
2 oz plain flour
1 tablespoon rice flour

Chocolate biscuit
  mixture
1 oz plain flour
1 oz rice flour
1 tablespoon cocoa
A little butter icing for
  decoration

For the bases
1 family sweet
  Italian-style vanilla
  ice cream

Cream the butter and sugar together. Add the egg yolk, well beaten. Divide the mixture in half. To one half add the 2 oz plain flour and 1 tablespoon rice flour, to the second half add the 1 oz plain flour and 1 oz rice flour and the cocoa. Work each mixture into separate doughs. Roll out separately to $\frac{1}{2}$-in. thickness. Cut various animal shapes in each. Bake on a greased baking sheet at 350°F, 180°C, Gas Mark 4, for 10–15 minutes. Cool on a wire rack. Pipe eyes, etc. in icing.

Using an ice cream or potato scoop, place small mounds of ice cream on a suitable serving dish. Place an animal on top of each mound. Surround with any animals left over.

Part VIII GARDENING FOR THE FREEZER

For any keen freezer-owner, it is worth planning the kitchen garden with the freezing programme in mind. While obviously the freezer is useful for preserving surplus produce (it is in fact the only safe way to keep most vegetables), it can be even more useful if the quantity and quality of that produce is controlled. Excellent results are only produced from seeds and plants carefully chosen at the planning stage. Most nursery catalogues now list those varieties which are most suitable for freezing, and their lists should be followed.

Not only should the varieties of fruit and vegetables be chosen carefully, but also the whole garden cropping plan should be considered. Winter greens and root crops need not be grown in such quantity as formerly, since they can be supplemented by many different types of summer vegetables. It is not normally worth freezing these winter vegetables, since they will stand in the ground, or can be clamped for storage. Peas, beans of all types, young carrots and beetroot, asparagus and sweetcorn, however, are all very successfully stored in the freezer. It is worth growing an early crop of peas, beans and carrots for immediate use, and then growing as many successional sowings as possible. These main crops can be used immediately, and stored by freezing. It is worth giving extra space to asparagus and sweetcorn, both of which have fairly short seasons and are fairly expensive to buy fresh or frozen.

Soft fruit and herbs should also be included in the garden freezer programme, since they are invaluable for winter use to supplement meals. If there is little space in the vegetable garden, they can be grown in flower borders.

All vegetables should be cropped and frozen when young and tender. It is better to pick and freeze a few each day than wait for a large crop to process, as some of the produce will then be overlarge and tasteless. Fruit should also be picked when just ripe, and easy to pick and process in small quantities. If there are glut crops of either fruit or vegetables, they will take up less space in the freezer in purée form.

RECOMMENDED VEGETABLES FOR FREEZING

Artichokes (Globe)

Artichokes are best grown from plants rather than seeds, and they may be propagated by suckers. These should be removed when 9 in. high, four weeks after the last frost, then replanted deeply and kept well watered. Plants should be protected in winter, after cutting off stems and large leaves, earthing up inner leaves, and covering with suitable litter. In the spring, when the plants are uncovered, only three suckers should be left, and well-rotted manure forked around the roots. Plants are best renewed after the third year. For large heads, remove all lateral buds as they appear or when no larger than an egg.

Asparagus

Asparagus does not like being transplanted, but raising from seed involves waiting four years for a crop, so that it is customary to buy plants. One-year plants transplant better than two-year or three-year ones, but this involves waiting for the crop also. When buying plants, it is important to make the time between unpacking and planting as short as possible, and the proposed site should be prepared well in advance.

Perfect drainage is essential, as stagnant moisture is fatal to the plants. Soil should be prepared three feet deep, with plenty of well-rotted natural manure, and annual dressings of the surface soil. A raised bed is essential on heavy clay subsoil, and in any case gives better drainage and warmth, and therefore earlier crops. The soil should not be trodden on once the plants are in place, and a bed 3 ft. by 2 ft. is the easiest to work; the roots spread, and the area round the bed should be kept free from weeds without disturbance of the roots. The bed should be prepared in the autumn with a view to planting the following spring.

Asparagus crowns should be put in 4 in. below the soil, and it is best to form a ridge on either side of which the long delicate roots can be spread out. These are numerous and very gentle handling is advised; they should not be exposed to sun or wind. Each shoot should be staked to prevent damage, as, if the foliage is blown about, the roots will suffer. An asparagus bed must be kept free of weeds, and given a dressing of well-rotted manure in the autumn and in spring. Soot can be applied at the rate of 2 lb. to the square yard. Salt makes the soil cold, and should only be used as a surface dressing once a month during the summer months, allowing 1 oz to 1 sq. yd.

Asparagus must be cut carefully to avoid injuring adjacent shoots, and is best cut about 4 in. below the surface soil. It should not be cut after mid-summer.

Broad Beans

Broad beans do best in rich ground. In mild areas, the seed can be planted in the early winter on a dry day when the ground is well broken up; some protection during cold spells is advisable. Broad beans need good hoeing during growing, and careful attention should be paid to black fly. As soon as the first flowers set, the tops should be pinched out to ensure an early crop; nipping off side shoots will strengthen the plants.

French Beans

French beans for freezing should be tender and young. They are an excellent crop for the freezer as they grow prolifically for a long season, and can be fitted in between rows of salad crops.

French beans like a light warm soil, and grow best in warm dry weather. It is possible to grow early crops under glass, but it is the later open-ground crop which will be of most use to the freezer-owner. Three sowings at 3-week intervals from late spring will ensure a long succession. For the first sowing, it is advisable to sow fairly thickly, about 3 in. apart, thinning the seedlings to 8 in. apart when in third leaf; slugs are a particular enemy of the seedlings. If seedlings are transplanted, it is important to keep the ball of earth round them intact, as the plants take a long time to recover if the roots have been exposed.

Runner Beans

These beans are very productive, and provide a useful crop for the freezer. Runner beans will grow in most soils, but need liberal watering as dry soil will cause them to drop their flowers and the pods will not set. The beans should be staked, and it is advisable to put in stakes before sowing as the roots of the beans are very brittle. Liberal watering is essential during growth, and mulching with well rotted manure is helpful. Tops should be taken off plants when they have climbed the stakes to make the plants more productive; also large pods should be removed every day or the plants will cease bearing.

Beetroot

Beetroot can be successfully frozen, but they must be selected and harvested carefully, and their preparation for freezing cannot be skimped.

Beetroot does best on well-cultivated sandy loam; heavy soils produce coarse growth and poor flavour and need to be lightened with wood ash, sand or leaf mould. Beetroot must not be sown on recently manured ground, or the roots will be forked and coarse. Care must be taken in hoeing so that the roots do not 'bleed'. They should be harvested as soon as ready, for if beetroot is left too long in the ground, it becomes 'woody'; roots should be taken up with a spade, and never pulled, and the leaves twisted off as near the crown as possible with a quick twist. The roots should not be cut, nor left exposed to the air longer than necessary.

Broccoli

Broccoli for freezing should have compact heads with tender stalks not more than 1-in. thick, and the heads should be uniformly coloured. Broccoli appreciates a well-dug rich soil and should be carefully handled at the seedling stage. Beds should be kept free of weeds, and the other plants grown at a distance of about 2 ft. from each other. Broccoli should not be watered unnecessarily. In a small garden, autumn and winter broccoli will be most useful for use when fresh and for filling the freezer.

Brussels Sprouts

It is most important only to freeze small compact heads of Brussels sprouts.
Good Brussels sprouts need careful growing. Young roots should not be exposed to sun and wind, lifted with insufficient earth, or left too long in the seed bed. They should be planted in firm ground which has been well manured for previous crop but not recently dug. The beds should be well hoed and weeded and kept free of rotting leaves and rubbish. When sprouts are gathered, they should be snapped off, never cut, and a few taken from each plant to ensure a long succession of growth. Tops of plants should not be removed until the plants have ceased production.

Cabbage

Frozen cabbage cannot be used as a salad vegetable while still raw, and must be cooked to be successful. Both white and red cabbage can be frozen, but the cabbage must be firm and solid for best results. Since this is not a particularly popular vegetable, it may not be worth using the freezer space, but better to use cabbage fresh as a seasonal change from other frozen vegetables. Red cabbage, however, is not commonly grown and is usually only sold for a short season, so it can be worth freezing to give variety to menus.
Cabbage grows well on light or heavy soil provided it is rich enough. Cabbage does not like poor loose soil, nor that which has insufficient lime. Cabbage should be planted out well apart, about 2 ft. between rows

and 2 ft. apart. Red cabbage can be grown in the same way, but the flavour is improved by a touch of frost. Pick cabbages for freezing when the heads are tight and compact.

Carrots

Only very young carrots should be frozen, and short horn varieties are very good.

Carrots grow best in good sandy loam. Clay soil has to be liberally lightened with leaf mould, sand, wood ash and green manure, and the soil must be thoroughly dug and well-prepared. Short-rooted and intermediate varieties are best on heavy soil. Early thinning of carrots is recommended, and the roots which are left must not be disturbed or they become prey to carrot fly.

Cauliflower

Small firm compact cauliflower heads may be frozen, but it is better to freeze in sprigs.

Cauliflowers are more tender than broccoli to grow and need care in cultivation. They grow best in very rich well-drained loam, and heavy soil must be thoroughly lightened. Cauliflowers need firm planting in firm soil. They need watering in a dry spell and throughout the growing season, with plenty of hoeing. Cauliflower heads deteriorate rapidly in dry weather with a hot sun and the heads are best protected with their own leaves. Heads should be gathered in the early morning before the dew has dried from them, and prepared quickly for the freezer.

Celery

Celery cannot be used raw after being in the freezer, but it is useful to freeze for future stews and soups, or as a vegetable.

Since celery has to be blanched while growing, it must be grown in soil that will not hold too much moisture. A heavy clay soil is not suitable unless well decayed stable manure and leaf mould are incorporated. Celery is a greedy feeder and likes plenty of well decayed manure, but for earthing up the soil should be sandy and free of manure. It thrives on acid soil and does not like lime. It must be grown in trenches, and 18 in. is the recommended trench width. The trenches should be 15 in. deep, and a 6-in. layer of manure should be trodden well down then topped with 4 in. of good sandy loam. Celery seedlings should be moved with great care, keeping each plant in a ball of soil, and they should not be planted out until 6 weeks after the last frost. They should be well watered in, and the soil firmed round them. The first earthing up is done when the plants are about 15 in. high, and is best done with a trowel or hand fork, leaving the soil loose enough for the heart to continue expanding. Three earthings-up will be necessary, the aim being to achieve complete darkness without any compression. Plants should be lifted about 6 to 8 weeks from the first earthing up.

Corn on the Cob

Corn on the cob can be successfully frozen, but it needs careful cooking afterwards for good results. It can be grown at home, but is not successful in a wet cold summer.

Fennel

The fennel herb can be frozen in sprigs or chopped in ice-cube trays, for flavouring sauces, but does not retain a good flavour in the freezer. Vegetable fennel (finocchio) however may be frozen like celery.
Fennel grows best in a rich moist soil, and the bases of the stems should be partially earthed up when they begin to swell. Plants should be kept well watered.

Kale

Kale will flourish in poor soil, with little attention, and is very hardy. It may not be considered worth freezing, as it is readily available in winter, and will not be particularly appreciated in the spring and summer months from the freezer when other fresh vegetables are available. Also, the more decorative varieties, so often grown now for their dual purpose as food and an adjunct to flower arranging, are more suitable for use in salads, which is not possible once they have been blanched for freezing. Although accommodating, kale is best grown in well dug and manured ground. An annual sowing in late spring will be enough for most needs, in an open sunny position, with protection from birds. Seedlings are best thinned out to 6 in. in a nursery bed, and planted in final positions when larger, about 3 ft. each way. A double transplanting gives good bushy roots. If kale is sown too early, especially after a mild winter, there will be a tendency to bolt.

Kohl-Rabi

Kohl-rabi grows well on light sandy soil, but good flavour is ensured if well-decayed manure has been dug in. Grow quickly for tenderness and good flavour, and sow from early spring through to summer.

Parsnips

Parsnips are best frozen when young and small. Older roots can be cooked and mashed before freezing.

Parsnips do well in most soils, but need some lime in the soil, which should not be very stony. If the roots come in contact with manure that has not thoroughly decayed, they tend to fork. Soil that is too light may cause 'rust'. The flavour of parsnips is best after one or two good frosts.

Peas

Peas freeze extremely well, and are among the most popular items prepared by commercial firms. Home-grown peas should be frozen when young and sweet.

Peas should be grown on good soil which has been well dug and manured for a previous crop; lime is essential, and peas like wood ash. The ground round peas should be kept well aerated, and supports provided which will also give additional protection to earlier varieties. If peas are to be productive, the fullest pods should be gathered daily or they will retard the progress of later pods.

Salsify

This vegetable is not commonly grown, and is rather a nuisance to prepare in the kitchen. It can be frozen, but discolours quickly so that special precautions need to be taken.

Salsify does well on a light soil manured for a previous crop. Newly manured ground will cause the roots to fork. The seedlings should be thinned out 1 ft. apart, but thinnings cannot be transplanted success-fully. The rows should be hoed, but not forked, as loose soil will also cause the roots to fork.

Spinach

Spinach is a useful vegetable in the freezer, for it freezes well when raw, but can also be frozen as Creamed Spinach which helps those who have to feed babies and old people.

Spinach grows best on rich, well-drained soil, but runs to seed quickly on light poor soil. Weekly waterings with liquid manure are helpful. Spinach should be thinned as soon as possible, kept well hoed, and given abundant watering in hot weather.

Turnips

Turnips should only be frozen when small, young and mild-flavoured. They are best sliced or diced, or prepared as a purée.

Turnips succeed in well-drained soil, but run to seed quickly in shallow soil. Light soil should be well enriched, and turnips like lime. Turnips can usually be sown from early spring onwards, with a main crop sowing in late spring. Turnips should not be grown too close together as the leaves are large and spreading.

Recommended Varieties of Vegetables and Fruit for Freezing

Beans, Broad
Carter's Green Leviathan
Green Longpod

French
Carter's Blue Lake
Masterpiece

Runner and Stringless
Crusader
Emergo
Emperor
Ne Plus Ultra
Tendergreen (stringless)

Brussels Sprouts
Cambridge No. 3
Cambridge Special
Irish Elegance
Jade Cross

Carrots
Carter's Early Gem
Carter's Improved Early Horn
Early Market
Early Nantes
Perfect Gem
Scarlet Intermediate

Cauliflower
Carter's Forerunner

Corn on the Cob
Early Xtra Sweet
John Innes Hybrid

Peas
Carter's Raynes Park
Dobie's Topcrop
Early Onward
Foremost
Johnson's Freezer
Kelvedon Wonder
Onward
Progress

Spinach
Carter's Goliath
New Zealand

Apple
Bramley Seedling

Blackcurrants
Blacksmith
Boskoop Giant
Laxton's Giant
Malvern Cross
Wellington

Gooseberry
Careless

Greengages
Cambridge Gage
Comte d'Althan's Gage
Jefferson

Plum
Victoria

Raspberries
Lloyd George
Malling Enterprise
Malling Jewel
Malling Promise
Norfolk Giant

Redcurrant
Red Lake

Strawberries
Cambridge Favourite
Cambridge Late Pine
Cambridge Rival
Cambridge Vigour
Royal Sovereign
Talisman

INDEX